ON COURSE for FIRST CERTIFICATE

STUDENTS' BOOK

Judy Garton-Sprenger

Simon Greenall

Heinemann Educational Books
London

ACKNOWLEDGEMENTS

The authors and publishers would like to thank the following for permission to use their material:

Miss A D Hatton, A D Peters & Co Ltd and Little Brown & Co for the extract from *Decline and Fall* by Evelyn Waugh (Chapman and Hall) copyright 1928 renewed 1956 by Evelyn Waugh; A D Peters & Co Ltd for the extract from *Fool's Paradise* (Pan Books) by Brian Moynahan; A D Peters & Co Ltd for the extract from *More Everyday Inventions* by Meredith Hooper (Angus and Robertson Ltd) – All extracts reprinted by permission of A D Peters & Co Ltd; Alan Hutchison Library Ltd; Anglia Television Ltd; Barclays Bank PLC; BBC; British Museum; British Railways Board; British Telecom; British Tourist Authority; Burroughs Machines Ltd; Camera Press; Campaway Holidays; Chrissie Roberts; Christopher Sainsbury; City of Glasgow Housing Department; Consumers' Association for the material from *Which?* (August 1982); Controller of Her Majesty's Stationery Office; Council of Forest Industries of British Columbia; Daimler Benz AG (Historical Department); Fisons Pharmaceuticals; Ford Photographic Unit; Mr Grant Williams; Alan Halliday; Hamish Hamilton for the extract from *The Hireling* by L P Hartley; Heinemann Educational Books for the extract from Social Geography by Dunlop & MacDonald; H J Heinz Company Ltd; Henry Grant; Hicks and Hayes Design Associates Ltd; Hodder & Stoughton for the extract from *The Romeo Error* by Lyall Watson (1974); Independent Broadcasting Authority; Island Sailing; J. Allan Cash Ltd; James Davis; Janine Wiedel; Japan Information Centre, London; Mr Jeff Page; John Topham Picture Library; Kodak Museum; Light Fantastic Gallery of Holography; London Transport Executive; London Weekend Television; Macmillan, London and Basingstoke for the extract from *Sociology* by Nobbs, Hine and Fleming (1975); Mary Evans Picture Library; Metropolitan Police Public Information Department; Mike Hindmarsh; Mrs Mole; Multimedia Publications (UK) Ltd; National Theatre; Nestlé Productions Technical Assistance Co Ltd; Notting Hill Housing Trust; Open University; Mr Paddy Hall; Penguin Books Ltd for the extract from *The School That I'd Like* Ed. Edward Blishen (Penguin Education 1969) Selection copyright Penguin Books and contributors (1969); PGL Adventure Ltd; Photographie Giraudon; Post Office; Press-tige Pictures Ltd; Portuguese National Tourist Office; QPL Express Couriers; Robert Bosch Ltd; Robert Hale Ltd for the extract from *The Day They Stole The Mona Lisa* by Seymour V Reit, also Summit Books, a division of Simon & Schuster Inc; Royal Aeronautical Society; Sailboard Mediterranean Holidays Ltd; Science Photolibrary; Severn House Publishers Ltd; Sports Council; Teddy Schwarz Travel Trade Photography; Thomas Nelson and Sons Ltd for the extract from *Different Worlds* People and Places Book 6 by Tony Crisp; Time Out; Toby Green; Tom Hanley of Bloomsbury; Tony Stone Photolibrary, London.

Note: Chrissie Roberts now has her own company called General Pattern and no further connection with Elephant Jobs.

Heinemann Educational Books Ltd
22 Bedford Square, London WC1B 3HH

LONDON EDINBURGH MELBOURNE AUCKLAND
HONG KONG SINGAPORE KUALA LUMPUR
NEW DELHI IBADAN NAIROBI JOHANNESBURG
PORTSMOUTH (NH) KINGSTON

British Library Cataloguing in Publication Data

Garton-Sprenger, Judy
On course for first certificate.
Students' book
1. English language—Text-books for foreign speakers
I. Title II. Greenall, Simon

ISBN 0-435-28014-7

First published 1983
Reprinted 1983, 1984 (twice), 1986 (twice), 1987

Teachers' Book 0-435-28015-5
Cassettes 0-435-28016-3

Designed and Typeset by Oxprint
Printed in Great Britain by
Thomson Litho Ltd,
East Kilbride, Scotland

CONTENTS

THE FIRST CERTIFICATE EXAMINATION

The Cambridge First Certificate in English Examination consists of five compulsory papers:

PAPER 1 Reading Comprehension (1 hour)

Section A 25 multiple-choice questions designed to test vocabulary and formal grammatical control.
Section B 15 multiple-choice questions based on three or more texts and designed to test comprehension of gist or detailed content.

PAPER 2 Composition (1½ hours)

Two compositions from a choice of descriptive, narrative or discursive topics, or based on prescribed texts. Candidates are expected to write not less than 120 words.

PAPER 3 Use of English (2 hours)

Section A Open-completion or transformation items designed to test active control of the language.
Section B directed writing exercise to test ability to interpret and present information.

PAPER 4 Listening Comprehension (approx. 30 minutes)

Questions of varying type (selection, re-ordering, blank-filling etc.) to test accurate understanding of spoken English, based on recorded material, including conversation, announcements etc.

PAPER 5 Interview (approx. 20 minutes)

A conversation using a picture stimulus, designed to test fluency and grammatical accuracy.

Reading aloud of a short passage (announcement, instruction or situation), to test pronunciation, stress and linking in phrases.

Structured communication exercise (role-play, discussion etc. on prepared and unprepared material), to test communicative ability and vocabulary.

GUIDE TO THE COURSE

On Course for First Certificate is divided into ten topic-based units each covering the five papers of the revised 1984 Cambridge First Certificate Examination. Vocabulary, structure and usage are practised throughout each unit in a variety of activities, with Key Language and Key Vocabulary presented clearly to help revision. The Structure Review at the back of the book provides grammatical explanations and exercises for further structure practice. Thorough attention is also given in each unit to the reading, writing, listening and speaking skills required for the examination. Each unit ends with an Exam Practice section. The table below shows the basic unit structure, and explains how particular sections relate specifically to the examination papers. The lines between the boxes show the relationship between the different activities within each section.

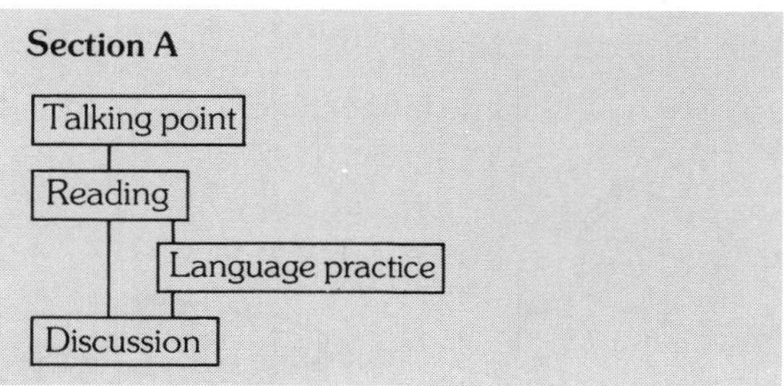

Section A introduces the topic of the unit and concentrates on vocabulary, structure and usage.

PAPERS 1 AND 2

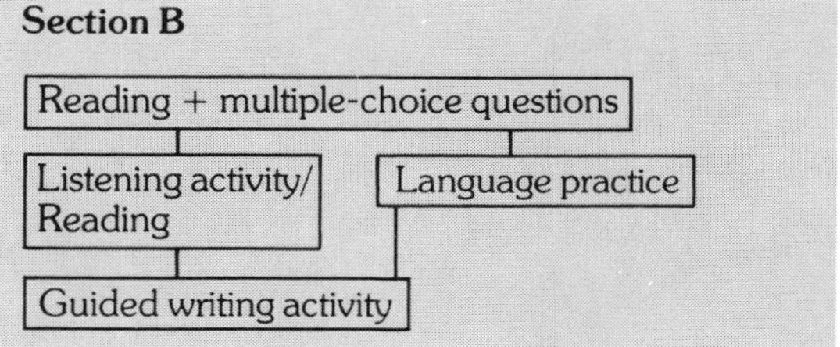

Section B begins with a reading passage with multiple-choice questions which test vocabulary and comprehension. The guided writing activity, based on a model text and on new information provided by a listening activity or further reading, gives practice in composition writing.

PAPER 3

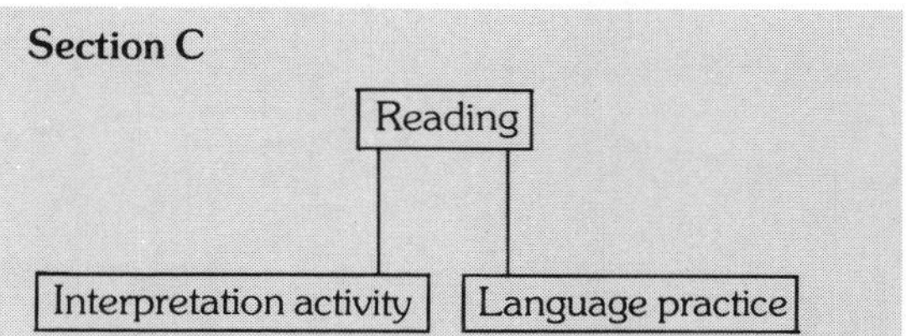

Section C opens with a reading passage which leads to an exercise to test the learner's ability to interpret and present information.

PAPERS 4 AND 5

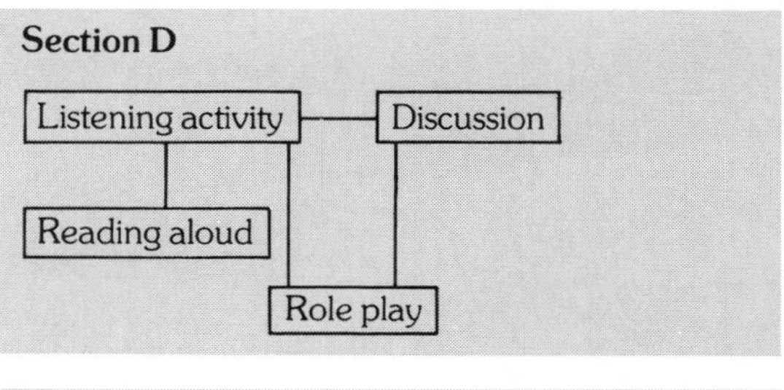

Section D provides practice in listening comprehension and speaking fluency, and includes a passage for reading aloud and a role play activity. The section is often introduced by a reading passage.

Exam practice

Suggestions for the exam

Practice questions

The **Exam practice** section concentrates on examination techniques and examination type questions, and encourages the learner to keep a close check on his or her progress.

The listening material is recorded on cassette and the transcripts are included in the Students' Book.

UNIT 1
PERSON TO PERSON

A DESCRIBING PHYSICAL APPEARANCE: FIRST IMPRESSIONS

TALKING POINT

None of these clothes or accessories would look out of place in even the most fashionable circles. But can you say what each one is called and which job or activity they were originally designed for?

Why do you think they have now become fashionable?

UNIT ONE

READING

The Language of Clothes

Clothes, decorations, physique, hair and facial features give a great deal of information about us. For instance, we wear clothes to keep us warm, because unlike animals we do not have a protective covering of hair. But for the purpose of communication, we dress in clothes of different colours, style and material; we wear jewellery and other valuables, we use cosmetics and perfume, we grow beards and sideburns; and we smoke pipes and carry walking sticks.

Strict rules govern the clothes we wear. We do not, for instance, wear football boots with a dinner-jacket, or a boiler suit to work in an insurance office. A worker in an office in the City of London or on Wall Street will wear more formal dress than someone in a similar job in a country town. Fashionable and smart clothes are associated with good qualities, and well-dressed people have been found to get more help and co-operation from complete strangers. A woman was given more offers of help with her broken-down car when she dressed attractively than when she dressed less appealingly.

Rebels consider themselves to be different from other people in society, and often alter their physical appearance to show this. In the last two decades in Britain there have been a number of youth movements with distinct uniforms – among them, hippies and punks. Hippies did not just wear simple clothes but dressed in a particular style that made them instantly recognisable. The punk rock craze has taken this even further, at least in a courageous few.

People also choose particular clothes to project their personalities. Sociable and extroverted types wear brighter colours than more introverted and reserved people. Some people wear odd combinations of clothes to express their individuality. For instance, someone might give an impression of high social status, eccentricity, Scottish origin and bad temper by an expensive suit with gold cuff-links, luminous green socks, a beret, tartan tie and bushy red beard.

a) 1 According to the text, what two purposes do clothes serve?

2 Why don't we wear football boots with a dinner-jacket?

3 Why might it be an advantage to travel in a suit rather than in jeans?

4 Why have many groups of young people adopted 'uniforms'?

5 Which group of rebels in society has worn the most extreme clothes?

6 What type of person wears reds, oranges and yellows?

7 What colours do introverted and reserved people wear?

8 According to the writer, what impression does a man with a bushy red beard give?

b) Find words in the text which mean:

make-up	fashion
control	brave
change	express
ten-year periods	peculiar
groups	unusual behaviour

LANGUAGE PRACTICE

1 **a)** Look at the people in the photographs, at their clothes, faces and hair. What impressions do you have of these people (personality – occupation – lifestyle)?
Describe them and give reasons for your impressions.

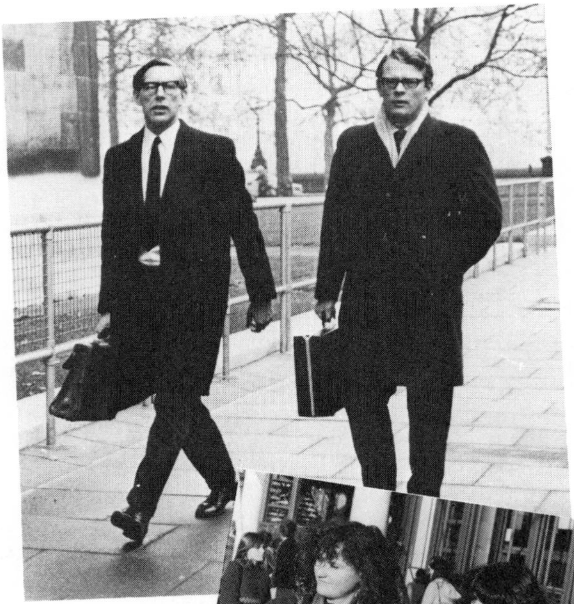

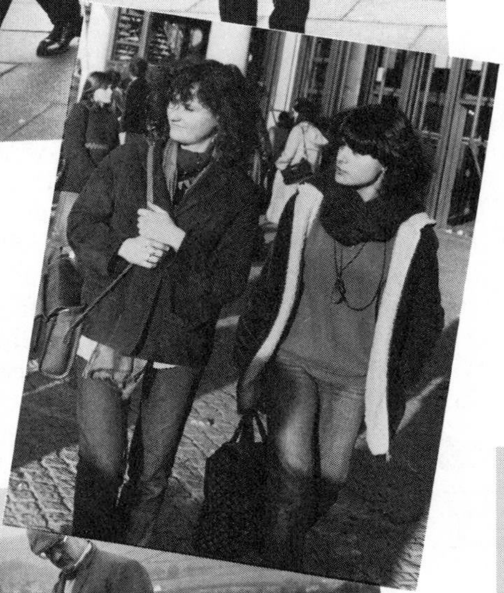

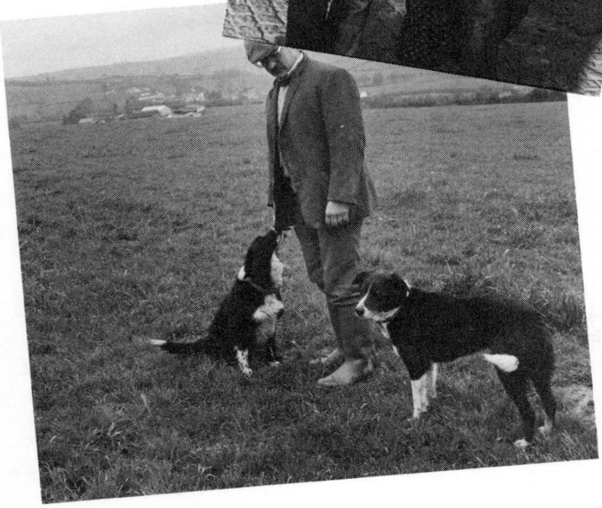

KEY LANGUAGE

Describing impressions (1)

look + adjective	She looks friendly.
look like + noun	He looks like a student.

Giving reasons:

because of + noun	. . . because of her smile.
because + clause	. . . because he's got long hair.

Modifying:

quite / *fairly* / *rather* / *very* + adjective	He's quite thin. She looks rather tired.
Suffix *-ish*	He's tallish.

b) What impressions do you have of people with the following?

long hair	a beard	thin lips
a round face	a high forehead	a red face
a long face	long fingers	

What other aspects of people's appearance give you clues about their personality?

2

Read the following sentences and decide what type of word is missing. Is it a noun, a verb or an adjective? Then choose the missing word from the list below.

KEY VOCABULARY

lining	nylon	match	
jumper	vest	waterproof	
belt	skirt	informal	
suit	fit	pocket	
casual	loose	bare	zip
smart	undress	fasten	bald
sleeves	tight	pyjamas	uniform

Remember that some of these words are both nouns *and* verbs or adjectives!

1 He rolled up his ______ and began the washing-up.

2 I thought my raincoat was ______, but I'm wet through.

3 The child ______ herself and climbed into bed.

4 Would you undo the ______ for me?

5 How lovely you look! Blue really ______ you.

6 Have you got a larger size? This one's a bit ______.

7 You can't go to the party in jeans. You're supposed to look ______.

8 I'm sure I had some matches. There must be a hole in my ______.

9 He's growing so fast that none of his clothes ______ him.

10 There's broken glass on the floor, so don't walk around with ______ feet.

3

Find the pairs and form twelve compound nouns. Check the compounds in your dictionary. Notice which compounds are one word, which are two words, and which are hyphenated.

KEY VOCABULARY

hand	shoe	over	
ear	dinner	jacket	
over	boiler	stick	hole
pull	walking	case	ring
cuff	suit	boot	coat
football		lace	links
button		suit	bag

4

Listen to the conversation in a shop and fill in the missing phrases below.

ASSISTANT: Can I help you, madam?
WOMAN: Yes, I'm . . . . something to wear in the summer.
ASSISTANT: Yes, of course. These are our lightweight jackets. What size do you take?
WOMAN: Er – size ten, I think. Oh, this one's lovely. Can I . . . . ?
ASSISTANT: Yes, of course. You're wearing rather a thick sweater. Do you want to . . . . ?
WOMAN: Er – I'm not sure.
ASSISTANT: Well, it *is* meant to be a summer jacket. Why don't you . . . . ?
WOMAN: Yes, perhaps you're right.
ASSISTANT: Here we are. Let me help you . . . .
WOMAN: Thank you.
ASSISTANT: Yes, it *does* suit you! It . . . . your trousers.
WOMAN: But it's much too tight. It really doesn't fit me.
ASSISTANT: Oh, don't worry. It'll be perfect once you've worn it a few times.
WOMAN: How can I wear it a few times if I can't even . . . . ? Have you got it in a larger size?
ASSISTANT: I don't think so.
WOMAN: Well, this one's no good. It's far too small. Oh, it's just my luck.
ASSISTANT: Never mind, madam. How about this one?

DISCUSSION

Which of these statements do you agree with, and why?

What do you think of fashion today? Do you try to be fashionable?

When do you wear smart clothes?

Which clothes do you feel most comfortable in?

What colours do you like wearing? What colours suit you best?

What assumptions do you make about people from the way they dress?

How important are clothes to you?

In my opinion she looks ridiculous.

SHE LOOKS LIKE SOMETHING FROM ANOTHER PLANET!

She shouldn't be allowed to dress like that.

I think she looks quite interesting.

EVERYONE HAS A RIGHT TO WEAR WHAT THEY LIKE!

Expressing opinions (1):

I think (that) . . .
In my opinion . . .
It seems to me that . . .

Agreeing:

I quite agree (with you).
I agree (entirely).
You're absolutely right.
Yes, definitely/exactly.
Yes, I think so.

Agreeing reluctantly:

I suppose so/not.
You may be right.

Disagreeing:

I'm afraid I don't agree/think so.
I'm sorry, I really can't agree with you.
I wouldn't say that.
You have a point there, but . . .
Yes, but don't you think that . . .

Note: All these expressions are polite.

B DESCRIBING PHYSICAL APPEARANCE: A CLOSER LOOK

READING

Pygmalion

Pygmalion is one of the most popular works by the famous playwright, George Bernard Shaw (1856–1950). In the play, Professor Higgins, an expert on phonetics, decides to train a poor flower girl, Eliza Doolittle, to speak and behave as an educated lady would. It was written in 1914 and the opening scene gives a wonderfully vivid picture of the contrasting styles of life in London at the time. Higgins and Eliza are very different when they first meet, and Eliza has much to learn!

The curtain rises on the scene in Covent Garden late one evening. The street is busy with people arriving to start work at the market, horses pulling carts piled high with vegetables, and carriages waiting for the audience who are just leaving the Opera House at the end of a performance. It is raining heavily, and people are running in all directions to avoid getting wet. The elegant opera-goers, wearing long evening dresses and jewellery, or tail coats and top hats, are in sharp contrast with the market workers, who are dressed in old trousers and dirty jackets, muddy boots and flat caps. The air is filled with shouts from porters warning bystanders to step back and make way for yet another barrow-load of apples, or cries from impatient young men trying in vain to find cabs to take them and their young ladies out of the rain and home as quickly as possible. In the middle of the crowds and confusion, nobody notices Eliza on the steps with her basket of flowers. She is such an unhappy figure. She must be between eighteen and twenty, but she looks older because of her poverty. She is wearing an old black coat with its collar turned up to keep out the rain, boots which are broken down at the heel, and a brown skirt which is soaked and stained by the mud of the streets. The water is running off her black hat onto her face, and she looks lonely and miserable. But when she offers her flowers to passers-by, her brown eyes become bright and lively and her frown is replaced by a cheerful smile. You can tell she is tall and slender under her shapeless coat, her cheeks are rosy, and the auburn curls falling from beneath her hat make her look quite pretty.

Standing behind a pile of barrels and boxes filled with cabbage leaves is one man who seems to be quite unaware of the noise and the crowds. He does not look like an opera-lover or a market worker, and appears to be very interested in Eliza. But instead of watching her, his head is tilted to one side as if he is listening, and when she cries, 'Who wants my lavender?', he takes out a notebook and pen from his overcoat pocket and writes something down.

Choose the best alternative to the following words or phrases in the text.

KEY VOCABULARY

1 CARTS
A carriages B lorries C barrels D wagons

2 PILED
A crowded B layered C heaped D raised

3 AVOID
A escape B prevent C defend D protect

4 SHARP
A painful B distinct C sensitive D sudden

5 IN VAIN
A with difficulty B without hope C without success D with pride

6 NOTICES
A glimpses B sees C warns D realises

7 STAINED
A damaged B coloured C dirtied D spoilt

8 UNAWARE OF
A ignorant of B annoyed by C separate from D unconscious of

Now decide whether the following statements are true or false.

1 The beginning of the play is set in Covent Garden.
2 The market sells fruit as well as vegetables.
3 People are in a hurry to leave the Opera House.
4 There are not enough cabs after the performance.
5 Eliza's figure is sad.
6 She looks old because she is poor.
7 She looks quite healthy.
8 The man behind the barrels and boxes has certainly been to the opera.
9 He is probably studying Eliza's speech.
10 Selling lavender makes Eliza cry.

LANGUAGE PRACTICE

Have you seen *Pygmalion* or its film version, *My Fair Lady* with Audrey Hepburn and Rex Harrison? If you have, describe the characters and the plot. If you haven't, talk about a film or a play you have seen recently and enjoyed.

KEY LANGUAGE

Describing dramatic events:

Present simple (historic)	Eliza meets Higgins in the market.

Describing background:

Present continuous	It is raining heavily.

GUIDED WRITING ACTIVITY

a) Read the description of Eliza again, and make notes about the following: age, clothes, expression, physique, facial features, hair.

b) The man who is so interested in Eliza is, of course, Professor Higgins. The director of *Pygmalion* has made some notes about Higgins' first appearance in the play.

Write a description of Higgins based on the notes opposite. Use the description of Eliza as a model.

c) Write a description of someone in your class or of someone famous. Leave out the person's name and see if the other students can guess the subject of your description.

Higgins

Age: In his early forties, looks younger (comfortable life)
Clothes: Informal tweed suit, heavy overcoat, soft hat, brown shoes splashed with mud.
Expression: Thoughtful & solemn, BUT when he talks to Eliza, eyes become humorous, good-natured smile.
Physique: Broad-shouldered, strong
Facial features: Handsome
Hair: dark, beginning to go grey - quite distinguished-looking.

KEY LANGUAGE

Describing people:

Present simple (state)	Her cheeks are rosy. He's got dark hair.
Present continuous (temporary)	She is wearing an old coat . . .
Adjectival phrase	. . . with its collar turned up.

Making deductions (1):

Modal auxiliaries *must* and *can't*	She must be eighteen.
You can tell + clause	You can tell she is poor (by/from/because of) . . .

Describing impressions (2):

look *sound* *seem* *appear* + adjective	He sounds French
look *sound* *seem* + *like* + noun	She seems like a kind person.
look *sound* *seem* + *as if* + clause	He looks as if he's in a hurry.
seem *appear* + *to* + infinitive	He appears to be interested.

Describing habits (1):

Present simple (habit) + adverbs of frequency	He wears smart clothes. He never loses his temper.
Present continuous + *always* (for irritating or suprising habits)	She's always breaking things.

C DESCRIBING PERSONALITY

READING

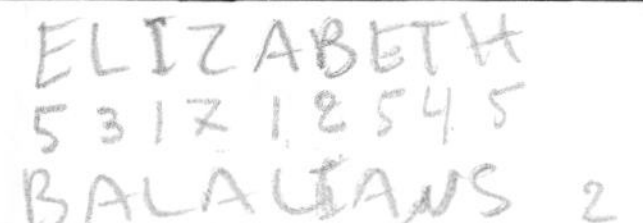

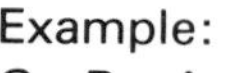

Figure it out!

Did you know that your name and date of birth are not just ways of identifying yourself on official forms? They can also be used to analyse your character and predict the future. And it's all done by numbers! Numerology is an old science which finds order and regularity in the confusing variety of events and influences which rule over our lives. It's based on two principles: firstly, that reality is mathematical and all things can be understood by numbers, and secondly, that your name is not just a label but in fact contains a description of your character. Here's how it's done. Each letter is given a number from 1 to 8.

1	2	3	4	5	6	7	8
A	B	C	D	E	U	O	F
I	K	G	M	H	V	Z	P
Q	R	L	T	N	W		
J		S			X		
Y							

To find the number of your name, write it down and give each letter a number, and then add them all together, and continue until you reach a single figure.

Example:

G R A H A M
3+ 2+ 1+ 5+ 1+ 4 +

W I L K I N S O N
6+ 1+ 3+ 2+ 1+ 5+ 3+ 7+ 5 = 49 4+9 = 13

1+3 = 4

Then refer this number to the table below.

Your full name indicates your personality. Apply the numbers to your nickname, and it will reveal the impression you give to the people who call you by that name. If you are a married woman, try the same procedure with your maiden name, and see how marriage has changed you! If you 'add up' the number of vowels alone, it will reveal your inner self, and the consonants alone, your outer self. Now try it with your date of birth.

Example:

17 July 1949 =
17.7.1949 = 1+7+7+1+9+4+9 = 38

3+8 = 11

1+1 = 2

This is your destiny, which will follow you all through your life, for better or for worse, and if it doesn't harmonise with your name number, there's a conflict in you! And finally, if you add the day and month of your birth to any year of your life, then the number will predict what will happen during that particular year. Try it yourself, and see what numerology can do for you. You could even try adding up all the money you have, but I don't predict that you'll become any richer!

1 powerful, aggressive, self-centred, ambitious, quick-tempered, lonely
2 passive, indecisive, shy, modest, charming, gentle
3 creative, bossy, versatile, optimistic, talkative, independent
4 solid, confident, steady, moody, practical, capable
5 nervous, attractive, impatient, lively, adventurous, irresponsible
6 loyal, affectionate, hard-working, friendly, balanced, self-satisfied
7 talented, serious, pessimistic, self-controlled, proud, sensitive
8 tough, efficient, materialistic, energetic, selfish, strong-minded
9 idealistic, romantic, impulsive, rebellious, determined, insecure

LANGUAGE PRACTICE

There are probably some unfamiliar adjectives in the table on page 14. Look them up in your dictionary to find out what they mean. Some of them are used to describe people favourably, while others are used for unfavourable descriptions. Make two lists from the following adjectives.

Examples:

Favourable	**Unfavourable**
adventurous	*aggressive*

adventurous
aggressive
bossy
capable
indecisive
efficient
friendly
hard-working
impatient
independent
irresponsible
lively
loyal
nervous
practical
quick-tempered
self-centred
selfish
self-satisfied
talented

INTERPRETATION ACTIVITY

Anna Maitland (born 29 January 1965) and Derek Barlow (born 6 November 1966) are both looking for jobs. Use numerology to analyse their personalities, and then choose the most suitable job for each of them from the advertisements. In each case write a paragraph giving reasons for your choice of job.

Begin: *The most suitable job for Anna . . .*

LOOKING FOR MORE THAN A 9 TO 5 JOB? We have opportunities for young people to work with children as adventure leaders at our outdoor activity centres. If you can instruct in either sailing, canoeing, pony trekking, rifle shooting, archery or hillwalking, or just enjoy contact with kids, we can offer you an informal happy working environment with the opportunity to meet all kinds of people. Interested? Write for further details to: Personnel Dept., PGL Young Adventure Ltd., 879 Station Street, Ross-on-Wye, Herefordshire HR9 7AH. Tel: Ross-on-Wye (0989) 64213.

CHARITY SHOPS ORGANISER

Energetic, enthusiastic organiser wanted to manage existing temporary charity shops and to find, set up and manage new shops throughout the London area. Must be a car driver. Confidence on telephone and ability to get on with a wide variety of people, including volunteers, essential. Must be able to work on own initiative. Preferably full-time, but hours possibly negotiable.
For details and application form please write or telephone

Rosemary Well,
NHHT,
26 Padenswick Rd.,
London W6 0UB.
Tel: 741 1570

ATTRACTIVE capable person required to manage glamorous photographic studio in Holborn area. Excellent salary and bonus. Previous experience one side of the camera or other an advantage. Call Sue, Studio London, 9 London Rd, London, SE1. 261 9681.

ASSISTANT COPYWRITER

Are you imaginative and versatile? Can you make quick decisions? Do you enjoy using words? Then you could be just the person for our expanding advertising agency. We are looking for a creative person to join our team of copywriters. For details & application form, write to: ATA, 26 King St, London, WC1.

SALES REPRESENTATIVE

Do you have that special spark? If you are dynamic, energetic, and efficient, then apply now for the opportunity of a lifetime and the chance of huge financial rewards. Ask for Robert Lasdon on 734 9599.

D DISCUSSING RELATIONSHIPS

READING

Here is the problem page from a magazine. People write in for advice on their personal problems. Amanda has replied to the reader's letters, but her replies have been accidentally mixed up. Match each reader's letter with the appropriate reply.

LISTENING ACTIVITY

a) Certain radio programmes also deal with personal problems. Listeners phone the radio station and discuss their problems on the air. Listen to the radio programme and take notes on the following points:

what Annie would like to do
what her parents think
what her present job is like
what she's worried about
what other people think

b) Listen to the radio programme again and write down the adjectives used to describe these people.

Annie   Annie's mother
Annie's father   Geoff   Mark
Annie's boss   Mrs Spencer   Jim
Annie's grandmother   Joan

KEY VOCABULARY

c) Now make nouns from the adjectives you have chosen.

Examples: *kind – kindness*
anxious – anxiety

★Amanda Dear answers your letters

GOSSIP

My husband and I live in a very friendly road. Everyone gets on well together because we all respect each other's private lives. However, a widowed lady has just moved into our street, and she's always discussing all our movements and problems with everyone else. Although she has a 22-year-old son, she must be quite lonely, and we're sure she simply wants to join in as much as possible. But some of us are a little annoyed by her gossipping. We don't wish to be unkind, but how can we ask her to be more discreet?

Congratulations for having the courage to contact him! Even in these liberated times, girls still don't want to seem too keen. But if he has such old-fashioned attitudes to women, he doesn't sound right for you. Good relationships depend on mental harmony as well as physical attraction. If his 'male' image is so important to him, I'd turn to someone less selfish and more sympathetic if I were you.

★

ATTRACTION

Six months ago, I broke up with my boyfriend. I was very upset for a few weeks, and then I met a rather strange but good-looking man who says he's in show business. We went out once or twice, then he didn't ring, so I called him. He sounded rather surprised, but agreed to meet me again. All evening he teased me about the fact that it was me who had got in touch. Now my former boyfriend has asked me to go back to him. He's very kind and unselfish, and I still care for him, but I'm more attracted to the other man. What do you think?

I understand your very natural concern but I doubt very much whether he will appreciate any help you want to give him. My advice is: don't interfere. This is something he must and will sort out on his own.

SHY

Every time I meet a girl, I start to blush. One girl I know meets my mother often and I feel relaxed with her, but when we meet at a party or at the pub, I'm too shy to say anything. I'd like to get to know her best friend, but I feel they are just laughing at me. I'm so embarrassed – how do I get over this?

You must first of all ask yourselves if your fears are exaggerated. She might seem bossy, but don't forget that others will realise this too. You could talk to your boss, but remember that people like this are usually lonely. How about inviting her out for a drink? Maybe she's nicer than you imagine.

INTOLERABLE

I find myself in an intolerable situation. My wife is so houseproud that I don't feel at home in my own house. Her mother who lives with us keeps interfering in our private lives. My daughter hardly ever speaks to me (when she does, she's rude) and her friends treat this place like a hotel. Now I've become very fond of a neighbour, and I'm sure she feels the same way about me. Should I leave while I'm young enough to enjoy myself?

Everyone has this problem at some time or other, and I do sympathise. But don't think that everyone is always talking about you! Have you thought of joining a local club, or going to evening classes? In this way, you'll meet new faces, but not just for social reasons. And the sooner you stop worrying, the sooner you'll have the confidence to talk to the girl you like.

BOSSY

My friend and I work in an office which is not very exciting but we manage to enjoy ourselves. But we have to put up with the behaviour of a colleague who thinks she's superior to us in every way, telling us to type her letters for her, checking on when we arrive and leave, etc. We've tried to ignore her, but recently she's been working very closely with our employer, and we're sure she's criticising us so that she can show how efficient she is. Now we're afraid of losing our jobs. What do you think we should do?

You sound a very sensitive and sensible person, and I'm sure you will do the right thing. Your friend must be very unhappy, and in the circumstances, you are probably the last person to be able to help. But contact the family, and try to arrange a meeting to discuss the matter and show that you're not as disagreeable as her father thinks. Ultimately, she is the only one who can make the decision.

DISAPPROVING

I'm planning to go abroad where I've got the chance of an exciting new career. I want my girlfriend to come with me, but her father disapproves of me. He's a violent man, and I think he drinks too much. Sometimes my girlfriend has red eyes and bruises; she says she's tired or has fallen over. She's old enough to live her own life but I don't want to force her to do anything she may regret. I love her very much, and only want to do the best for her. The question is, what?

You don't say if you have much of a life outside the house. It's a good idea to get out as much as possible and show your independence. Are you quite sure that you are the cause of his unpleasant attitude? Perhaps there is something worrying him at the moment which you don't know about. In any case, you should talk to him about your feelings. You might be imagining things.

CAUTIOUS

My son has got to know a charming young lady who often visits me to chat and talk about herself, as she comes from a rather troubled home. He never says anything about his feelings but I feel that he is not brave enough to ask her out. He never asks her to visit but he obviously enjoys her company. How do I encourage him to be a bit more bold?

You have obviously thought about all this very carefully, and I'm sure the situation is difficult. But is it all so intolerable that any change will be for the better? As for your proposed new life, can you be sure that it is going to be so very different from your old one? I suggest that you get to know this new friend better before you decide anything.

UNWANTED

My son-in-law is making the autumn of my life very difficult. I live with him and my daughter because my husband died three years ago and I had to sell our house. My daughter is very kind, and I know it can't be easy to have an old person around the house. But her husband is always rude to me, particularly when I try to comfort my granddaughter who is often upset by his awful behaviour. It is hard for me to leave, but I sometimes wonder if that would be the best thing to do.

It is very hard to start a new life in a close community like yours. The newcomer is obviously interested in you all because she wants to make friends. You may think she should mind her own business, but she certainly deserves some sympathy and it's important not to hurt her feelings. Why don't you try talking to her son? He might be able to make her understand without offending her.

READING ALOUD

a) Listen to part of the radio programme and follow the tapescript below. As you listen, mark those words which are stressed with a dot •. These are usually the most important words in the text.

EVE SCOTT: How old are you, Annie?
ANNIE: I'm nineteen.
EVE SCOTT: And Geoff?
ANNIE: Twenty-four.
EVE SCOTT: And if you go to America, what will you do there?
ANNIE: Well, Geoff thinks he's got a job. He met some musicians from the States last year when they were over here on holiday. They've stayed in touch and they've invited him and his friend Mark to join a band they're forming.
EVE SCOTT: Yes, but what will *you* do?
ANNIE: Well, I'll be with Geoff, and perhaps I'll get a job as a secretary, because I work in an office at the moment. But I'm a bit shy really, and I'm not very good at interviews. I wouldn't mind looking after kids, or something like that.

b) Now practise reading the text aloud with a partner. Change roles when you have finished. Listen carefully for the stressed syllables in longer words, e.g. *musicians*. You can mark these as well, with a line ¯.

DISCUSSION

a) What do you think Annie should do?

b) All the characters in the magazine problem page are mentioned by Annie during the phone-in. Decide who is writing about whom.

c) There are photographs of four of these people opposite. Name the people in the photographs and give your reasons.

Example: *I think this one is Mrs Spencer, because she's middle-aged and she looks very sympathetic.*

ROLE PLAY

a) Choose one of the characters in the photographs and discuss Annie's problem from his or her point of view.

b) **New information.** Now listen to Eve Scott's advice and take notes on the suggestions she gives.

c) Continue the role play by giving your opinions on Eve Scott's advice.

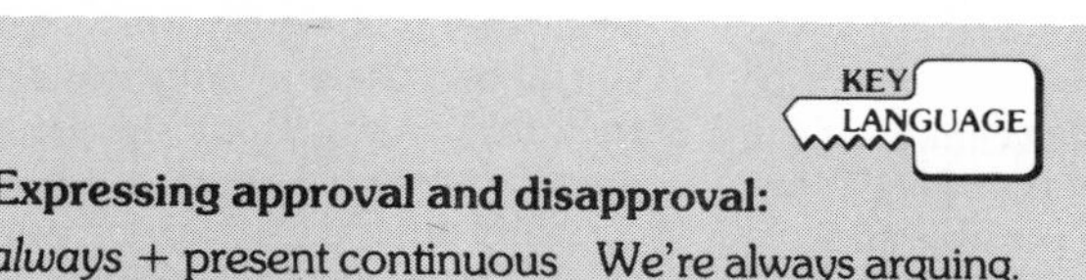

KEY LANGUAGE

Expressing approval and disapproval:

always + present continuous	We're always arguing.
keep + -ING	She keeps interfering.
such (a) + (adjective) noun	You talk such nonsense.
so + adjective	She's so houseproud.

KEY LANGUAGE

Giving advice:
If I were you, I'd . . .
Why don't you . . . ?
How about + -ING . . . ?
What about + -ING . . . ?
Try + -ING . . .
You (really) ought to/should . . .
Have you thought of + -ING . . . ?
You must . . .
You could . . .
My advice is . . .
I suggest (that) you . . .

EXAM PRACTICE

PAPER 1: READING COMPREHENSION

Section A

Suggestions for the exam
In the exam you will have about 15–20 minutes to complete this section. Try and answer every question; you can always make an intelligent guess if you are not sure by eliminating those choices which are not possible and then deciding between those that remain. Remember to read through your answers before going on to the next section. Above the questions are the instructions you will see on the exam paper. Read them now, but read them again during the exam.

Instructions
In this section you must choose the word or phrase which best completes each sentence. For each question, 1 to 25, *indicate on your answer sheet* the letter A, B, C or D against the number of the question.

1 She's ________ interrupting me while I'm talking.
A sometimes B never C always D just

2 He was ________ by his son's behaviour.
A shy B embarrassed C nervous
D impatient

3 When it started to snow he ________ his overcoat.
A put on B put in C took off D took out

4 He's only in his twenties but he's already going ________.
A smooth B bare C bony D bald

5 She's ________ a kind person that she can never say no to anyone.
A so B quite C very D such

6 He ________ a policeman; he's much too short.
A can't be B must be C looks like
D should be

7 The student worked ________ a barman during his holidays.
A at B as C like D as if

8 When it's very hot, you may ________ the top button of your shirt.
A untie B undress C unwrap D undo

9 I was ________ by my telephone bill.
A anxious B shocked C bad-tempered
D serious

10 It's a smart restaurant and men have to wear a ________.
A coat B blouse C dress D jacket

11 He left his ________ at the station and went sight-seeing.
A handbag B purse C case D sack

12 He's so ________ about his success that he doesn't like to talk about it.
A thoughtful B modest C honest
D sincere

13 He forgot how ________ he was and hit his head on the low doorway.
A tall B high C large D great

14 I haven't seen my aunt for ages; I suppose I ________ go and see her.
A ought B need C needn't D ought to

15 After her diet, she looked very ________ and healthy.
A thin B skinny C hungry D slim

16 You'll have to ________. I can't hear you at all.
A cry B call C shout D scream

17 He was so wet after the storm that he went upstairs to ________ his clothes.
A change B alter C wear D put on

18 She was so depressed that there was ________ I could do to cheer her up.
A something B anything C nothing
D everything

19 He lives ________ in his bachelor flat in Mayfair.
A lonely B lone C himself D alone

20 It ________ to me that her ideas are very good.
A thinks B seems C agrees D looks

21 Her ________ in her work is very encouraging.
A interest B attention C thought
D concern

22 When her father retired, her ________ brother took over the company.
A older B eldest C oldest D old

23 She wore a beautiful ________ of pearls round her neck.
A string B ring C band D bracelet

24 He arrived wearing a suit, but he put on his ________ when he went into the workshop.
A underclothes B overcoat C overalls
D overwork

25 I think it would be ________ to take an umbrella.
A sensitive B thoughtful C understanding
D sensible

PAPER 3: USE OF ENGLISH

Section A, Question 1

Suggestions for the exam
In the exam you will have about 25–30 minutes to do this question. Above the text are the instructions you will see on the exam paper. Read them now, but don't forget to read them again during the exam. Then read the text ***all*** *the way through before you begin, to try and get the general sense. You will probably think of a number of possible answers, but you can check them by deciding if the missing word is a noun, a verb, an adjective, etc. Then choose a word which will fit more or less in the context. Finally decide whether the word is* ***appropriate*** *in the general sense of the text. When you have finished, read through the text again and see if it all makes sense!*

Instructions
Fill each of the numbered blanks in the following text. Use only *one* word in each space.

He came to the café every day at four o'clock, sat down ________ (1) the same corner table, and ordered black coffee and ________ (2) bacon sandwich. No one knew who he was, and no one ________ (3) asked. We ________ (4) him 'Topper' because ________ (5) the hat he always ________ (6), but his ________ (7) name, as we discovered later, was Jamieson. He looked ________ (8) a painter or a musician ________ (9) had known better days. He was obviously ________ (10) a rich man, but his old clothes were elegant. He had a neat grey moustache ________ (11) curled up at the ends, and his brown ________ (12) were kind. He was always alone.

And then, one autumn day, he was joined by a young woman. Topper ________ (13) to be very anxious and he drank several ________ (14) of black coffee. Suddenly, he got ________ (15) and walked out of the café, leaving his companion to pay the ________ (16). We never saw him ________ (17).

A few days later, ________ (18) police were asking questions ________ (19) a man wearing a grey top-hat. Apparently he had shot his wife. We were shocked and puzzled, because he didn't look ________ (20) if he could hurt a fly.

PAPER 4: LISTENING COMPREHENSION

Suggestions for the exam
In the exam you will be asked questions on a number of recorded texts, which may include radio-type sequences of news or features, situational dialogues, announcements, etc. There will be a variety of question types, such as blank-filling, labelling, re-ordering, and multiple choice selection. Some of the questions will test general comprehension; others will refer to specific points in the text. You will have time to look at the questions on your question paper, and you will normally hear each piece twice. So ***don't*** *panic if you aren't sure of the answers after the first hearing!*

Instructions
For questions 1–6 fill in the information you hear on the form below. Number 1 has been filled in for you.

DESCRIPTION OF LOST BAGGAGE

1 Surname: TAIT Initial: P Mr/Mrs/Miss
2 Passenger from ________
to ________
via ________
3 Flight No: ________
4 Departure date: ________ Time: ________
5 Arrival date: ________ Time: ________
6 When was the item of baggage last seen by the owner?
____

For each of the questions 7–9 put a tick (✓) in one of the boxes, A, B, C or D.

7 What colour is the missing suitcase?

A greenish
B greyish
C blue-ish
D brownish

8 How big is it?

A small
B medium-sized
C large
D bulky

9 How many shirts did Tait pack?

A a couple
B about six
C about twelve
D He doesn't know.

PAPER 5: INTERVIEW

Part (iii)

Suggestions for the exam
The third part of the interview will involve **one** *of the following activities:*

- *A straightforward situation is outlined in which you are expected to ask specific questions or make comments encouraged by spoken or written prompts. Since the exercises will be based on conventional situations (e.g. customer talking to sales assistant), you must remember that the language should be formal and polite. You will not have a choice, but for practice, three examples are given in 1 below.*
- *Finding out information, such as the name of a town, a person, etc., by asking questions with Yes/No answers. ('Twenty Questions')*
- *Giving definitions or opinions on specific topics, e.g. electric irons, ice cream.*
- *Discussion of specific 'problem' situations, giving opinions and suggesting a possible solution.*
- *A short talk on a topic of general interest (see example 2 below). You will be given a few minutes to prepare this topic, and you will be expected to talk for 3 or 4 minutes and then answer a few questions in a general discussion. Write your ideas down in note form; you will not have time to prepare enough ideas in connected sentences, and marks will be deducted if the examiner sees that you are reading your script.*
- *Discussion of one of the optional prescribed texts.*

It is possible that you will be examined in groups of three for this part of the interview, if not for the whole interview.

1 You ask a colleague or someone at your school to meet a relative of yours at the station.

Explain: When he or she is coming
Where he or she is coming from
What he or she looks like
Where to bring/take him or her

You are invited to a formal party by people you do not know very well. Thank them and accept the invitation.

Ask about: Dress
Time the party starts
Possibility of bringing a friend

You are in a shop and you wish to try on an article of clothing.

Ask about: Price, size, type of material
Availability of another size, colour
Changing rooms

Having tried on the garment, you decide not to buy it. Explain why.

2 Prepare a short talk on one of the following subjects:

The father's role in the family
Women's fashion in your country
Your favourite actor or actress

UNIT 2

TIME OFF

A TALKING ABOUT LIKES AND DISLIKES, AND MAKING COMPARISONS

TALKING POINT

Look at these objects. What hobbies or leisure activities are they used for? Think of a leisure activity and mime it to the others in the group. Think about how you spend your free time. Ask the others what they do in their free time.

Does anybody have an unusual hobby? Do you know of anybody who has an unusual way of spending their free time?

KEY LANGUAGE

Asking about likes and dislikes:

What do you like doing in your free time?
(How) do you like / *What do you think of* + noun/-ING?
Do you ever + infinitive?
Do you mind + noun/-ING?

Talking about likes:

I (do)/(really) like/enjoy/love/adore + noun/-ING
I'm (very) fond of / *I'm (really) looking forward to* + noun/-ING

Talking about dislikes:

I don't like/hate/can't stand/can't bear + noun/-ING
There's nothing I hate more than + noun/-ING

Expressing preferences:

I prefer + noun/-ING
I'd sooner/rather + infinitive

READING

Look at the extract opposite from a survey on leisure activities published in a consumer magazine in Britain. Find the answers to the following questions.

Which leisure activity/activities

1 is the most expensive?
2 is the cheapest?
3 is the most time-consuming?
4 encourage the whole family to join in?
5 are the best for meeting people?
6 can help you save money?
7 is the most relaxing?
8 attract both men and women?

BOATING

Mostly men, particularly 35 to 55

Time spent: 10 hours a week; almost a third did it all year

Running costs: £410 a year

Family participation: Most wives, all husbands, many children

Exceptional for: Most read books and buy magazines, belong to a club and enter competitions

Hints: Gain experience crewing before buying a boat; buy a second-hand inexpensive boat

Comments: 'Never leave the boat in an emergency until it leaves you'

'Be prepared to spend 2 out of 3 annual holidays involved in it'

CAR MECHANICS

All men, mostly 25 to 55

Time spent: 3½ hours a week

Running costs: £105 a year (but you save on garage bills)

Family participation. Some sons, a very few wives

Exceptional for: Having financial spin-offs; most read books and magazines; some time spent in less enjoyable aspects (cleaning up?)

Hints: Buy a workshop manual, don't be afraid to ask for advice, make notes when you take things apart

Comments: 'The only way to learn is through expensive mistakes and losing lots of skin from knuckles'

DANCING

(from ballroom and ballet to morris and square dancing)

Men and women, mostly over 35

Time spent: 5 hours a week

Running costs: £118 a year

Family participation: Most wives, many husbands and a few daughters; but very few sons

Exceptional for: Most belong to a club and attend classes; good for meeting people; satisfying without taking too much time

Hints: Join a club; take beginners' classes; don't feel shy, get discouraged, or take it too seriously

Comments: 'As a single female one does not feel at all out of place going Scottish dancing!'

'My mother made me go'

FISHING (all types)

Nearly all men, most started when under 15

Time spent: 7 hours a week

Running costs: £129 a year

Family participation: A few wives; many sons, but very few daughters

Exceptional for: Being relaxing; many belong to a club

Hints: Don't spend too much on equipment to start with; be patient

Comments: 'There is competitiveness between you and the fish'

'More equipment is produced to catch fishermen than fish'

'It is a reason to be in the air, to walk to remote lakes and rivers, to understand water life . . .'

SKIING

Men and women; mostly under 55

Time spent: About 6 hours a day for less than one month in year

Running costs: £573 a year, but this includes part of annual holiday

Family participation: Most wives, all husbands; many sons and daughters

Exceptional for: Can be risky; physically taxing; some time spent in less enjoyable aspects (queuing for lifts?)

Hints: Get fit before going, hire equipment at first, then buy boots

Comments: 'You don't improve if you don't fall down'

'It also helps to be rich with plenty of available holiday time'

SWIMMING

Men and, particularly, women

Time spent: 3 hours a week

Running costs: £56 a year

Family participation: Most husbands, many wives, sons and daughters

Exceptional for: Good for health, satisfying without taking too much time

Hints: Start as young as possible, have tuition at first; go regularly; use public baths at off-peak times

Comments: 'It also does away with "hanging around street corners with nothing to do"'

'I swim lunch times about 2 miles per week. Thus achieving maximum exercise in minimum time'

TENNIS

Men and women (but more men) up to 65

Time spent: 6 hours a week

Running costs: £79 a year

Family participation: Many wives and sons; some husbands and daughters

Exceptional for: Most belong to a club; good for meeting people; physically taxing

Hints: Start young; join a club, get proper coaching; play regularly

Comments: 'Sometimes you can play a shot as well as Borg (but not quite as often)'

'. . . there is a crying need for indoor courts'

WINE/BEER MAKING

Mostly men

Time spent: 2 hours a week

Running costs: £51 a year

Family participation: Many wives and husbands: a very few sons

Exceptional for: Most read books; satisfying without taking too much time; a portion of time spent is less enjoyable (cleaning up?)

Hints: Start with a kit; take great care with sterilisation; keep careful records so success can be repeated; be patient – keep for as long as possible before drinking

Comments: 'Do not tell your friends it is home-made until they are on the second bottle!'

LANGUAGE PRACTICE

1 Make sentences comparing the leisure activities shown on page 23.

Examples: *Skiing is the most expensive activity.*
Fishing is more relaxing than tennis.

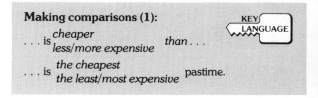

Making comparisons (1): KEY LANGUAGE

. . . is *cheaper* / *less/more expensive* *than . . .*

. . . is *the cheapest* / *the least/most expensive* pastime.

2 Write a short description of a leisure activity which you enjoy, using the survey notes as a model.

3 Listen to these four people talking about their favourite pastimes. In each case, decide which activity they're talking about.

4 a) The diagram below gives some information about a number of hobbies and leisure activities. Does your hobby appear among the examples? If not, where should it go?

b) Place the activities mentioned in the survey and in the listening text on the diagram.

c) Place the following activities on the diagram: KEY VOCABULARY

judo	watching TV	football
yacht racing	bird-watching	riding
cooking	flower arranging	hang-gliding

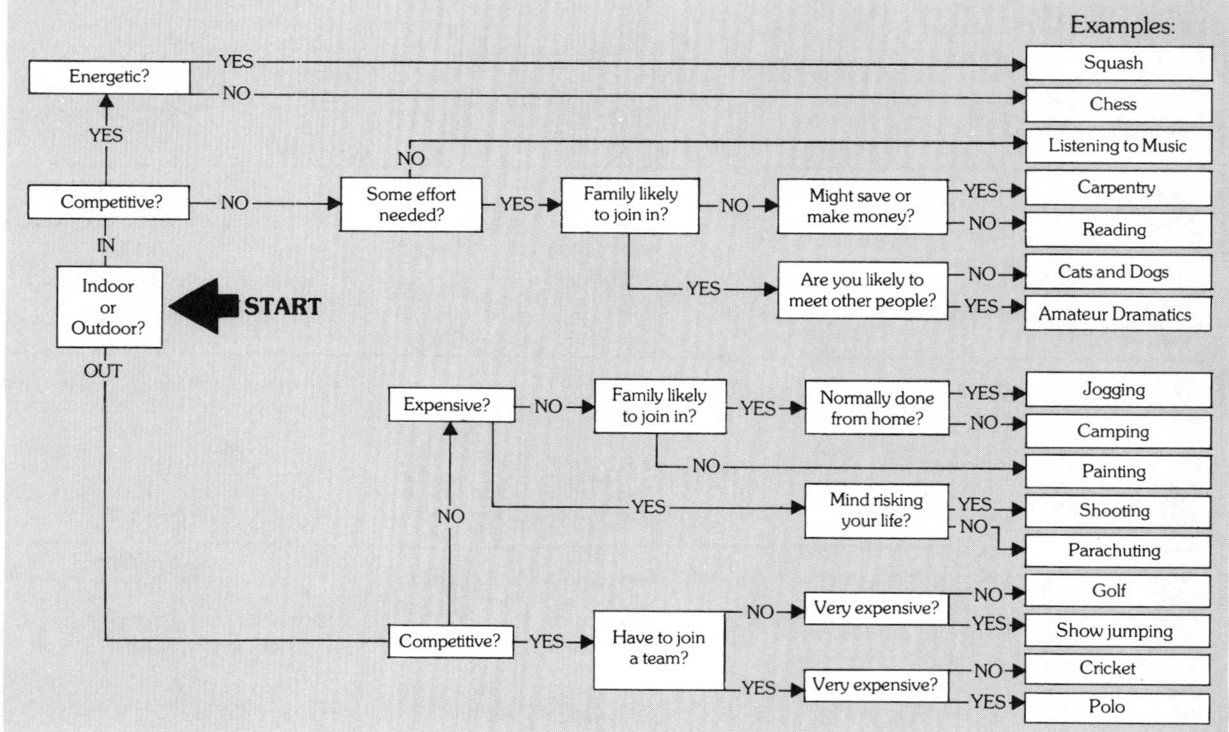

5 a) In no more than ten questions, try and guess the favourite hobbies or pastimes of the others in your group. They can only answer 'yes' or 'no'.

b) Which is the most popular pastime in the group?

c) What do you think is the most popular pastime in your country?

6 a) Read the following sentences and decide what type of word is missing. Is it a noun, a verb, an adjective or a gerund (-ING form)? Choose the missing word from the list below.

KEY VOCABULARY

record	sail	programme
match	joke	novel
sketch	tour	opera
print	frame	amateur
fishing	museum	player
cards	humorous	bet
relaxing	tent	review
film	fiction	circus

1 Reading is the best way I know of ______.
2 I can't take any more photos as I've run out of ______.
3 The local ______ dramatic society is performing in the village hall tonight.
4 He's gone to watch the football ______ at the stadium.
5 No, I prefer light reading, something ______ to make me laugh.
6 Have you got the latest ______ by John Fowles? It's just been published.
7 He loves ______ but he never catches anything.
8 I usually invite some friends for a game of ______ at least once a week.
9 We only went to see it because it had a very good ______ in the paper.
10 We love camping, but the ______ is too small for the whole family.
11 That horse is the favourite to win the race. I'll put a ______ on it.
12 The local artist has drawn a delightful ______ of the village.

b) Some of these words can be two parts of speech; for example, they can be nouns *and* verbs.

Example: *Could you lend me your new Supertramp* **record**?
They're going to **record** *the music of their latest tour.*

Which other words above can be two parts of speech?

c) Some words can have more than one meaning.

Example: *He's gone to watch the football* **match** *at the stadium.*
She struck a **match** *and lit a cigarette.*

Which other words above have more than one meaning? Use your dictionary if necessary.

DISCUSSION

In the future, machines will do most of our routine work, and we will have more time to ourselves. Are you looking forward to this?
How will you spend your free time?
Do you think that the government should develop more leisure facilities?

Making predictions about the future (1):

KEY LANGUAGE

I (don't) think / expect / suppose / imagine I'll . . .
I'll probably . . .
I probably won't . . .

B EXPRESSING CRITICAL OPINION AND MAKING INVITATIONS

READING

Events on this week

FILMS

The French Lieutenant's Woman: The complicated but highly enjoyable novel by John Fowles is successfully transformed into a beautiful and well-directed film. With great attention to the detail of the nineteenth-century setting, the story shows the social and moral restrictions of Victorian life against the background of a twentieth-century love affair. See it and then read the book again. Filmcenta, Charing Cross Road, 7.30 p.m.

Pink Floyd – The Wall: The best selling record and the sensational stage show is turned into a film of very little subtlety by Alan Parker's excited and violent direction. The story is developed by the songs, Gerald Scarfe's animations and a series of images taken from documentary films, old commercials, and news reports. Probably better to buy the album. Empire, Leicester Square, 9.25 p.m.

MUSIC

Rolling Stones: Twenty years on and the Stones are still rolling! This is their first concert for six years in Britain, as part of a two-month European tour. The band still plays the songs that made them so popular with the same energy as before, but it's Mick Jagger who attracts the crowds as surely the most spectacular rock artist on stage at the moment. In case they don't play for another six years in this country, go and see them on Friday and Saturday at 9 p.m. at Wembley Stadium.

Musical Youth: Many music lovers would think that a group whose players are so young hardly deserves to be taken seriously. But they all play their own instruments and they *do* show a real skill in writing and arranging their songs. Well worth seeing. Battersea Arts, all this week, at 8 p.m.

THEATRE

Guys and Dolls: The long-awaited revival of this masterpiece which shows the American Dream in its most romantic as well as most depressing light. It is a triumphant success not just because of the four stunning lead performers, but also because of the rest of the cast who dance with such energy that you are tired out just watching them. Olivier, Monday–Thursday at 7.15 p.m.

Pirates of Penzance: The real fans of Gilbert and Sullivan's operas will see this as a clumsy imitation of the original, and after its very successful run in New York, the London production sometimes goes a little too far with its energetic and disrespectful interpretation. But in the end, you cannot help being delighted by the superb staging and the enthusiasm of the performers. Drury Lane, Evenings 7.30 p.m., matinees on Wednesday and Saturday at 3 p.m.

KEY VOCABULARY

a) Choose the best alternative to the following words from the text.

1 COMMERCIALS
A magazines B posters C advertisements D shops

2 POPULAR
A current B general C well-liked D common

3 ARTIST
A actor B performer C painter D comedian

4 SKILL
A ability B experience C knowledge D talent

5 CAST
A band B company C crew D group

6 IMITATION
A repetition B reflection C model D copy

Now decide whether the following statements are true or false.

7 The reviews are taken from an American newspaper.

8 The novel *The French Lieutenant's Woman* is based on the film of the same name.

9 The review of *The Wall* suggests that it's a very good film.

10 The Rolling Stones are playing in a number of different countries.

11 Musical Youth are playing every day.

12 *Guys and Dolls* is a new musical.

13 The production of *The Pirates of Penzance* will disappoint the real fans of Gilbert and Sullivan.

14 There are no evening performances of the opera on Wednesday and Saturday.

b) For each review, make notes on the following:

event
place and time
opinion (acting, direction, etc.)

LANGUAGE PRACTICE

1 What's on in your town at the moment? Discuss with a partner which films, plays, groups, etc. are worth seeing.

Look in the newspaper, and find out which events are reviewed. Do you usually agree with the reviewers?

Expressing opinions (2):

KEY LANGUAGE

Personal

I've never seen such (a) + (adjective) noun
What (a) + (adjective) noun
I thought . . .
I did think . . .

I liked . . .
I did like . . .
It's well / really / not (really) worth + -ING

Impersonal

It's said/meant to be . . .
Apparently, it's . . .
Everyone says it's . . .

2 Listen to members of the audience at the annual International Entertainment Awards talking about who they think will win this year's Best Film Award.

a) In each case decide what type of film they're talking about, choosing from the list below.

KEY VOCABULARY

western	comedy
thriller	science fiction film
horror film	musical

b) Listen again and fill in the table below. Some of it has already been filled in.

Title of Film	*Type*	*Opinion*	*Comment*
A.D. 1999		writing - excellent brilliantly imaginative	
What Goes Up			Highly amusing
Two Hearts As One	Musical		
Western Sunset			
The Beast In Us All			
The Sicilian Connection			

c) Rewrite the following sentences using an adverb and a past participle.

Example: The writing was excellent.
It was excellently written.

1 The direction was very clever.
2 The staging was brilliant.
3 The photography was beautiful.
4 The design was magnificent.
5 The acting was superb.

d) Look at the following words and put a plus (+) if you think they are favourable, and a minus (−) if you think they are unfavourable. Use your dictionary if necessary.

appalling	careless	tasteful
unimaginative	outstanding	boring
remarkable	clumsy	dull
delightful	sensitive	powerful
impressive	depressing	
awkward	exciting	

GUIDED WRITING ACTIVITY

1 a) Write a short review of one of your favourite films, using some of the vocabulary and phrases from Language Practice 2.

Remember to mention: the type of film
what you most like about it
a particularly enjoyable scene
a final comment

b) Listen to the presentation of the award for the Best Film.

c) Your favourite film is this year's winner of the Best Film Award. Write the speech you will give when you present the director with the award.

Remember to include: opening remarks
why you chose this film as winner
a description of a scene you particularly enjoyed
concluding remarks
the presentation

Making a speech/Giving a talk (1)

Opening remarks:

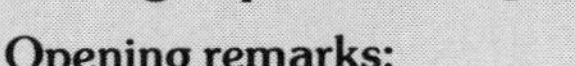

Good morning/afternoon/evening, ladies and gentlemen . . .
I'm delighted/very pleased to be here to . . .
It's my great pleasure to be here today to . . .
I'm here today to . . .

Summing up (1):
So, to finish, I'd just like to say . . .
In conclusion, ladies and gentlemen . . .
So the moment we've all been waiting for . . .
Well, I won't go on any longer!

Making a presentation:
On behalf of . . .
I'm delighted/very pleased to present you with this . . .
As a token of our respect/thanks, . . .
I hope you'll accept this award/trophy/cup/token of our respect . . .

2 a) Listen to the acceptance speech made by the director of the winning film.

b) You are a film director who is hoping to win the Best Film Award. Prepare an acceptance speech just in case!

Remember to include: your thanks for the award
your delight in receiving the award.
your pleasure in working with your colleagues
concluding remarks

Making a speech/Giving a talk (2)

Thanking (1):
I should like to thank . . . for . . .
I should like to take this opportunity to say thank you to . . .
I'm very grateful for . . .
Thank you from the bottom of my heart.

C DESCRIBING HABITS AND GIVING ADVICE

READING

SPORT FOR ALL

Take a walk round your local park – slowly now, there's no need to overdo things! If you feel a little breathless, sit down and have a look around you. If all you can see is one or two people taking a breath of fresh air, a dog playing with a stick, the trees and the birds, you can relax; the health and fitness craze has yet to reach your town. But the chances are that you will be surrounded by people running, playing football, and doing the kind of exercise usually reserved for athletes at the Olympic Games! You now have a choice: either you can light up another cigarette and find the nearest bar, or you can join in.

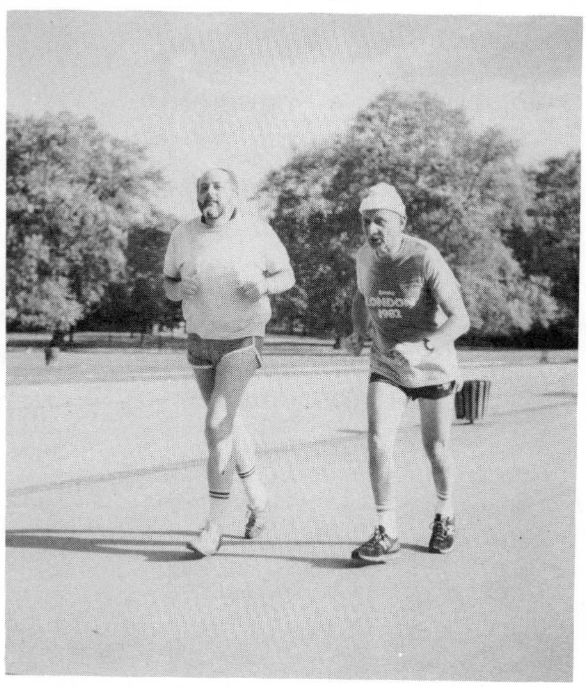

'If you can't beat them, join them', as the saying goes, and you certainly won't be in the minority if you do. In the last ten years, recreational sport has become extremely popular, and, according to doctors, is absolutely essential for a long and healthy life. In America, for example, there are now 36 million joggers and 32 million tennis-players. In 1982 the London marathon attracted over 16,000 entries, and nine out of ten of them arrived at Westminster Bridge after running 42 kilometres.

The reasons for this enormous interest in sport of all kinds are varied, but when you ask people why they spend so much time, effort, and sometimes money, they will talk about the physical benefits (feeling fit, sleeping better, the chance of living a more active life), the psychological benefits (self-discipline and respect, a sense of personal achievement) and the social advantages (meeting people with similar interests, the team spirit). However, the social aspect seems to be more important for men than for women. Very often, enjoying a drink with friends after the match is as important for the former as the physical activity itself. The latter generally see sport as a way of keeping fit rather than anything else.

Often the healthiest sports are the cheapest. If you take up jogging, for example, all you need is a T-shirt, a pair of shorts and some gym shoes. Swimming only costs you the entrance to the pool, although it's advisable to take your swimming costume with you! In Britain, sports clubs for tennis, football, basketball, judo, table tennis and squash are plentiful. You usually have to become a member, but as long as the club isn't very fashionable, it's not likely to be very expensive. It's only when the sport requires complicated equipment, or when the facilities are a long way away, that it starts to cost a lot more. Riding when you live in a city can pose problems, and it's better not to take up skiing if you're not very rich and live in a hot country with no mountains!

Whatever sport you choose, go carefully at first. You can do more harm than good if you try to run a marathon without slow and steady training. Don't forget to spend a few minutes warming up before you start. Look after any injuries, and if you're not feeling well, wait until you get better. You should see your doctor if you're over 35 and have never done much sport. And, above all, choose a sport which you'll enjoy, and not one which just makes you sweat.

So join the health and fitness craze; you'll be in very good company!

This list of sports is placed on a 100-point scale to reflect the energy used, the strength needed, and the skill required. It shows how much effort is involved, and/or how difficult it is to do well.

Sport	Points	Sport	Points
Boxing	95	Table tennis	55
Swimming	87	Skating	50
Football	79	Golf	24
Basketball	79	Rowing (slow)	20
Tennis	66	Walking	15
Jogging	63	Bowling	15
Skiing	59		

Explain what the underlined words refer to.

1 . . . you won't be in the minority if you do.
2 . . . nine out of ten of them arrived . . .
3 . . . is as important for the former . . .
4 The latter generally see sport . . .
5 . . . it's not likely to be very expensive.
6 . . . and not one which just makes you sweat.

LANGUAGE PRACTICE

1 Do you take physical exercise? What kind of exercise do you take? How often? Work in groups to produce a physical fitness survey of your class.

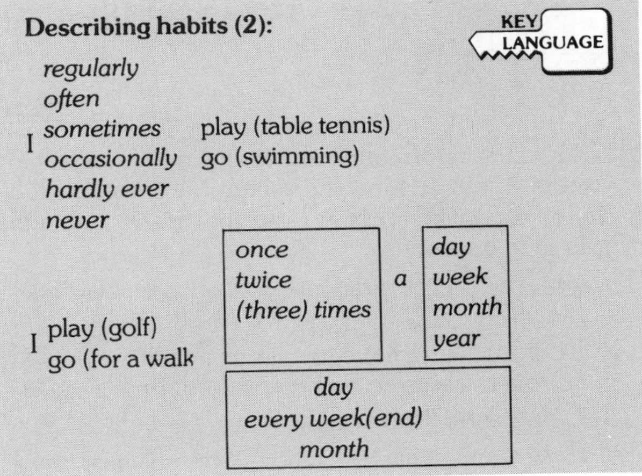
Describing habits (2):

KEY LANGUAGE

I *regularly* / *often* / *sometimes* / *occasionally* / *hardly ever* / *never* play (table tennis) / go (swimming)

I play (golf) / go (for a walk) *once* / *twice* / *(three) times* *a* *day* / *week* / *month* / *year*

every *day* / *week(end)* / *month*

2 Look at the list of sports in the text. How many compound nouns can you make by adding the words below? Some words can be used several times. Check the compounds in your dictionary.

KEY VOCABULARY

pitch	racket	boots
bat	boat	alley
rink	gloves	court
ball	pool	net
club	match	ring
course	trunks	track

Which word could be used for every sport?
Which compound has two meanings?

3 Make adjectives from the nouns opposite by adding the suffix *-ful* and/or *-less*. Check the adjectives in your dictionary. Note: In words of more than one syllable, a final *y* changes to *i* when a suffix is added.

Examples: care – care*ful*, care*less*
plenty – plenti*ful* (not *-less*)
breath – breath*less* (not-*ful*)

beauty
doubt
end
fault
fright
harm
hate
help

home
hope
mercy
pain
peace
regard
respect
sense

shape
sorrow
success
use
value
waste
wonder
worth

INTERPRETATION ACTIVITY

a) Listen to three people talking, and make notes on their age, situation, and state of health. Which sport do you think is the most suitable for each of them? What other advice would you give? Write a short paragraph for each person giving reasons for your suggestions.
Begin: *I think the student should take up . . .*

b) Using information from your physical fitness survey, discuss in groups whether you take enough physical exercise. Given your age, situation, and state of health, which sport should you take up?

D ASKING FOR AND GIVING INFORMATION

READING

a) Look at the information sheet for English-speaking visitors about leisure and cultural activities in the city of Lyon in France. Find the answers to the following questions.

1 What is there to do in Lyon on Saturday evenings?
2 Do you always have to reserve a table when you go to a restaurant?
3 Can you buy food on Sundays?
4 How can you find out where the smaller cinemas are?
5 Where can you go dancing?
6 What is there to do on Sunday afternoons?

b) Write notes about the leisure and cultural activities in Lyon.

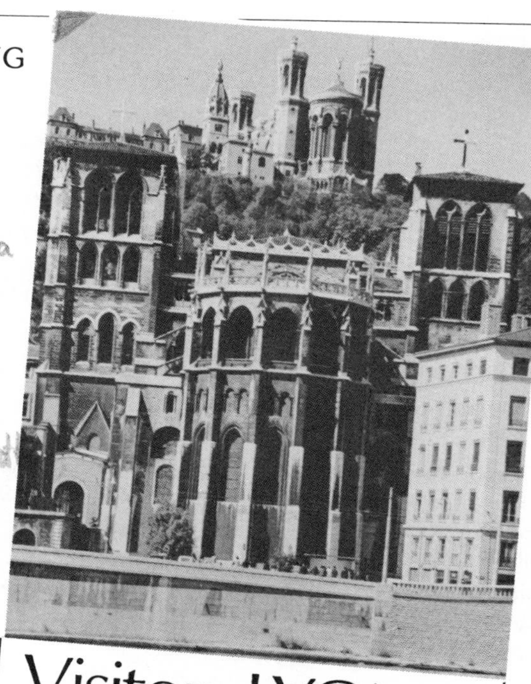

Visitez LYON ...
LYON vous étonnera.

You will be happily
surprised by LYON

TIME OFF IN LYON

LYON is one of France's oldest, largest and most important cities. As well as being the capital of the region, with a population of over a million, and a major banking and industrial centre, it also has great historical interest with its perfectly preserved Renaissance streets and fascinating Roman ruins. The city provides a wide variety of entertainment and leisure facilities; in fact, there's almost too much to do! It's impossible to give a complete list of everything you can do to make the most of your spare time in Lyon, but here are some suggestions.

Restaurants

Lyon is well known for its excellent food, a reputation which is based not only on the fact that a number of famous chefs live and work in the region, but also on the numerous little restaurants to be found everywhere in the city centre. Just go for a stroll and take your pick; the choice is enormous. Some restaurants are closed on Sundays, and it's always a good idea to book on Fridays and Saturdays.

Shopping

Try the pedestrian precincts just off the main square, or the magnificent shopping centre, which is the largest in Europe and has all you could possibly want under one roof. Whichever you choose, shopping is a wonderful experience in Lyon. Big stores are closed on Sundays and are very busy on Saturdays. Don't miss the fruit and vegetable markets on Sunday mornings.

Cinemas

There are plenty of cinemas showing the latest French and international films. But, as the home of the Lumière brothers who invented the techniques of the moving picture, Lyon also has a number of smaller cinemas which specialise in less commercial, more artistic films. They're usually hidden down little streets in the old part of town, so buy the local paper for their addresses. Programmes usually run from midday to midnight.

Nightlife

After finishing your meal, you might like to try one of the first-rate nightclubs or a discothèque. If you find nothing that appeals to you in the Old District, go along the River Saône, where by day the quayside is a sleepy suburb, but by night everybody wakes up and enjoys themselves. If you're a jazz fan, go to the Hot Club or one of the many small bars much loved by musicians and their audience. Wherever you go, Lyon is never livelier and more exciting than by night!

Music

For those of you who like classical music, Lyon has plenty to offer. The Maurice Ravel Auditorium is the home of the famous Lyon Symphony Orchestra, and there are concerts most nights of the week, particularly on Thursday and Saturday evenings. The Opera attracts some of the most famous singers and ballet dancers in the world and tickets are not at all expensive. The composer Berlioz was born nearby, and there's a concert in his honour every September.

Museums

Lovers of museums and galleries can't leave Lyon without visiting the fascinating collection of Roman treasures displayed in the striking setting of the Gallo-Roman museum built on the hillside overlooking the amphitheatres. The Museum of Fine Arts has a marvellous collection of works by the Lyon school of painters as well as a great deal of modern art. Closed Mondays.

Sport

Lyon football club is one of the best in France, and the stadium is in the south of the city. Matches in the evenings and on Sunday afternoons. If you wish to participate rather than just watch, the University campus has some very good facilities to offer.

Parks

If you need to escape from the city for a moment, go to the park on the River Rhône where you can relax in the beautiful Rose Garden, visit the zoo, or take a rowing boat on the lake for an hour or so. If you're looking for somewhere more deserted, try the park at Miribel in the north east of the city. Closes at 6 p.m. in the winter, 11 p.m. in the summer.

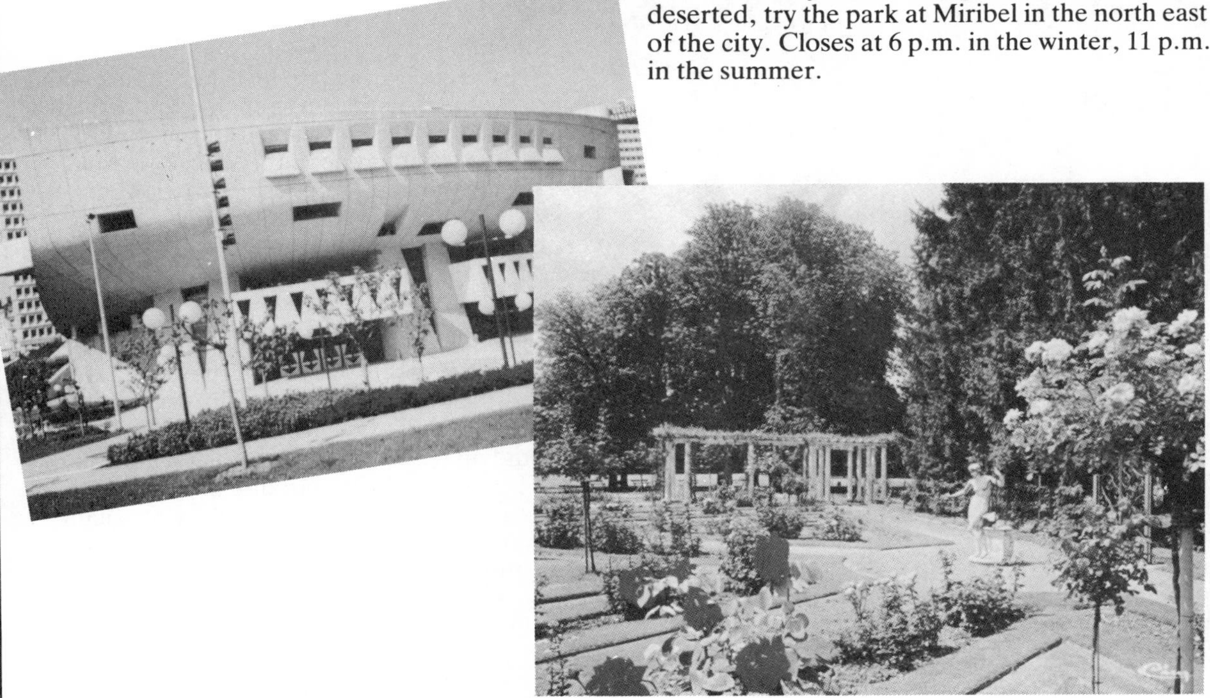

LISTENING ACTIVITY

a) Listen to the radio programme about Lyon. Look at the map and the list of places. Try and identify the places which the speakers mention. Mark the correct number against the name of each place.

b) Listen to the programme again, and take notes about any extra information on specific points which isn't mentioned in the information sheet.

c) Listen to six people talking about their impressions of Lyon. What have they just seen or done in the city?

d) The six visitors made the following comments:

KEY VOCABULARY

I was rather disappointed by the place.
Really, I was quite moved by the sight.
Frankly, I was quite bored by the performance.
I was amused by some of the jokes.
I was tempted by the seafood.
I was fascinated by some of the old portraits.

Rephrase each sentence in such a way that it means exactly the same thing, using an adjective ending in -ING.

Example: I was very interested in the Renaissance architecture.
The Renaissance architecture was very interesting.

LYON – The view from the hill

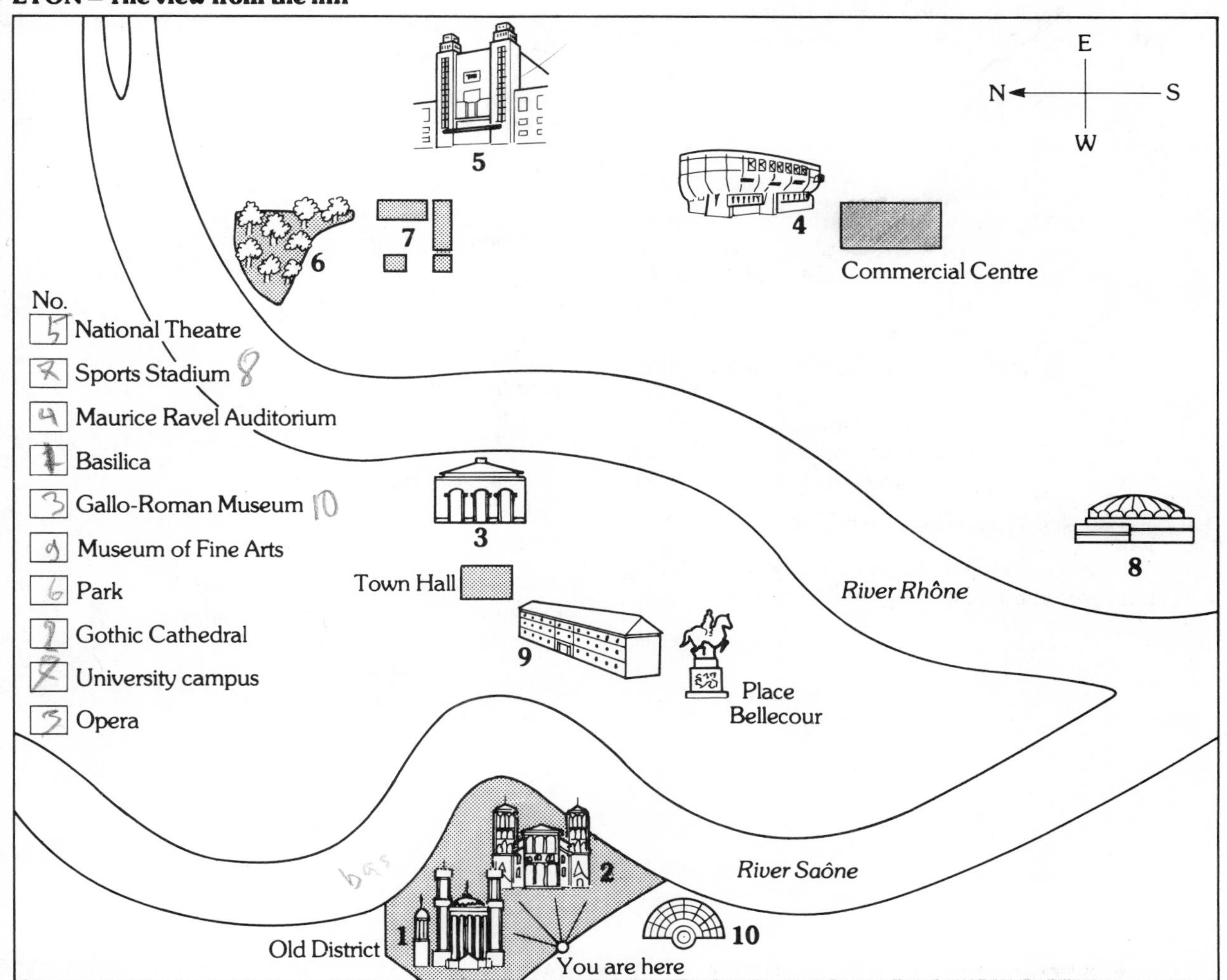

READING ALOUD

a) Listen to the first speaker and follow the tapescript below. As you listen, notice how the voice rises and falls. Mark the intonation like this ╱ if it rises on a particular word, and like this ╲ if it falls.

I must say I was rather disappointed with the place. I was told that I had to go there, particularly as I don't really like the usual tourists sights, you know, churches and museums and so on. There was certainly a great deal of choice, but it's all so expensive. I mean, can you imagine a plain blue skirt costing the equivalent of forty pounds and of such poor quality! No, tomorrow I think I'll just sit in a café and watch the world go by. I'd rather save my money until I get home.

b) Now practise reading the text aloud. Listen carefully for stressed words and syllables. Mark these in as you did in Unit 1.

DISCUSSION AND PROJECT

a) Does your town have as much to offer as Lyon? With a partner who knows the town as well as you do, write notes about its cultural and leisure activities. Think about the variety of entertainment it offers, times of opening, ticket prices, things for the visitor to buy which are typical of the town or region, etc. Use the headings that appear in the information sheet on Lyon.

b) Use these notes to prepare an information sheet about your town.

ROLE PLAY

a) You are EITHER: a tourist information officer for the town you've chosen. Use the information sheet you've prepared to answer questions about this town.

OR: a tourist seeking information about a town you don't know. Ask the tourist information officer for advice about what there is to see and do.

b) Change roles when you have finished.

c) Return to your original partner and invite him or her to take part in the activities you have chosen.

KEY LANGUAGE

Making invitations:

Would you like to . . . ?
I was wondering if you'd like/care to . . .
Why don't we . . . ?
Shall we . . . ?
What/How about | *Do you feel like* | *Do you fancy* + noun/-ING?

Accepting invitations:

Thanks, I'd love to.
That's a good idea.

Refusing invitations:

I'm sorry, I'm afraid I can't. I'm + present continuous (future arrangements)
I'm not sure, actually . . .
I don't really feel like + noun/-ING

EXAM PRACTICE

PAPER 1: READING COMPREHENSION

Section A *(Suggestions for the exam – see Unit 1)*
In this section you must choose the word or phrase which best completes each sentence. For each question, 1 to 25, *indicate on your answer sheet* the letter A, B, C or D against the number of the question.

1 In his first game for Newcastle, Keegan ________ a goal after 58 minutes.
A scored B won C earned D gained

2 During the ________ he was relaxed, but he was very nervous on the first night.
A rehearsal B repetition C performance D production

3 We're thinking of going ________ holiday to Spain.
A in B at C for D on

4 Because both teams came from the same town, the stadium was packed with ________.
A playgoers B public C spectators D audience

5 I must remember to put that dinner invitation in my ________.
A agenda B diary C record D journal

6 His roses won first ________ in the local flower show.
A cup B price C prize D reward

7 I just can't ________ the winter so I can go skiing again.
A wait for B look forward to C expect D await

8 The ________ of Turner's paintings finishes at the end of the week.
A demonstration B spectacle C exhibition D show

9 Manchester United are playing ________ Leeds this Saturday.
A with B against C opposite D facing

10 I found the last scene extremely ________ and particularly well-directed.
A pathetic B sympathetic C pitiful D moving

11 Beethoven's Seventh Symphony will be ________ by Herbert von Karajan.
A conducted B produced C directed D lead

12 I was greatly disappointed ________ the poor leisure facilities offered.
A of B by C for D against

13 The box office is open ________ for ticket sales.
A daily B a day C in day D daytime

14 The critic gave them a very ________ review.
A favourite B favourable C preferable D preferred

15 Have you been able to book us a tennis ________?
A pitch B court C field D ground

16 The Iffley Road running ________ is where the first mile under 4 minutes was run
A track B course C circle D ring

17 It was raining too hard for us to ________ up our umbrella.
A lift B put C make D turn

18 He succeeded ________ improving on his fastest time of last season.
A in B on C at D to

19 Have you finished eating, sir? Shall I bring you the ________?
A cheque B ticket C bill D addition

20 I've got to stay at home doing the decorating ________ going away on holiday.
A in spite of B instead of C because of D on behalf of

21 During the fourteen-day cruise, seven will be spent ________ sea, and seven in port.
A at B by C to D over

22 His latest novel was only ________ a few weeks ago, and it's already a bestseller.
A broadcast B printed C written D published

23 They've gone on a ________ of the Alps.
A turn B tour C route D round

24 There's nothing better than taking a ________ on the lake in the park for the afternoon.
A ship B boat C liner D cruiser

25 With every ________ he took, he got more and more tired.
A walk B march C step D foot

PAPER 3: USE OF ENGLISH

Section A, Question 1 *(Suggestions for the exam – see Unit 1)*

Fill each of the numbered blanks in the following text. Use only *one* word in each space.

When people are asked why they choose _______ (1) live in big cities, most of them usually talk about the variety of entertainment to be _______ (2) there. But I wonder how _______ (3) of them actually feel like _______ (4) to the theatre or a concert after a hard day _______ (5) the office and a crowded ride home on the Underground. And how many of them visit the famous galleries and museums other than _______ (6) they're caught in the rain without an umbrella?

Meanwhile, those tourists _______ (7) make shopping and travel _______ (8) the centre of town so difficult in the summer months, are visiting the sights which the inhabitants are so proud of, but don't quite have the time _______ (9) see. It was only _______ (10) moving to the country that I realised how to enjoy my free time. Living there _______ (11) me aware that legs are not intended simply to _______ (12) you _______ (13) your front door to your car! Evenings are filled _______ (14) little more _______ (15) a leisurely drink with friends who'd _______ (16) talk about darts than discothèques. Of course, there are days when I'm tempted _______ (17) the entertainment page of the national newspaper to go up _______ (18) town, but when you have to take the dog _______ (19) a walk across the fields, talk to the postman, and see the amateur dramatic society's latest production, you're far _______ (20) busy to find the time!

Section A, Question 4

Suggestions for the exam
You should allow yourself about 15 minutes for this exercise. Question 4 is often a completion exercise, of which the skeleton sentences below are a typical example. The sentences should be completed by putting the verbs in the correct tense (adding auxiliary verbs if necessary), and by adding words, such as articles, prepositions, and pronouns. Don't forget to read through the final version to check that it all makes sense!

Instructions
Make all the changes and additions necessary to produce, from the following eight sets of words and phrases, eight sentences which together make a complete letter. Note carefully from the example what kind of alterations need to be made.

Example: I wonder/you like/come/ballet with me/tomorrow night?

Answer: *I was wondering if you would like to come to the ballet with me tomorrow night?*

Dear Robert,

Thank you/letter/I receive/when/get home/last night.

a) ______________________________

I be pleased/hear you/after such/long time.

b) ______________________________

I love/go ballet/with you/but I/not be free/until 6.30 p.m.

c) ______________________________

How about come/my flat/and have/something/eat/before/go?

d) ______________________________

I/not want/take my car/because it be/difficult/find somewhere/park.

e) ______________________________

Why/we not go/taxi?

f) ______________________________

Let hope/dancing be/good as/reviews say.

g) ______________________________

I look forward/see you/tomorrow night.

h) ______________________________

Love,

Jackie

PAPER 4: LISTENING COMPREHENSION

(Suggestions for the exam – see Unit 1)

For questions 1–6, fill in the information you hear in the notebook below. Number 1 has been filled in for you.

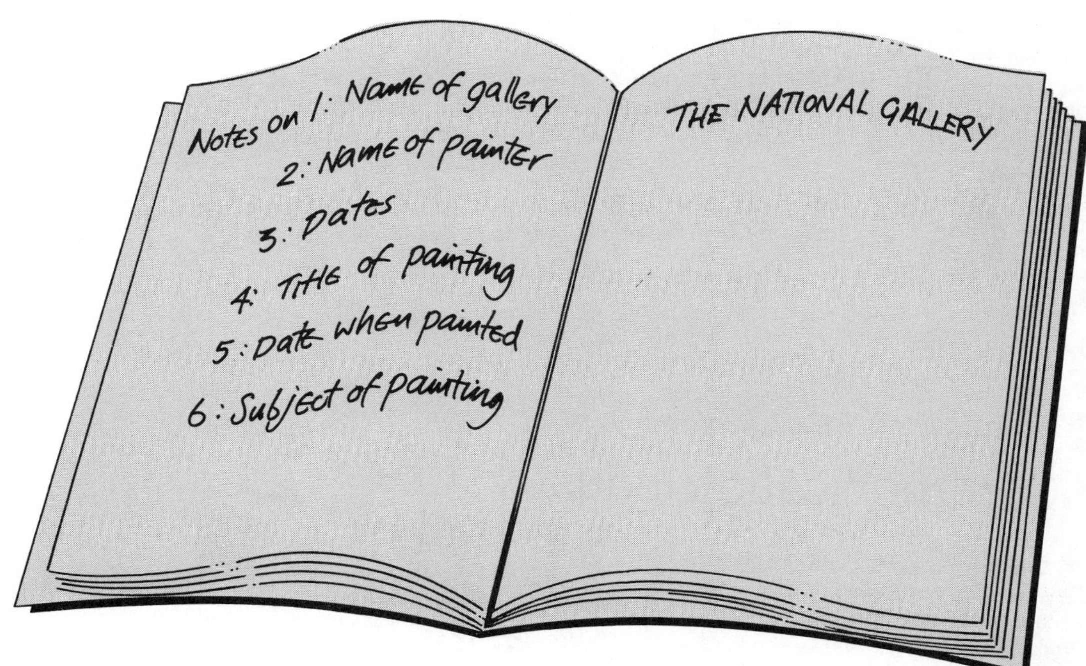

Notes on 1: Name of gallery
2: Name of painter
3: Dates
4: Title of painting
5: Date when painted
6: Subject of painting
THE NATIONAL GALLERY

For each of the questions 7–9 put a tick (✓) in one of the boxes, A, B, C or D.

7 This painting

A is Turner's first major work.
B shows one of Turner's famous sunsets.
C has a subject which is different from his other paintings.
D shows a different steam train from other paintings.

8 Turner's principal interest was

A factories and chimneys.
B colour and light.
C trains.
D the industrial age.

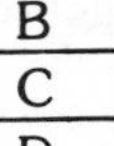

9 Turner finished this painting

A as he watched the train.
B in his studio, using studies.
C in poor weather conditions.
D just using his creative imagination.

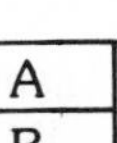

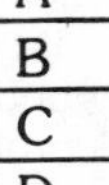

UNIT 3

THE SHRINKING WORLD

A COMPARING AND CONTRASTING

TALKING POINT

A recent survey has found that married couples in the USA spend, on average, 27½ *minutes a week* talking to each other. That's about 1% of the time the TV set is on in the typical American living room.

How much time do *you* spend talking to family or friends? (at home – on the phone – at work – in social situations)

How much time do you spend watching TV?

READING

The Communication Industry

British stamps for Information Technology Year

Clearly if we are to participate in the society in which we live we must communicate with other people. A great deal of communicating is performed on a person-to-person basis by the simple means of speech. If we travel in buses, stand in football match queues, or eat in restaurants, we are likely to have conversations where we give information or opinions, receive news or comment, and very likely have our views challenged by other members of society.

Face-to-face contact is by no means the only form of communication and during the last two hundred years the art of *mass communication* has become one of the dominating factors of contemporary society. Two things, above others, have caused the enormous growth of the communication industry. Firstly, inventiveness has led to advances in printing, telecommunications, photography, radio and television. Secondly, speed has revolutionised the transmission and reception of communications so that local news often takes a back seat to national news, which itself is often almost eclipsed by international news. The Israeli raid on Entebbe airport, Uganda, in 1976 was followed by six books about the subject and two films within months of the event.

No longer is the possession of information confined to a privileged minority. In the last century the wealthy man with his own library was indeed fortunate, but today there are public libraries. Forty years ago people used to flock to the cinema, but now far more people sit at home and turn on the TV to watch a programme that is being channelled into millions of homes.

Communication is no longer merely concerned with the transmission of information. The modern communications industry influences the way people live in society and broadens their horizons by allowing access to information, education and entertainment. The printing, broadcasting and advertising industries are all involved with informing, educating and entertaining.

Although a great deal of the material communicated by the mass media is very valuable to the individual and to the society of which he is a part, the vast modern network of communications is open to abuse. However, the mass media are with us for better, for worse, and there is no turning back.

a) 1 What examples are given of person-to-person communication?

2 What are the two main reasons for the development of mass communication?

3 Why is the cinema less popular than it was forty years ago?

4 Apart from information, what other material is communicated by the mass media?

5 Which industries are concerned with producing this material?

KEY VOCABULARY

b) Find words in the text which mean:

take part in	present-day	rich
amount	brought about	lucky
carried out	nearly	affects
turned into	a few people	enormous

LANGUAGE PRACTICE

1 These are some of the advantages and disadvantages of mass communication.

- People are much better informed than ever before.
- People are conditioned by the controllers of the media.
- Mass production has led to material of poor quality.
- A great deal of superficial material is communicated.
- A wide variety of material is available to cater for all tastes.
- Experiences previously enjoyed by the minority are available to the masses.

Make two separate lists showing the advantages and disadvantages. Can you add to the lists? Think about TV, radio, the press, and advertising.
Write sentences contrasting the advantages with the disadvantages.

Expressing contrast (1): KEY LANGUAGE

People are better informed, *but* they . . .
Although people are better informed, they . . .
People are better informed. *However*, they . . .
(*On the one hand*) people are better informed. *On the other hand*, they . . .

---

2 There are many milestones in the development of communications. Some of these are listed below.

1690 First newspaper printed regularly
1829 Typewriter invented
1830 Letters first carried by train
1876 First telephone conversation held
1886 First petrol-driven car built
1890 First moving picture made
1903 First regular airline flights began
1936 First regular TV broadcasts made

De Havilland bomber, converted for passenger flights

The first telephone

The first petrol-powered car

a) Ask each other questions about the events above.

Example: *When was the first newspaper printed regularly?*
About three hundred years ago.

b) What was life like without newspapers/typewriters/trains, etc?

What did people use to do? How is life different today?

Discuss the effect these developments had on people's way of life.

Write sentences comparing the past with the present.

Comparing past and present habits: KEY LANGUAGE

People *used* / *didn't use* *to* . . . , but *now/today* we . . .
+ present simple

We don't . . . any more/longer.
We no longer . . .

3 The table shows the division of programmes on ITV (commercial TV channel in Britain).

a) According to the table, how much TV time is given to:

news and current affairs?
children's programmes?
general entertainment?

What proportion of programmes are informative?

Compare the amount of TV time given to different types of programmes.

Which programmes are given the most/least time?

b) Use the ITV table to complete the paragraph below.

Programmes of fact and information represent ________% of ITV transmissions, a total of over ________ ________ a week. ________ programmes, comprising drama, films made specially for ________, and feature films, represent a ________ of the output. ________ and ________ account for about 20%, and sport for just over ________%.

c) What is the division of TV programmes in your country? Work in groups, and list a week's programmes for one channel. Using the ITV table as a model, work out how much time each type of programme is given. Do you think the balance of programmes is reasonable?

d) Write a paragraph describing the balance of your TV programmes using **b)** as a model. How does your TV channel compare with ITV?

WEEKLY TRANSMISSION HOURS OF THE AVERAGE ITV COMPANY 1980–81

	hrs. mins.	
INFORMATIVE		
News	10.56	10½%
Current affairs, documentaries	13.47	12¾%
Religion	2.27	2½%
Education	10.34	10¼%
Children's informative	2.22	2¼%
NARRATIVE		
Plays, drama, TV movies	24.45	24¾%
Feature films	7.23	8¼%
ENTERTAINMENT		
Children's non-factual	7.45	7¼%
Entertainment and music	13.43	13¼%
SPORT	10.07	8¼%
TOTAL ALL PROGRAMMES	103.49	100%

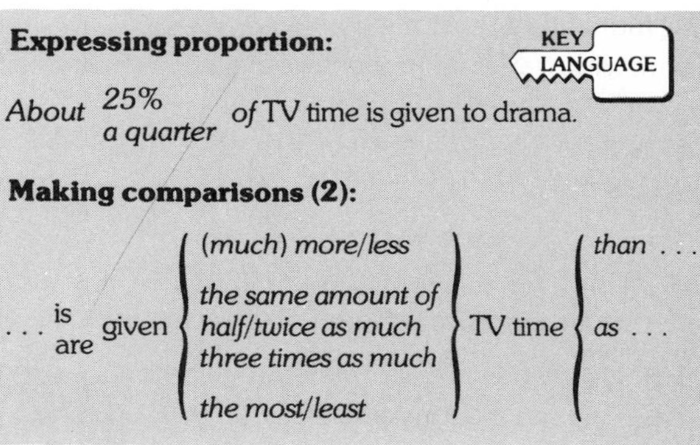
Expressing proportion: KEY LANGUAGE

About 25% / *a quarter* of TV time is given to drama.

Making comparisons (2):

. . . is / are given { (much) more/less | the same amount of | half/twice as much | three times as much | the most/least } TV time { than . . . | as . . . }

SATURDAY

ITV

8.45 T J Hooker
KING ON THE HILL
Second in this new American police drama series. Sgt T J Hooker speeds into action when he believes an old racing friend has been wrongfully arrested. Originally scheduled for transmission on Saturday 9 April.
Hooker William Shatner
Officer Romano Adrian Zmed
Cpt Sheridan Richard Herd
Rookie Stacy Sheridan Heather Locklear

9.45 Tales of the Unexpected
COLIN BLAKELY
BERNARD CRIBBINS
JUDY GEESON
THE MEMORY MAN
BY HENRY SLESAR, DRAMATISED BY DENIS CANNAN
Penniless and in danger of losing his beautiful girlfriend, ace memory man Colin Mearns tries to exploit his one asset. The first client for his advertised memory training classes is Charlie Krebs, a highly dubious character who wants to remember just one thing — the station locker number where he has left valuable property. Can Mearns help Krebs? Or is this a golden opportunity for Mearns to help himself to a quick fortune?
Colin Colin Blakely
Tobacconist John Biggerstaff
Mary Judy Geeson
Charlie Bernard Cribbins
Police Inspector John Judd
DESIGNER JANE MARTIN
DIRECTOR PETER DUFFELL
PRODUCER JOHN ROSENBERG
EXECUTIVE PRODUCER JOHN WOOLF
Anglia Television Production

Memory man Colin Mearns (Colin Blakely) can't afford to forget Mary (Judy Geeson). *Tales of the Unexpected*, 9.45.

10.15 ITN News and Sport

10.30 The Big Match
BRIAN MOORE
JIM ROSENTHAL
Featuring one of today's FA Cup semi-finals, plus news of all the other major stories.
PRODUCTION TEAM RICHARD WORTH, TONY MILLS
EDITOR JEFF FOULSER
DIRECTOR TED AYLING
London Weekend Television Production

11.30 London News Headlines
followed by

7.45 Race, Rhetoric, Rastafari
Makeda Lee, the former Barbara Blake, lived and worked in Britain in the Sixties as the first black TV reporter. Returning from Jamaica, where she has lived for the p : 9 years, she takes a loo.. at Britain from her particular perspective — as a Rastafarian. Music by Ras Messenger.
CAMERA PHILIP CHAVANNES
EDITOR KEITH LAKHAN
PRODUCER MAKEDA LEE
Jamaica Media Production

8.45 World of Animation
The Great Cognito by American animator Will Vinton, presented by Ricl ard Evans.

9.0 Malu — A Woman Now
HERE WE GO AGAIN
Malu becomes involved n an affair with Mario, an ol l friend from her marriec days. But how to overcome the difficulties, the fears, the feelings of guilt that this creates?
Malu Regina Duarte

Join *The Late Clive James* for words, wit and wisdom, 11.0

Rupert Warner Roland Curram
Cassie Manson Sheila Allen
DESIGNER FRANK NERINI
DIRECTOR/PRODUCER TONY WHARMBY
EXECUTIVE PRODUCER REX FIRKIN
London Weekend Television Production

11.0
NEW SERIES
The Late Clive James
A weekly series in which journalist and television critic Clive James takes an individual view of people and events — and invites his studio guests to explain, discuss and even argue over the topics he raises.
See page 71
RESEARCH LORNA DICKINSON, MICHELLE DE LARRABEITI, MARK REDHEAD, HELEN WRIGHT
DIRECTOR

4 The following nouns are all connected with different aspects of communications: television, the press, and telecommunications. Arrange the nouns in three groups according to topic. Use your dictionary if necessary.

KEY VOCABULARY

announcer	dial	
article	directory	
broadcast	documentary	
call	headline	receiver
channel	issue	review
circulation	magazine	telegram
code	operator	screen
column	programme	set

5 Look at the sentences below and decide what type of word is missing.

Example: *ENTERTAIN*
entertainer—concrete noun
entertainment—abstract noun
entertaining—adjective

Fill in the blanks with a suitable word formed from the word in capitals.

1 PERFORM
There was an interesting ______ of *Hedda Gabler* on TV last night.
Shirley MacLaine is a talented ______.

2 INVENT
Television was the ______ of John Logie Baird.
Gugliemo Marconi was the ______ of radio telegraphy.

3 EDUCATE
Some people think there should be more ______ programmes on TV.
There is no doubt that the mass media have improved ______ all over the world.

4 INFORM
The Times is a serious and ______ newspaper.
For further ______, telephone the airport.

5 SPEAK
The principal ______ at the conference was Dr Abbott.
The Prime Minister made a ______ on information technology.

6 RECEIVE
The shop will change undamaged goods if a ______ is shown as proof of purchase.
To make a call, pick up the ______ and wait for a dialling tone.
She turned off the car radio because the ______ was so bad.

7 VARY
The Open University in Britain broadcasts programmes on a wide ______ of subjects.
The government was criticised by ______ newspapers.

8 PRODUCE
The worldwide ______ of video cassette recorders in 1981 was 9 million.
Orson Welles is not only an actor; he is also a writer, director and ______.
If manufacturers want to sell a ______, they have to advertise it.

DISCUSSION

Which newspaper do you prefer reading? Why?
What types of TV programme do you enjoy watching most?
What is your favourite TV programme?
What effects does TV have on children?
Have you ever been influenced by a play or novel? If so, how were you influenced?
Have you ever been influenced by advertising?

B GIVING AND UNDERSTANDING INSTRUCTIONS

READING

British TELECOM **Blue Payphone**

Charges may differ slightly from other payphones
No change given from partly used coins
Only wholly unused coins returned

 **2p**  **10p**  **50p**

Have money ready **Minimum fee – 8p**

1 Lift handset
Listen for dial tone. (Continuous purring or new dial tone – high-pitched hum).

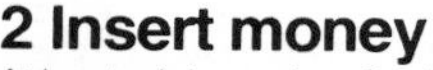

2 Insert money
At least minimum fee. Credit display stops flashing on insertion of minimum fee.

Do not insert money for operators or SOS-Emergency (999) calls.

If dial tone stops before you start to dial, press blue follow-on call button, listen for dial tone, then dial number.

3 Dial number
Listen for ringing tone. Speak when connected.

Failed call? New call with remaining credit? Do not replace handset. Press blue follow-on call button, listen for dial tone, then re-dial. (Minimum fee still applies. Insert more money if necessary)

To continue a dialled call – when you see display flashing and hear paytone (rapid pips), or anytime during call, insert more money.

4 Replace handset
Value showing on credit display is not always returnable.
Only wholly unused coins returned.

No change given from partly used coins.

Nowadays, thanks to the telephone, it is possible to have instant contact with someone on the other side of the world. Look carefully at the instructions for payphones in Britain.

Choose the best informal alternative to the following words in the payphone instructions.

KEY VOCABULARY

1 LIFT
A hold up B hold C carry D pick up

2 HANDSET
A headphone B receiver C caller D listener

3 INSERT
A put in B pay in C fill in D hand in

4 VALUE
A price B cost C worth D amount

5 WHOLLY
A fully B completely C all D mainly

6 RETURNED
A changed B put back C given back D turned back

Now choose the best answer.

7 You want to make a local call and you have a variety of coins. How much should you insert?
A 2p
B 1p, 2p and 5p
C 10p
D 50p

8 If the line is engaged, and you want to try another number, you should
A hang up and start again.
B put in more money.
C listen for the ringing tone.
D press a button and dial again.

9 You put in three 10p coins and use 16p worth. How much do you get back?
A Nothing
B 10p
C 14p
D Only new coins

LANGUAGE PRACTICE

Printed instructions like those for the payphone are usually *formal* and *impersonal*. Imperatives are used. Articles and auxiliary verbs are often omitted. Phrasal verbs are avoided.

a) Read the payphone instructions again. Imagine that you are in Britain, and a tourist has asked you how to use the payphone. Explain, using *informal* language. Remember to include the article where necessary, and use phrasal verbs where possible.

Begin: *First you pick up the receiver . . .*

b) Explain to a foreigner in your country how to make a call from a public phone.

Giving instructions: KEY LANGUAGE

Sequencers: *first, next, then, after that, finally*

Impersonal *you* + present simple.
Then you dial the number.

if/when/as soon as + clause.
If you want to go on talking, put in more money.

LISTENING ACTIVITY

Richard lives in New Orleans, USA. Sally has invited him to come and stay with her in London. He telephones her about arrangements.

a) Look at Sally's part of the conversation, and at her diary notes. Decide what Richard says.

SALLY: 435 8447
RICHARD: . . . . ?
SALLY: Speaking
RICHARD: . . . .
SALLY: Hi, Richard! How are you?
RICHARD: . . . . ?
SALLY: I'm fine too. When are you coming over?
RICHARD: . . . .
SALLY: The weekend after next! That's great. How long are you going to stay?
RICHARD: . . . . ?
SALLY: Yes, of course it's OK. My flat's enormous, and there's plenty of room. What time do you arrive in London?
RICHARD: . . . .
SALLY: Oh, that's a pity. I'd like to meet you at the airport, but I'm working till lunchtime. . . .
RICHARD: . . . . ?
SALLY: No, it's quite easy to get to, but it's a bit complicated to explain over the phone. Look, I'll write to you giving you directions from the airport. By the way, which airport do you arrive at?
RICHARD: . . . .
SALLY: OK, I'll work out the best way of getting here from Gatwick, and send the letter off today.
RICHARD: . . . .
SALLY: So am I! Till a week on Saturday, then. Bye.
RICHARD: . . . .

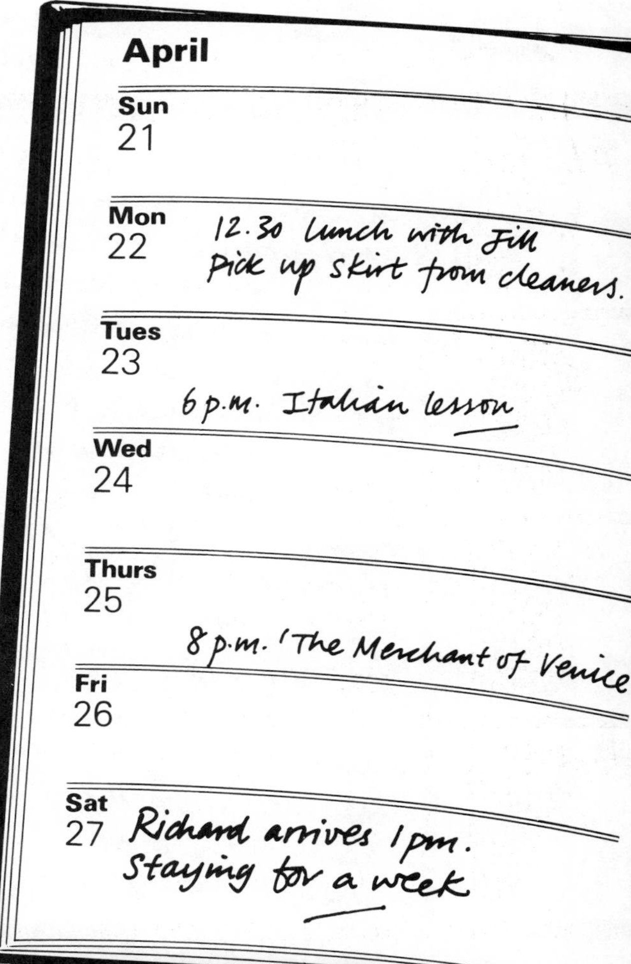
April
Sun 21
Mon 22
12.30 Lunch with Jill
Pick up skirt from cleaners.
Tues 23
6 p.m. Italian lesson
Wed 24
Thurs 25
8 p.m. 'The Merchant of Venice'
Fri 26
Sat 27
Richard arrives 1pm.
Staying for a week

b) Listen to the complete conversation and fill in Richard's part.

READING

Read Sally's letter to Richard, and make notes on how to get to her flat.

21D Antrim Road,
London NW3 2EJ

15 April 1983

Dear Richard,

It was great to hear from you again, and I'm delighted that you're coming to London for a week.

It's quite easy to get to my flat, and the best way is to come by train. First you take a train from Gatwick to Victoria in central London, which takes about forty minutes. Then you take the underground from Victoria. You should take the northbound Victoria line to Euston, where you change to the Northern line. Be careful because there are two branches going north from Euston, and you want the Edgware branch. You should get off at Chalk Farm. When you come out of the tube, turn left and walk up the hill a few hundred yards until you come to a pub called the 'Sir Richard Steele'. After that, you take the next turning on the left, and the first turning on the right into Antrim Road. I live halfway along, on the left.

I hope you can follow my directions! If you get lost, you can always telephone me. I expect it'll take you about two hours to get here from Gatwick, so you'll probably arrive some time between 3 and 4 p.m.

I'm very much looking forward to seeing you again!

with love,

Sally

GUIDED WRITING ACTIVITY

a) Make notes on how to get to your home from the nearest airport.

b) A friend from abroad is coming to stay with you and doesn't know how to get to your home. Write a letter giving clear directions based on your notes. Use Sally's letter as a model, and organise your paragraph content as follows:

Paragraph 1: Opening with reference to letter/phone call
Paragraph 2: Directions
Paragraph 3: Estimated time of arrival at your home
Paragraph 4: Conclusion

Giving directions:

It's easy/hard/difficult to . . .
The best way is to . . .

		bus		
		train		*a bus*
go	*by*	*taxi*	*take*	*a train*
come		*tube*		*a taxi*
		underground		*the underground/tube*
		car		

You should . . .
take the (first) turning on the left/right
. . . until you come to . . .
It takes about (ten minutes)

Writing informal letters:

Look carefully at Sally's letter.

1 Notice the **position** of:
Sally's address.
the date.
the beginning of each paragraph.
'Dear Richard', the ending ('With love,') and the signature.

2 Notice the **punctuation.**
Remember that contractions should be used in informal letters.
Example: *I'm, you're,* etc.

3 Notice the **beginning** and **ending.**
Begin: 'Dear . . .' and the name you use when you speak to the person. End with a phrase appropriate to your relationship, for example:

(With) kind regards,
(With) best wishes,
Yours, } followed by your signature.
(With) love,
All my love,

Never write your name at the top of the letter.

The LONDON CONNECTION

Rail, Underground and Bus travel in and around London

C DESCRIBING A SYSTEM AND EXPLAINING HOW IT WORKS

READING

Among the latest developments in telecommunications are viewdata systems which use both telephone and television. The extract below is from a brochure advertising *Prestel.*

Welcome to Prestel

Prestel is the first of a new kind of information service. It is currently being used by thousands of customers in Britain and overseas, large businesses, small firms, colleges, farms, hotels, high street shops and in a growing number of private homes. They find Prestel a quick and very easy way to get the information they need every day, as well as offering powerful two-way communications.

An adapted television set and an ordinary telephone line link Prestel customers to an enormous range of computer-held information. To call up an item from the thousands available, you simply press the numbered buttons on a keypad the size of a pocket calculator.

The information on Prestel is organised in 'pages' – a page is a screenful of information. As soon as you ask for a particular page, the computer sends it instantly down the telephone line and it appears on the screen of your set. Prestel can store hundreds of thousands of pages, but finding the information is easy. There are special index pages on Prestel to help you, and also printed directories. You can learn how to use the system in a few minutes without any special training.

The information on Prestel is supplied by hundreds of independent organisations called Information Providers, who are in direct contact with the central computer and edit their pages to keep them constantly up-to-date. Prestel is therefore an important medium for fast-changing information like foreign exchange rates, the availability of airline seats, or the latest sports results. It can of course bring you business information, the latest news, detailed guides to the

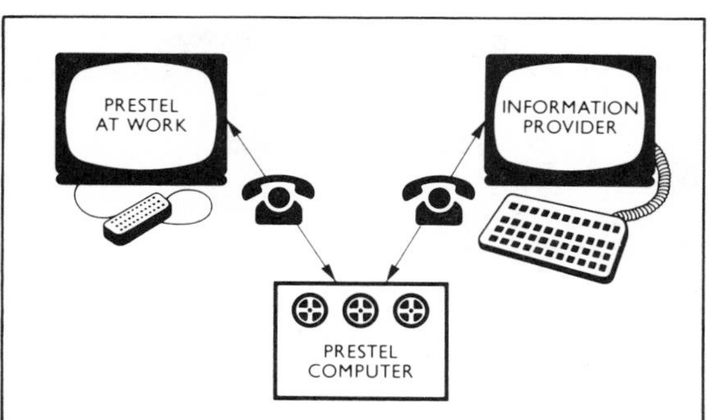

countries of the world, office space to rent, theatre and cinema guides, and more.

The first group of people to take to Prestel in a big way were travel agents, and there are now over 200 tour operators, ferry companies and airlines on Prestel detailing fares, timetables and up-to-date availability, all at the press of a button. Such information can be invaluable when planning holidays and business trips.

With its vast range of topics, Prestel can be thought of as an electronic publishing medium. But it is more than that. As well as receiving information, users can send messages both to each other on a special computer, and to Information Providers using Response Pages. These allow you to order goods via Prestel, book a hotel room, or reserve a seat at the theatre.

How do you use Prestel?

When you call up your local Prestel computer, the first page you see is the one that welcomes you individually. You can then either go straight to the page you want or you can work your way through the index pages. These show lists of information headings each with a number. As soon as you key that number, Prestel sends you the page with that topic on it. The last page in the sequence is a response page. This can be used for a variety of messages – reservations, ordering of goods (with credit card number in many cases), requests for further information, etc. All you need to fill in this 'electronic coupon' are the normal buttons on your keypad. The computer inserts your name and address automatically.

LANGUAGE PRACTICE

1 The advertisers claim that: 'Simplicity and speed have proved to be the winning characteristics of *Prestel*'. In the brochure extract, there are several words and phrases which emphasise the *simplicity* and *speed* of the system. Make a list of these words and phrases.

Example: *all at the press of a button*

2 **a)** Look at the linking words in the box. Find examples of each in the brochure extract, and notice how they are used. Underline the two ideas that are linked in each case.

> KEY LANGUAGE
>
> **Expressing addition:**
>
> He *both* reserved his flight *and* booked a hotel room.
> *As well as* reserving his flight, he booked a hotel room.
> He reserved his flight, and *also* booked a hotel room.
>
> **Giving alternatives:**
>
> You can *either* write *or* phone.

b) The brochure extract describes the various uses of *Prestel* in different situations. In the notes opposite, half the information is missing.

i) Supply an *addition* to each statement (using only information from the text).

Example: *Prestel* is used in Britain.
Prestel is used both in Britain and overseas.

Prestel is used in business organisations.
Customers find it a quick way to get information.
There are special index pages on *Prestel*.
The system can bring you business information.
It is useful for planning business trips.

ii) Give an *alternative* to each statement.

Example: You can make reservations.
You can either make reservations or order goods.

You can go straight to the page you want.
You can receive information.
You can use *Prestel* in the office.

INTERPRETATION ACTIVITY

a) You are trying to sell *Prestel* to an interested travel agent. Answer the travel agent's questions.

TRAVEL AGENT: Does *Prestel* need special equipment?
YOU: . . . .
TRAVEL AGENT: I see. Is it difficult to use?
YOU: . . . .
TRAVEL AGENT: Really? What kind of information can you get from *Prestel?*
YOU: . . . .
TRAVEL AGENT: And who supplies all this information?
YOU: . . . .
TRAVEL AGENT: How do you get a page of information?
YOU: . . . .
TRAVEL AGENT: But I don't see how you find the page of information you want.
YOU: . . . .
TRAVEL AGENT: Wait a minute, is *Prestel* just an information receiver?
YOU: . . . .
TRAVEL AGENT: What exactly is a Response Page?
YOU: . . . .
TRAVEL AGENT: That's useful! What kind of people use *Prestel?*
YOU: . . . .
TRAVEL AGENT: And what are the main advantages of the system?
YOU: . . . .

b) Look at the *Prestel* General Interest index page. Which number should you key first if you want:

to sell your hi-fi equipment?
to find out the population of Alaska?
to check flight-times to Los Angeles?
advice on insurance?
to join a tennis club?
to find out about secretarial courses?
to find out who wrote *The President's Child?*

D TALKING ABOUT THE FUTURE: ARRANGEMENTS, PLANS AND INTENTIONS

LISTENING ACTIVITY

a) Listen to the extract from a radio programme. During the programme, you will hear short interviews with twelve people at the airport. For each person interviewed, make notes on the following:

		Destination	*Occupation* (if stated)	*Reason(s) for travelling*
Example:	1	Rome	Student	Going home

b) Listen to the extract again, and complete the flight information.

FLIGHT NO.	DESTINATION	INFORMATION
BA 193		
	AMSTERDAM RAWALPINDI	
	ROME BAHRAIN HONG KONG	
BA 175		
		Go to Gate 14

c) How many of the people interviewed are travelling on business?
How many are travelling to New York?

The announcements affected all the people who were interviewed. *Six* of these people are delayed. What is their flight number? What are the flight numbers of the other people?

READING ALOUD

a) Listen to two of the interviews, and follow the tapescript below. As you listen, mark those words which are stressed with a dot.

ANGIE: There's a gentleman over here with a wonderful sun tan! Where are you going, sir?
PASSENGER 4: I'm flying to Kuwait.
ANGIE: Why Kuwait?
PASSENGER 4: I'm an engineer—and I'm going out for a few months to develop an oilfield.
ANGIE: You look as though you spend a lot of time in the sun. Have you been before?
PASSENGER 4: Not to Kuwait, no. But I've spent a lot of time in the Middle East. It pays the bills, you know.
ANGIE: I can imagine. And here's a very happy-looking couple—where are you off to?
PASSENGER 5: We're going to the States – our son's getting married in New York tomorrow.
ANGIE: How exciting! Have you been over before?
PASSENGER 6: No, we couldn't afford it. But we've saved up for this trip, and we're going to stay a fortnight. We can't believe it, really.
ANGIE: Well, have a wonderful time—I'm sure you will.

b) Listen to the interviews again, and mark the intonation like this ↗ when the voice rises, and like this ↘ when it falls. What differences in intonation do you notice when you compare the engineer with the couple? What does their intonation tell you about their feelings?

c) Now practise reading the text aloud in groups. Change roles when you have finished.

DISCUSSION

Where was this picture taken?

Why are the people standing in a queue?

Who is the person sitting behind the desk?

What happens at the desk?
(ticket – baggage – boarding card)

What do you do after you have checked in?
(passport control – customs – departure lounge – flight call – gate – aircraft)

What happens if the flight is seriously delayed? Have you ever been seriously delayed? What did you do?

ROLE PLAY

During the interviews at Heathrow airport, we heard that Flight BA 175 was delayed due to technical problems. Some passengers on this flight are very worried about the delay.

a) Look at the notes you have made about six of the passengers on Flight BA 175. Choose one of these characters, and explain why you are anxious to get to New York.

b) **New information:** Now listen to two further announcements.

c) Continue the role play. You are one of the six people who did not confirm the flight. You are determined to get on the plane, and argue with the other five passengers about your right to a seat.

KEY LANGUAGE

Expressing obligation and necessity (1):

I/we *must* / *need to* / *have (got) to* + infinitive

We've got to get on the plane . . .

Talking about future arrangements:

Present continuous
. . . because our son's getting married tomorrow.

Present simple (timetables)
When does the next flight leave?

Talking about plans and intentions (1):

I'd/we'd like to

I/we *want* / *intend* *to* + infinitive

I'm/we're going to
We're going to stay a fortnight.

EXAM PRACTICE

PAPER 1: READING COMPREHENSION

Section A *(Suggestions for the exam—see Unit 1)*

In this section you must choose the word or phrase which best completes each sentence. For each question, 1 to 25, *indicate on your answer sheet* the letter A, B, C or D against the number of the question.

1 Shy people often find it difficult to ______ group discussions.
A take place in B take part in C get on with D get in touch with

2 ______ he was tired, he played brilliantly.
A However B But C Although D Because

3 The government hopes to ______ its plans for introducing cable TV.
A carry out B turn out C carry on D keep on

4 He doesn't travel as much ______ he used to.
A that B than C as D what

5 You can look up the number in the phone ______.
A index B register C dictionary D directory

6 Some people ______ at least four hours a day watching TV.
A take B use C spend D last

7 Laurence Olivier gave an excellent ______ in the film.
A performance B play C act D character

8 One ______ of riding a bicycle is that it's cheap.
A credit B advantage C advance D value

9 Careless driving ______ many accidents.
A affects B influences C results D causes

10 Do you mind waiting while I ______ a phone call?
A have B make C do D give

11 Can you ______ the radio—I'm trying to work.
A turn down B turn out C turn back D turn up

12 Could you give me some ______ about train times?
A news B education C advertisements D information

13 I read a newspaper every day to keep ______ with current affairs.
A modern B present-day C contemporary D up-to-date

14 The manager has flown to Switzerland on a business ______.
A journey B travel C voyage D trip

15 I see them more than I ______.
A use B use to C used to D didn't use to

16 Walk down the street ______ you get to the cross-roads.
A when B until C as far as D unless

17 The best way to get there is ______ the underground.
A to take B taking C to taking D take

18 There's a very interesting ______ in the paper about robots.
A documentary B article C programme D news

19 The Kremlin and the White House are in ______ contact through the 'hot-line'.
A fast B straight C direct D latest

20 I tried phoning, but the line was constantly ______.
A occupied B engaged C used D full

21 Do you enjoy travelling ______ plane?
A with B on C in D by

22 You need ______ a passport and a visa.
A either B as well as C both D each

23 Do you know who ______ the electronic computer?
A discovered B invented C founded D realised

24 The newsreader reported the ______ information about the election.
A last B late C latest D newest

25 What time does the 4.50 train from Manchester ______ to London?
A reach B get C come D arrive

Section B

Suggestions for the exam
In the exam, you will have about 40 – 45 minutes to answer 15 multiple-choice reading comprehension questions based on three or more texts. One of these is likely to be an advertisement, a notice, a set of instructions, etc. For each question, only **one** *of the four suggested answers is correct. Begin by reading the passage at least twice, and try to guess the meaning of unfamiliar words and phrases from their position in the sentence and from the context. You should only look at the questions when you have a clear understanding of the passage. Some of the questions will test general comprehension, while others will refer to specific points in the text. Remember that, since only* **one** *answer is correct,* **three** *of the four suggested answers must be wrong. You should be able to find the correct answer by eliminating those you can prove wrong. When you have made your choice, read the passage again and check that your answer accurately reflects the information given.*

Instructions

In this section you will find after the passage a number of questions or unfinished statements about the passage, each with four suggested answers or ways of finishing. You must choose the one which you think fits best. For each question, *indicate on your answer sheet* the letter A, B, C or D against the number of the question.

Passage

Next to his car, the telephone was the most important thing in Leadbitter's life, and perhaps his greatest friend; of all the sounds he heard, mechanical or human, its summons was the one he welcomed most. He sat in his furnished bed-sitting-room with his ear glued to it, and he sometimes lay awake at night, hoping to hear it ring. However tired he might be, and often he was very tired, his face relaxed when he lifted the receiver and his voice, announcing his number, glowed with warmth. Even when it woke him up at night, or in the cat-naps that he snatched by day, he felt no animosity towards it, and he would smile into it, to the voice which spoke to him, smiles that the owner of the voice seldom, if ever, saw. If the voice was one he recognised he was pleased, if it was strange to him he was still more pleased, for it meant another customer.

One morning when he was shaving, a ritual he performed meticulously, sometimes twice a day, for to be better shaved than other men was part of his defence against the world as well as a commercial asset, the telephone bell rang. Almost the only time that he resented being rung up was when he was shaving. It was a moment of deep relaxation; if the ritual was disturbed and he had to begin again, it was never quite the same—to say nothing of the waste of time. So his voice was a shade less cordial than usual when he picked up the receiver and announced his number: 'Hopewell 4126'.

'This is Lady Franklin's butler speaking,' he was told. 'Her ladyship wishes to know if you can take her ladyship to Canterbury on Thursday, February 10th. Her ladyship would be starting at 10.30 in the morning and would be returning in the late afternoon.'

What a lot of ladyships, Leadbitter thought. He glanced at his engagement list which he kept in a large silver photograph frame beside the telephone. It had once enshrined the picture of the woman with whom he had lived longest, and was almost the only memento of his past life that he allowed himself.

'Yes, I can do that. Where shall I pick her up?'

'Pick her ladyship up?' The butler sounded shocked. 'Will you call for her at her residence, 39 South Halkin Street.'

'Right,' said the driver, scribbling on his pad. It was really an unnecessary precaution; he had a phenomenal memory for names, addresses, dates and destinations and seldom needed telling twice.

'You won't be late, will you? You car-hire drivers are sometimes late,' the butler said. 'You try to fit in too many jobs. You won't be late, will you?'

'Not on your life!' said Leadbitter and put down the receiver. You wouldn't be alive, he thought, if I could get at you. It took him several minutes to recover from the insult.

1 Leadbitter's telephone
A was his most valued possession.
B was necessary for his business.
C prevented him from sleeping.
D was attached to him.

2 When Lady Franklin's butler rang, Leadbitter
A was relaxing.
B was very pleased.
C felt rather annoyed.
D was wasting time.

3 The butler sounded shocked because Leadbitter
A offered to carry Lady Franklin.
B offered Lady Franklin a lift.
C didn't know Lady Franklin's address.
D used informal language.

4 When the butler gave the address, Leadbitter
A had to write it down.
B needn't have written it down.
C didn't bother to write it down.
D realised he had been there before.

5 When the conversation was over, Leadbitter
A was rude to the butler.
B wanted to kill the butler.
C felt quite ill.
D felt depressed.

6 What does the passage tell you about Leadbitter?
A He is punctual and hard-working.
B He is cold and unfriendly.
C He is proud and rather shy.
D He is poor and unhappy.

PAPER 2: COMPOSITION

Suggestions for the exam

In the exam, you will be asked to write **two** *compositions in 1½ hours. Four of the questions will be based on descriptive, narrative, or discursive topics, and one question will be based on prescribed reading. The first four questions are likely to include a letter, a talk or speech, an account, and a discussion of advantages and disadvantages.*

First read all the composition questions **very** *carefully. When you have decided which compositions to write, make notes on your ideas. Then you can organise and expand your notes. Make sure you have a clear* **introduction** *and* **conclusion**, *and that the* **'body'** *of the composition develops logically. Look for useful idioms and linking words. Decide whether the style should be* **formal** *or* **informal**, *and choose appropriate language. For each composition, you should allow about fifteen minutes for planning in note-form. Finally, be sure to leave enough time for checking each composition at the end. Pay particular attention to prepositions and tenses!*

Instructions

Your answers must follow exactly the instructions given, and must be of between 120 and 180 words each.

1 Write a letter inviting a friend to spend a long weekend with you, and give details of what is planned. You should make the beginning and ending like those of an ordinary letter, but the address is not to be counted in the number of words.

2 A famous person is coming to give a talk at your school or institute. Write the speech you would make to welcome him/her.

3 Describe a play or a film which you have particularly enjoyed.

4 A television in every home—what are the advantages and disadvantages?

PAPER 3: USE OF ENGLISH

Section A, Question 2

Suggestions for the exam
This question will be a sentence conversion exercise of the type given below. The exercise is designed to test your knowledge of English structure patterns, and is likely to include constructions involving comparison, passive/active forms, direct/indirect speech, conditional forms, inversion after negatives, etc. You should allow about 15 minutes for this question.

Instructions

Finish each of the following sentences in such a way that it means exactly the same as the sentence printed before it.

Example: There's nothing I can do.
Answer: There isn't *anything I can do*. . . . .

a) David didn't enjoy the film as much as Anne.
Anne . . . .

b) He plays the guitar, and he also writes songs.
As well as . . . .

c) People travel more than they used to.
People didn't . . . .

d) I used to listen to the radio.
I don't . . . .

e) The film was so exciting.
It was such . . . .

f) The town was too small to be marked on the map.
The town wasn't . . . .

g) Colour TVs don't cost as much as they used to.
Colour TVs cost . . . .

h) I've arranged to go to the theatre tonight.
I'm . . . .

i) He searched everywhere, but he couldn't find the ticket.
Although . . . .

j) My advice is: take the train.
If I . . . .

Section A, Question 3

Suggestions for the exam
This question is usually a vocabulary exercise which may involve word-building, or choosing the correct vocabulary or structure within associated areas, as in the example below. You should allow about ten minutes for this question.

Instructions

Complete the following sentences with the appropriate phrase made from TURN.

Example: I applied for a job at the BBC, but they *turned me down*.

a) Please . . . the photocopier before leaving the office.

b) It . . . that the suspicious-looking man was a journalist.

c) The book was . . . a film.

d) Oh, I love this song—would you . . . the radio?

e) The pilot decided to . . . to the airport because of the weather.

UNIT 4

DOWN TO EARTH

A DESCRIBING CAUSE AND EFFECT

TALKING POINT

Where do you think this picture was taken?

Does your country suffer from natural disasters of this kind?

Are there any seasons when you can predict the weather conditions with accuracy?

READING

The Tragedy of the Floods in Florence

On 4 November 1966, after extremely heavy rain, the River Arno in Northern Italy finally overflowed its banks and caused great loss of life and destruction of homes, as well as extensive damage to the countless art treasures which the city contained. It was not only one of the country's most serious natural disasters; it was also an event of tragic proportions for those people all over the world who saw this beautiful city as the very symbol of Western culture.

Although flooding on this scale has occurred only twice before in the history of Florence – in 1333 and in 1344 – it was clear that it could happen again. Consequently, the city council had to take certain measures.

- Give better warning of floods by improving alarm system.
- Stop river from overflowing by building higher river banks.
- Stop landslides in Arno valley by planting trees.
- Improve co-operation between dam authorities and city council by organising special committee.
- Store seasonal rain by building new water reservoirs.

1966

October
An extremely wet month throughout Italy. Streams and rivers full.

1–2 November
Fresh winds clear showers and cloud; 2 days of sunshine.

3 November
Heavy rain, with river rising at rate of 1 metre per hour. Serious flooding and landslides in Arno valley.

3–4 November (night)
After one-third annual rainfall in 24 hours, dam gates opened to control flood, but too much water released.

4 November (morning)
Water overflows banks; streets in Florence flooded to depth of 5 metres.

4 November (morning)
Narrow streets act as channels; water forced through at speeds of up to 130 kilometres per hour.

4 November (afternoon)
Central heating fuel tanks burst open; serious damage from combination of mud, water and oil.

5 November
Rain stops, river level begins to fall. Inhabitants of Florence begin to realise full extent of damage.

Damage caused

33 lives lost in Florence
127 lives lost in surrounding countryside
12,000 families made homeless
6,000 shops destroyed
No electricity, fresh water, telephones
Reconstruction of buildings and services = **£300 million**

Rare books, manuscripts, paintings, sculptures ruined
Galleries, churches, museums damaged
Restoration of art treasures = **£???**

a) 1 What combination of events caused the floods in Florence?
2 Why were the dam gates opened?
3 Why did the water rush through the streets at such speed?
4 What was the effect of the floods on the people of Florence?
5 Were the floods expected?

b) Find words in the text which mean:

enormous	residents
in every part of	total
speed	obvious
yearly	as a result
mixture	prevent

LANGUAGE PRACTICE

1 Make sentences explaining the causes of the floods in Florence.

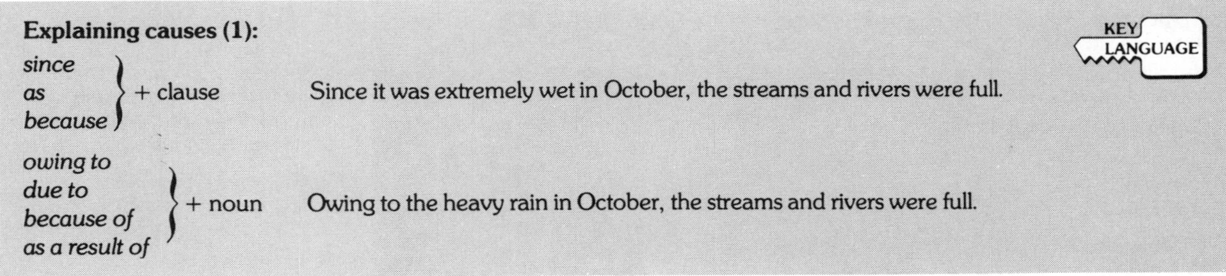
KEY LANGUAGE

Explaining causes (1):

since / *as* / *because* } + clause — Since it was extremely wet in October, the streams and rivers were full.

owing to / *due to* / *because of* / *as a result of* } + noun — Owing to the heavy rain in October, the streams and rivers were full.

---

2 Write sentences describing what measures the city council had to take to prevent such a disaster happening again.

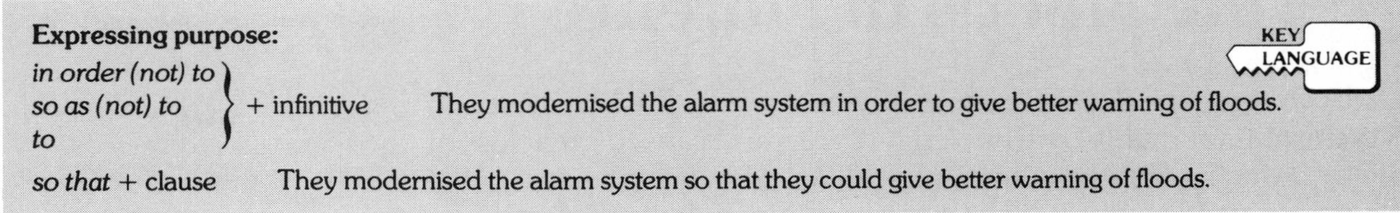
KEY LANGUAGE

Expressing purpose:

in order (not) to / *so as (not) to* / *to* } + infinitive — They modernised the alarm system in order to give better warning of floods.

so that + clause — They modernised the alarm system so that they could give better warning of floods.

---

3 Look at the notes opposite, and explain how these natural events occur.

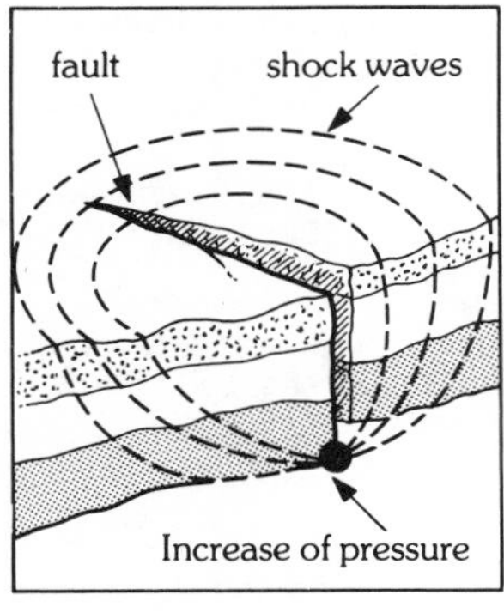

EARTHQUAKES
Natural movement deep inside earth
Weak spot (fault) in surface
Shock waves break through fault

Example: *Earthquakes occur when there is a natural movement deep inside the earth, and a fault in the surface. As a result, shock waves break through the fault.*

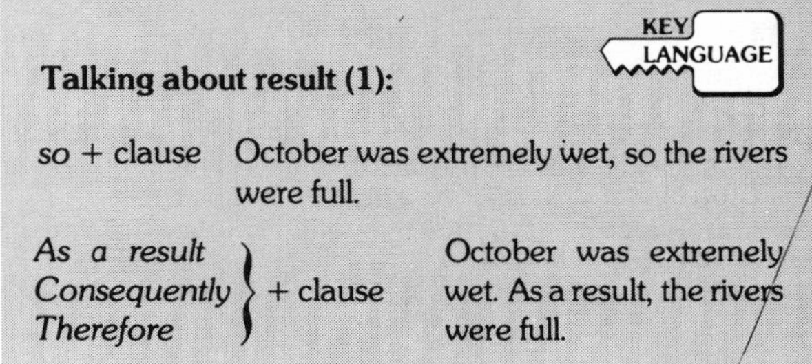
KEY LANGUAGE

Talking about result (1):

so + clause — October was extremely wet, so the rivers were full.

As a result / *Consequently* / *Therefore* } + clause — October was extremely wet. As a result, the rivers were full.

AVALANCHES
Snow begins to thaw because of rise in temperature
Vibrations such as voices, passing train
Sudden downward movement of snow

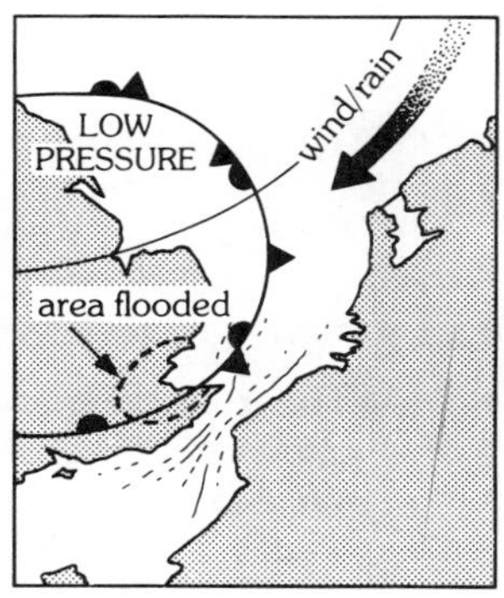

FLOODS
Low pressure leads to heavy rain
Sea level rises
If water cannot pass into open sea, floods coastal areas
Can also be caused by earthquakes

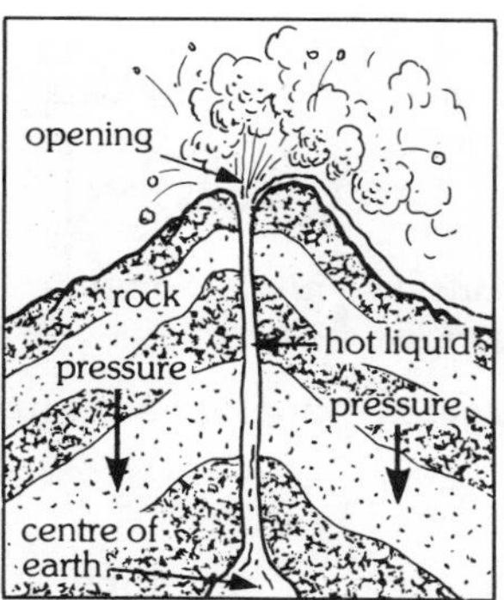

VOLCANIC ERUPTIONS
Rock made liquid by heat at centre of earth
Liquid rock forced upwards by pressure of rock on top
Rock, lava, and ash erupt through opening in surface

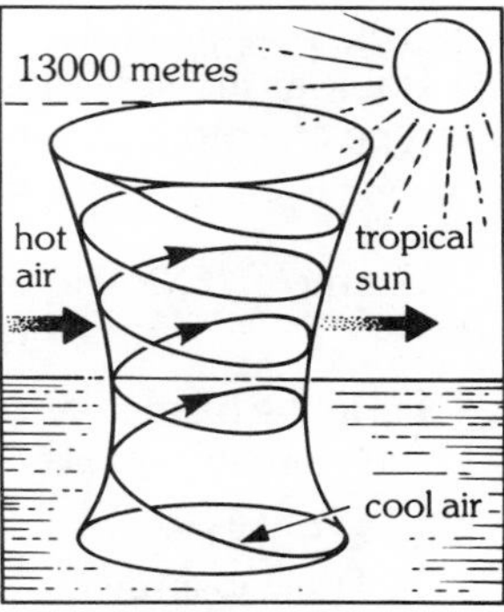

HURRICANES
Cool air heated by tropical sun
As warm air rises, replaced by more cool air, and so on
Circling column of air formed

---

4 Disasters may be either natural or caused by man. Read the following news reports, and decide who or what was responsible. Describe the causes of each event, and choose the appropriate vocabulary from the sets of words below.

KEY VOCABULARY

hurricane/coast/tidal wave/flood/seaside town
explosion/chemicals/factory/give out/poisonous gas
oil tanker/wreck/rocks/discharge/cargo
avalanche/skiers/shout/snow/slide
cigarette end/set fire to/dry leaves/wind/flames

A

Thousands of birds are lying on the beach, unable to move. Volunteer rescue workers are trying to save them but only a small number are expected to live. The effects of the pollution on the fish is not yet known, but it is supposed that many fishermen will find themselves without work for a few years. Tourism will be hit as well, since the beaches are covered in thick, black sludge.

B

120 homes and 200 square kilometres of land are said to have been destroyed in the South of France over the weekend and the danger is now moving north. Police are advising tourists to avoid the region and to take great care with cigarette ends and camping stoves, particularly in forest areas.

C

and the village has been completely buried with three quarters of the population dead or missing. Further down the valley, troops are trying to save the passengers of a train who have been trapped for twenty-four hours.

D

The thick white cloud settled on homes and gardens, killing pets and poisoning crops. Many people are suffering from nausea and sore spots on the skin. Authorities have ordered a total evacuation to protect the inhabitants from further harm, and are burying or burning all contaminated materials. No one knows if the effects are temporary or not.

E

trees were scattered around like matchsticks, cars were lying on their sides, half-buried in mud, and houses were completely flattened. A spokesman says that the water level which had risen to ten metres is now dropping but there is a major risk of disease and starvation if supplies do not get through soon.

5 Look at the sentences below, and decide what type of word is missing.

KEY VOCABULARY

Example: EXPAND *expansion – abstract noun*
expansive – adjective

Fill in the blanks with a suitable word formed from the word in capitals.

1 EXPLODE
There was an ______, as the volcano erupted.
Dynamite is a highly ______ material.

2 DESTROY
The pollution from cars can be quite ______ to the stones of buildings.
After the hurricane, it was the tidal wave which completed the ______ of the city.

3 CONSTRUCT
The government has given priority to the ______ of new houses.
His opinions were interesting and extremely ______.

4 PROTECT
The policeman surrounded the President to give him ______.
Workers in the nuclear power station had to wear ______ clothing.

5 THREATEN
The heavy rain and high tides posed a ______ to the safety of the region.
The black clouds looked particularly ______.

DISCUSSION

Which are the most dangerous to the human race – natural disasters or those caused by people?
What can be done to reduce the dangers of such disasters?
When disasters occur, what practical aid can more fortunate countries give?
Where do you think is the safest place to live in the world?
Have you ever been in a situation where your life has been threatened?

B DESCRIBING A COUNTRY

READING

1 **a)** Read the extract from the tourist brochure opposite, and mark the safari route on the map.
b) Choose the best alternative to the following words in the tour description.

KEY VOCABULARY

1 LODGE
A hotel B town C room D balcony
2 BORDER
A edge B frontier C margin D boundary
3 STOP
A break B finish C holiday D visit
4 PEAK
A point B slope C summit D plain
5 REMOTE
A small B crowded C isolated D strange
6 BUSH
A tree B shrub C hedge D countryside

Now choose the best answer.

7 In all, the number of nights spent in Kenya is
A 15 B 14 C 13 D 12
8 Nairobi National Park
A is on the outskirts of Nairobi.
B is some way from the city centre.
C costs nothing to visit.
D is in the centre of the city.
9 To get to Treetops, the route
A misses out Nyeri.
B goes west to Lake Nakuru.
C takes all day.
D passes through Nyeri.
10 Holiday prices do not include
A breakfast while on safari.
B lunch and dinner while on safari.
C lunch and dinner in Nairobi.
D lunch and dinner in Mombasa.

UNIVERSAL TOURS presents

The 'Best of Kenya' Safari

An exciting tour which takes you through the very heart of some of Kenya's most stunning natural scenery.

Day 1
Leave England and the rain on the evening flight direct to Mombasa on the Indian Ocean.

Day 2
Morning arrival. Coach to the luxury hotel of Taita Hills set in a wildlife sanctuary near Tsavo Park. Afternoon at leisure beside the swimming pool. Lunch, dinner and overnight stay.

Day 3
Drive through Tsavo, Kenya's largest game park with an estimated 20,000 elephants, into Amboseli, a reserve famous for its variety of animal and birdlife. Overnight stay in a lodge close to the border with Tanzania and just below Mt Kilimanjaro. The mountains provide fresh water for the springs of the park and so attract a permanent concentration of wildlife, with the snow-capped peaks making a perfect background for photography.

Day 4
After breakfast, continue through Masai country to Nairobi, the modern capital of Kenya.

Day 5
Free day for shopping and sightseeing, or a visit to Nairobi National Park on the city limits.

Day 6
Early morning start northwards to the Aberdares. Stop for lunch at the famous Mt Kenya Safari Club with its wonderful gardens spread out below the snowy peak of Mt Kenya. Then north again into the semi-desert region lying in the Samburu National Park. It is as remote now as it has been for hundreds of years, an unspoilt world of broad horizons, nomadic tribesmen herding cattle, goats and even camels. Overnight stay at the River Lodge.

Day 7
Morning drive to Treetops via Nyeri to spend the afternoon relaxing by the pool or fishing for trout. The lodge overlooks a floodlit waterhole where, from early evening and throughout the night, the wildlife comes out of the bush to drink. Overnight stay.

Day 8
West to Lake Nakuru to admire the extraordinary number of different birds. Overnight stay.

Day 9
A morning drive along the Rift Valley to Kisumu where you will stay for three nights. Afternoon relaxing on the bay, then an evening cruise on Lake Victoria to watch the sunset.

Day 10
A day free to explore the shore, with optional excursions to its unspoilt fishing villages or to the crater lake.

Day 11
Early morning start to the Masai Mara Game Reserve with yet more elephants, lions, rhinos and birds. Late arrival in Nairobi. Overnight stay.

Day 12–14
Flight to Mombasa and transfer to your beach hotel where you will spend 2½ days at your leisure. The hotel is set in a tropical garden with a swimming pool. All rooms are air-conditioned, with balconies facing the Indian Ocean.

Day 15
Morning departure for London by direct flight.

Holiday prices include air travel to Mombasa, sightseeing and transport on safari, transfers between airports and hotels, all meals while on safari, full board in Mombasa, but breakfast only in Nairobi, local taxes and service charges.

2 Most people want to know something about places they are going to visit. Look at this extract from a book about Kenya.

Write notes about the following:

population	landscape
capital city	climate
main port	sightseeing
resources	other activities

Kenya

SITUATED IN EAST AFRICA, with a coast on the Indian Ocean, Kenya is a vast country of ½ million square kilometres and with a population of 16 million people. It stretches from the sea with its sandy beaches, across the plains and forest land, to the mountains which rise to heights of over 5,000 metres. The capital, Nairobi, which is less than a hundred years old, is the most important business and conference centre in Africa.

The climate is very pleasant, although there is heavy rain in April, May and June. This type of weather is particularly suitable for growing bananas, sugar, cotton, tea and above all, coffee. Much of this produce is taken to Mombasa, the largest port in the country, and exported all over the world. Most tourists come to see the wonderful national game parks, taking safari tours through the bush to see the scenery and the wildlife – elephants, lions, giraffes, rhinos and monkeys. There are also plenty of opportunities for fishing or relaxing on the beach.

3 What information does this map of Egypt show?

For example: What is the main produce of Egypt?
Which is the principal port?
What kind of landscape does Egypt have?

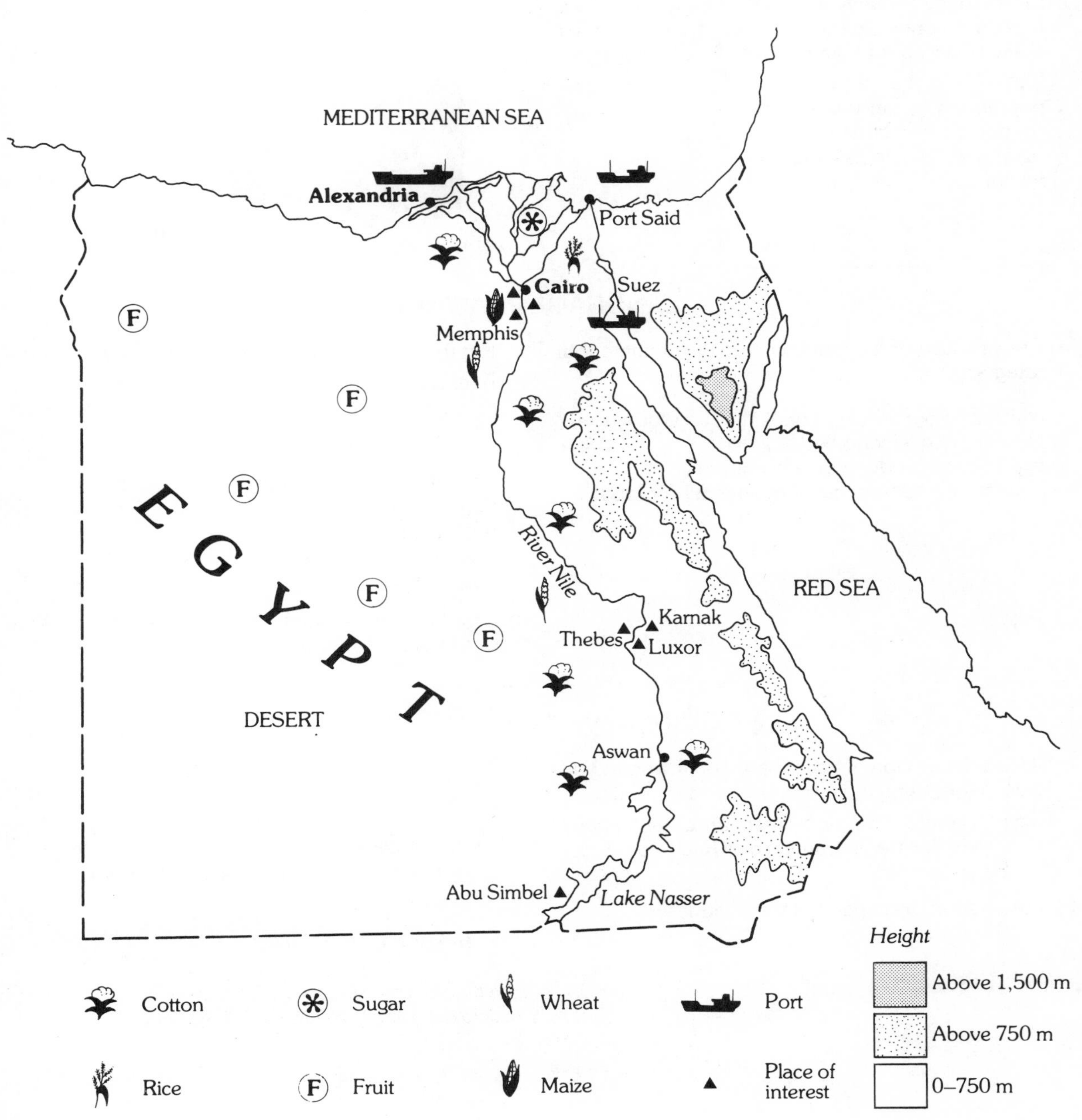

LISTENING ACTIVITY

George has just been on a tour of Egypt called 'The Treasures of the Pharoahs'.

a) Listen to his conversation with Paul, and mark the route he took on the map of Egypt on page 63.

b) Listen to the conversation again. Using information from the conversation and from the map above, make notes about Egypt under the following headings:

population	landscape
capital city	climate
main port	sightseeing
resources	other activities

Ramesses II

LANGUAGE PRACTICE

a) The produce of a country can be divided into four categories:

KEY VOCABULARY

Natural resources (e.g. coal)
Industry (e.g. electronics)
Agricultural production (e.g. cotton)
Livestock breeding (e.g. farm animals for food)

Put the words below in their categories.

beef cattle	goats	sheep
cars	gold	shipbuilding
chemicals	grapes (wine)	silver
coffee	iron	tea
copper	machinery	textiles
corn	oil	tobacco
dairy cattle	pigs	vegetables
electrical equipment	poultry	wood

b) Egypt produces mainly agricultural products. What does your country produce?

GUIDED WRITING ACTIVITY

a) Write a description of Egypt based on the notes you have made, using the text on Kenya as a model.

Begin: *Situated in North West Africa, with coasts on the Mediterranean and Red Seas, Egypt is . . .*

b) Write a short description of your country.

Describing position: KEY LANGUAGE

on the coast/plain/ocean *in the hills/mountains/valleys* *by the sea*	Lying in the hills, . . .
to / in the north/south/east/west	Situated in the west of of the country, . . .
along the river/shore *across the forest land/fields*	It stretches across the forest land.
not far from *close to* *near (to)* *a long way from* } + noun	

C TALKING ABOUT FUTURE CHANGE

READING

Loch Kyle, on the west coast of Scotland, is a long narrow stretch of water with an opening onto the sea to the south, and is said to be one of the most beautiful lakes in the country. It is surrounded by wooded hillsides and mountain peaks which are very popular with walkers and mountaineers. Ben Craggach (1,100 m) is usually climbed from here, a long but not difficult walk, offering magnificent views of the Highlands to one side and the ocean to the other. The village of Crannog consists of a single street containing a few houses, a small hotel, a general store and a church. The villagers are either sheep farmers or fishermen; the loch provides a safe harbour for six or seven fishing boats. The village's meagre income is supplemented in summer by tourism and the sale of craft goods.

BOC to build new Scottish oil terminal

THE BRITISH OIL CORPORATION announced yesterday its intention to construct a new deep water oil terminal in Loch Kyle on the west coast of Scotland which will be large enough to take the new 500,000 ton supertankers. At the same time it plans to lay a pipeline to connect the new terminal with the oil refinery at Howeskirk on the east coast.

When BOC were asked why they needed a new terminal, a spokesman said, 'It is essential if we are to meet Britain's requirements for imported oil in the 1990s. If we don't build it, we cannot supply the necessary oil – it's as simple as that. There are few sites around Britain which are deep enough to accept these new ships. It has to be Loch Kyle, otherwise they'll have to unload on the Continent and transfer the oil onto smaller tankers. And it's not far from Howeskirk which must expand its refinery or it'll lose its place in the world petro-chemical industry. If that happens, then large-scale unemployment in this region, which is already economically depressed, is inevitable. Obviously, the tankers have to unload their cargo quickly and storage tanks at Crannog are the only answer. And we must accept that roads and a heliport will have to be built, otherwise communications will be very difficult.'

Asked whether BOC was concerned about the disruption to the village of Crannog and the damage to the environment, the spokesman replied, 'Inevitably we'll meet some local opposition and probably some resistance from conservation groups, but we're hoping that people will understand why this new terminal is necessary. It will create about 900 jobs, most of which will be in Crannog. It really is in the interests of the country as a whole.'

Friends of Scotland

The BOC have just revealed their plans for the new west coast oil terminal and they have chosen Loch Kyle and Crannog as the site.

What they plan to do

- **Pull down part of Crannog to build new offices, storage tanks and living accommodation.**
- **Dig up the fields and hillsides to lay a pipeline to Howeskirk.**
- **Destroy the east shore of the lake by building a new road.**
- **Pollute the loch and ruin the fishing by building a deep water harbour for 500,000 ton tankers.**
- **Disrupt the peace of the Highlands by putting a heliport in the middle of Crannog.**
- **Threaten the traditional Highland way of life by creating hundreds of new jobs and bringing in workers from outside.**

They say the Crannog terminal is essential.
We say it is NOT! WE MUST RESIST THESE PLANS!

Crannog today

Crannog tomorrow?

INTERPRETATION ACTIVITY

You are the spokesman for BOC. Answer the journalist's questions.

JOURNALIST: Where will the new terminal be built?
YOU: ....
JOURNALIST: Why did you choose Loch Kyle?
YOU: ....
JOURNALIST: Why is a new terminal necessary?
YOU: ....
JOURNALIST: Why does it have to be close to Howeskirk?
YOU: ....
JOURNALIST: I see. And exactly what do you intend to build at Crannog?
YOU: ....
JOURNALIST: Why is the pipeline necessary?
YOU: ....
JOURNALIST: Why are the storage tanks necessary if you're going to lay a pipeline?
YOU: ....
JOURNALIST: Do you think the changes will disrupt the Highland way of life?
YOU: ....

LANGUAGE PRACTICE

1 **a)** Make nouns out of the following verbs from the texts. Check your list of nouns in the dictionary.

KEY VOCABULARY

reveal	announce	accept
choose	reduce	lose
connect	expand	surround
pollute	create	contain

b) Make verbs out of the following nouns.

intention	storage
opposition	conservation
refinery	requirement
resistance	development

2 **a)** You are the owner of the hotel in Crannog. You realise the consequences of the new terminal for the old style of life in the village, but you are aware that the plan will create a lot of business for you, as well as a great number of new jobs in the area. Talk about the planned changes, and give your opinion.

b) Look at the *Friends of Scotland* hand-out. Talk about the changes the terminal will bring.

Example: *If they build new offices, they'll pull down part of Crannog.*

c) Now look at the newspaper article. Talk about the consequences if they don't build the terminal.

Example: *Unless they build a new terminal, they won't be able to meet Britain's oil requirements.*

Talking about the likely future: KEY LANGUAGE

If not / *Unless* } + present simple . . . . *will/won't* + infinitive

INTERPRETATION ACTIVITY

You are the local Member of Parliament. You are aware that the plan will create jobs for the villagers who have difficulty in making a living, but you are also aware that Britain's North Sea oil will reduce oil imports from other countries in a few years, and the Crannog terminal will no longer be necessary.

Write the text of the talk you must give to the villagers, summarising the arguments for and against the plan, and giving your opinion.

Begin: *Good evening, ladies and gentlemen, and thank you all for coming to this meeting. I'm sure you all know why we are here . . .*

D MAKING DEDUCTIONS

LISTENING ACTIVITY

Many countries have a rich collection of mysterious stories and legends. They are usually tales which have been passed from parent to child and may neither be true nor have any explanation.

a) Chris and Emma are on a cycling tour of the Keverne peninsula. Listen to their conversation, and take notes.

b) Decide whether the following statements are true or false.

1 Azuris is said to be an underwater city.
2 The city was flooded as a punishment for the people who lived there.
3 Ash Kelso is like Atlantis.
4 Overmouth was the scene of a battle in the fourteenth century.
5 The King's soldiers were beaten by the rebel army.
6 Jack Carver was a taxman in Penberry.
7 The taxmen took too much money from the villagers.
8 Jack Carver was hanged at Penberry.

READING ALOUD

a) Listen to part of the conversation again and follow the tapescript below. As you listen, mark those words which are stressed with a dot.

LANDLORD: Well, Rich Harold, as he's called, died in 1895. He was said to be richest man in the region, but he never spent anything, so everyone thought he was mean. Perhaps he wasn't rich at all, I don't know. Anyway, on the wall in the church where he was buried, he left a series of clues, a kind of riddle. If you can solve it, you'll find exactly where he left his money. Nobody has ever succeeded, though.

CHRIS: Oh, that sounds interesting. We'll have a look at that.

EMMA: Yes, I'd love to solve it.

CHRIS: We could go there now, and have something to eat at the same time.

EMMA: Yes, that's a good idea. Let's go. Bye!

LANDLORD: Enjoy yourselves – and come back here when you've found the treasure!

b) Now practise reading the text aloud in groups. Change roles when you have finished.

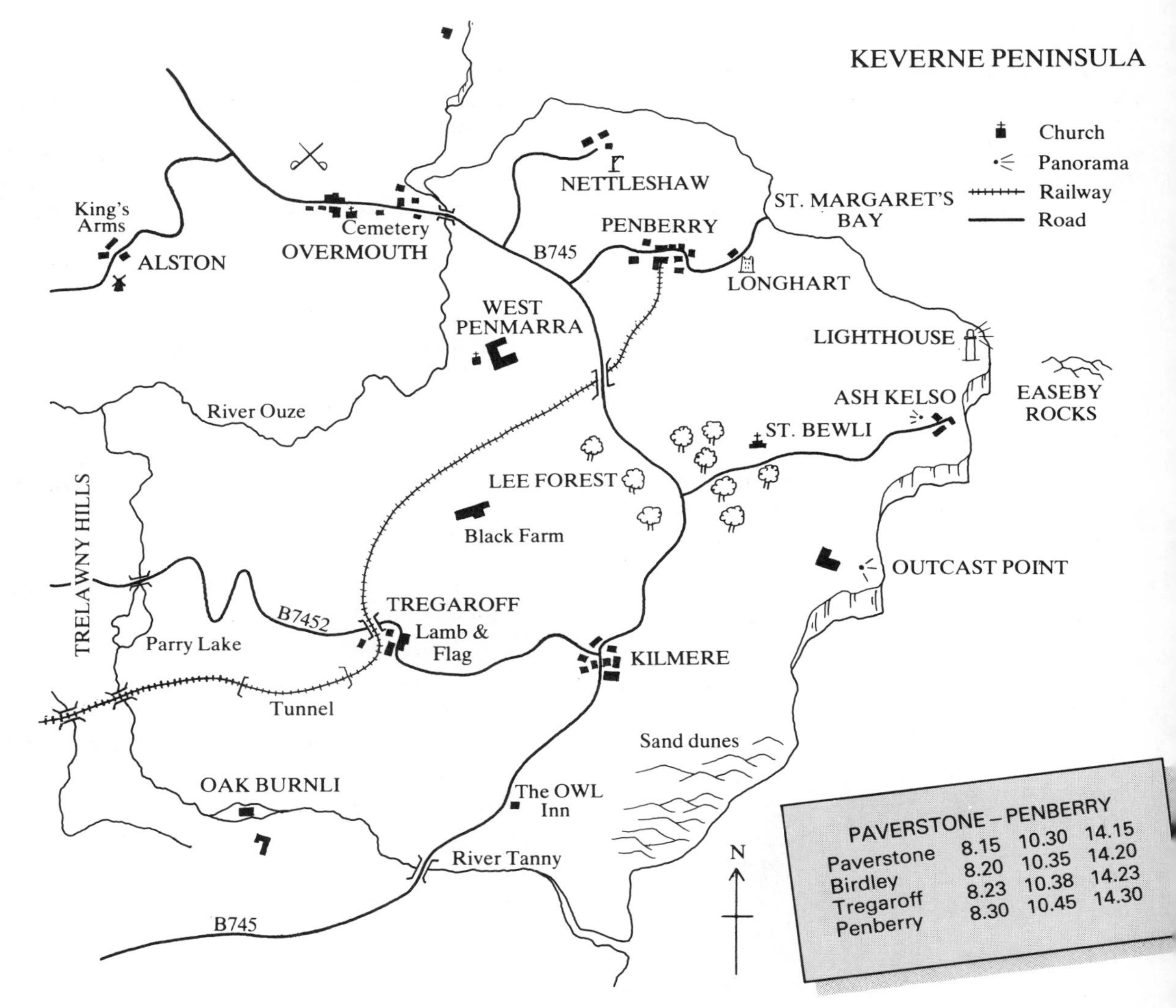

PAVERSTONE – PENBERRY			
Paverstone	8.15	10.30	14.15
Birdley	8.20	10.35	14.20
Tregaroff	8.23	10.38	14.23
Penberry	8.30	10.45	14.30

West Country Legends –
Keverne Peninsula

At Longhart, or Lone Heart as it once was, there is nothing left except the Bell Tower. It is said that the bell rings when a ship is about to be wrecked on the EASEBY Rocks.

OAK BURNLI

Once a village with ten houses, only the farm and the watermill remain. The farm serves wonderful cream teas to visitors. The mill's position on an island on the River Tanny allows it to use the water power on both sides.

South West England –
Walk 22: 3½ or 6 miles

Follow the path across the fields, through gate and towards sea. It is here that the submerged city of AZURIS is said to lie. On your left is OUTCAST POINT where escaped prisoners used to be brought when recaptured to spend the rest of their lives in isolation.

ASH KELSO

A fine view back across the fields and moors, the favourite resting place of Sir Joseph Stone who gave the bench here to the community. Sit down and enjoy the view.

GOOD PUB GUIDE

	Rooms	Atmosphere	Food
Lamb and Flag Tregaroff	**6**	★★	★★★★
King's Arms Alston	**NONE**	★	★★
The Owl B745	**12**	★★★	★★★
The George Craybourne	**NONE**	★	★★

WEST PENMARRA Abbey
Visiting hours to abbey ruins:
9.30–12.30 1.30–5 Tues–Sat
2–5 Sundays and Holidays.
Mondays closed.
Please do not walk on the Abbot's cross and the gravestone.

Here I, rich Harold, lie six feet down,
A man much envied by all in town.
Now, when I died, I went to heaven
But left my riches somewhere in Keverne.
So read the lines which below this stand
And look for place names in this sweet land.
Then what in life you thought I was worth,
In death you'll find is like nothing on earth.

My first stands lonely and swings in the wind
Kind Jack's last stand against those who have sinned.
My second is as near as the nose on your face,
For here men died when a battle took place.
My third is a place where brothers once prayed;
Now all there remains is a cross on a grave.
My fourth lies silent and still all year
Except for those days when tragedy is near.
My fifth keeps running but always stands still,
A house on wheels stands under a hill.
My sixth is a break from this lengthy chase;
Take refreshment and advice in a bird-like place.

Are you now ready for the next set of clues?
My seventh lies there where artists once drew.
My eighth lies near darkness with light at both ends,
Light-dark, dark-light as you come round the bend.
My ninth stands high and faces the sea
Where bad men suffered in their wish to be free.
My tenth is the site where a foreigner stood
And fought off the demons who came from the wood.
My eleventh lies under a watery light,
A cruel fate for sailors on a dark moonless night.
My twelfth is my last and here you may rest
And watch the world end as you look to the west.

And before I bring these lines to a close,
Write down the names of each place you choose.
For the first letter says where *you now must seek,*
And the last is what; *if you find you may keep.*

ROLE PLAY

a) You and a friend are visitors to the Keverne peninsular, and have overheard Chris and Emma's conversation. You have also found the riddle that Rich Harold left on the church wall in Overmouth. Read it all the way through, and then try to find where he left his fortune. Some of the clues to the riddle can be found on or around the map. Others have been mentioned in Chris and Emma's conversation.

b) **New information**: Now listen to a further conversation. Now you should have all the clues you need to solve the riddle.

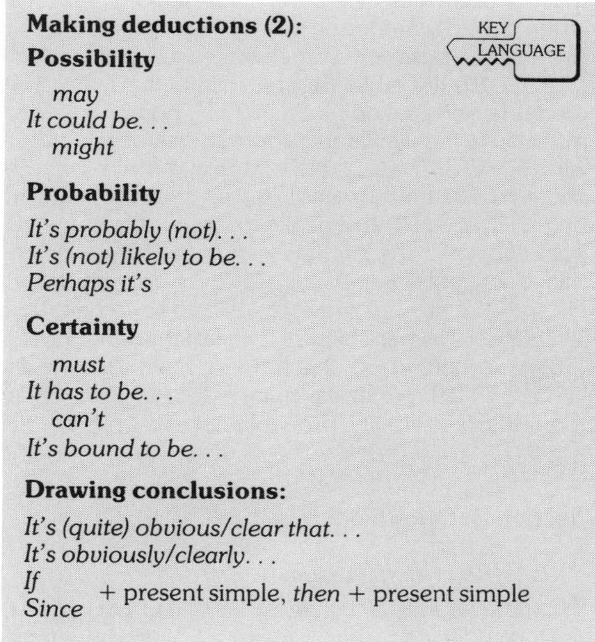

Making deductions (2):

Possibility

It could be... may / might

Probability

It's probably (not)...
It's (not) likely to be...
Perhaps it's

Certainty

It has to be... must / can't
It's bound to be...

Drawing conclusions:

It's (quite) obvious/clear that...
It's obviously/clearly...
If / *Since* + present simple, *then* + present simple

DISCUSSION

Does your country or region have any legends or stories?

EXAM PRACTICE

PAPER 3: USE OF ENGLISH

Section A, Question 1

(Suggestions for the exam – see Unit 1)
Fill each of the numbered blanks in the following text. Use only *one* word in each space.

Stephen woke ________ (1) and looked around, shaking ________ (2) head in confusion. He was lying on ________ (3) floor in a small room, which ________ (4) only a small table and a chair. The walls ________ (5) lit by a strange red glow, and his first ________ (6) was that the place was ________ (7) fire. He got ________ (8) in terror and went to the door. It was locked. He was obviously a prisoner. There was a small high window ________ (9) the table. Stephen climbed ________ (10) the table and looked ________ (11), hoping to recognise some familiar landmark. He was disappointed. All around, as ________ (12) as the eye could see, were snow-covered mountains. The ________ (13) was setting ________ (14) the peaks to his right, spilling red-gold light over the icy landscape, and he realised he had been unconscious ________ (15) several hours. He fell helplessly onto ________ (16) chair, and ________ (17) where he was. The last thing he ________ (18) was getting off the train in Paris. 'This place ________ (19) be miles away ________ (20) Paris,' thought Stephen. 'It's probably not even in France!'

Section B, Question 5

Suggestions for the exam

You are advised to spend about 40 minutes on this section. Section B is a directed writing exercise where you are asked to read and interpret information which may be given in the form of a dialogue, a map, a timetable, notes, a diagram, a letter, etc. You have to extract certain information and reproduce it in the form of a summary, a letter, a dialogue, etc.

First read the text(s) very carefully, and make sure you understand how you are required to present your answer. Read the text(s) again to get a general idea of the information you will include in your answer. Take notes or underline the points you have selected, making sure you include **only** *information that is appropriate to the writing task you have been given. Then order your notes, and write connected sentences. You should try to express the ideas differently from the way they are put across in the text(s). Do not introduce your own ideas unless you are asked to in the instructions.*

Instructions

Using the information given below, continue each of the three paragraphs in the spaces provided. Use no more than 60 words for each paragraph.

Mr Jackson is going to retire in about six months' time. He and his wife would like to leave their house in the south of England, but have not yet decided where they want to go. They both love the countryside and the sea. They also love the sunshine. They have lots of friends in the south whom they will be sorry to leave, but they would also like to see more of their daughter. Mrs Jackson does not like living in a flat. Mr Jackson loves his golf and Mrs Jackson enjoys going to the shops now and then. They cannot afford to spend too much on their new home.

Lanzetta, Spain
- Sunshine 9 months of the year – Long way to shops – Few English-speaking people
- Countryside inland – dry & mountainous
- Beautiful flat near golf course
- Completely new life – Are we too old?

Broughton Regis
- South Coast town, only 1 hour from old house by car – 15 minutes walk from daughter
- Very close to town centre – Walks in hills
- Very pretty – Small but attractive house
- Quite cheap – Golf course nearby

Hawkesthwaite, North of England
- Pretty cottage – very cheap – Hills and valleys, wonderful for walking – Active and friendly community – Nearest town 1 hour away – few buses – Weather cold and rainy – Long way from old home

I think that . . . would be the best place for Mr and Mrs Jackson because . . .
I also think they might be happy in . . . because . . . .
I don't think they would be happy in . . . because . . .

PAPER 5: INTERVIEW

Part (i)

Suggestions for the exam
In the first part of the interview, you are asked to talk about a picture which the examiner will show you. About 5 minutes discussion is developed, where you will be asked to comment on the picture and talk about the topic in a general way. You may be asked to refer the topic to your own experience. This might seem difficult, but will always make this part of the interview more interesting for both you and the examiner.

1 Where do you think this is?

2 How would you describe the landscape?

3 What do you think are the main occupations of the people who live here?

4 Have you ever been to a place like this?

5 Do you think that tourists come here? How can you tell?

Related topics
The effects of tourism
Living in a small village
The ideal climate

Part (ii)

Suggestions for the exam
In this part of the interview, you will be given a few minutes to prepare a text which you will read aloud to the examiner. It will be an announcement, a situation, or instructions. Try and imagine that you are the person speaking in real life. You won't have time to mark the stress and intonation, so spend the preparation time in understanding the text and thinking about the situation and the role you have to play. You will be asked to say what you think the situation is, and who is speaking.

Well, if you're a beginner, Davos in Switzerland has plenty of slopes where you can learn. All the instructors speak English and I advise you to take some lessons. As for the non-skier, the town is quite large, and there are plenty of things to do, lots of bars, restaurants, and so on. The hotels are very good, and they don't mind if you bring your children with you. And we have a special arrangement with them, so if you book your holiday with us, there's a 15% discount on the total price.

Part (iii) *(Suggestions for the exam – see Unit 1)*

You may be asked *one* of the question types below.

1 Choose one of these topics:
Town or country?
Adventure holidays (e.g. safaris)
Conservation of the countryside
World shortage of food
Living in a foreign country

Be prepared to answer questions on the topic, or discuss it.

2 Define and discuss natural disasters.

3 You are at a travel agent's and you are enquiring about a country you don't know.
Ask about:
Hotels
Weather
Places to visit etc.

UNIT 5

JUST THE JOB!

A DESCRIBING PROFESSIONAL SKILLS AND PERSONAL QUALITIES

TALKING POINT

What is work?
All the activities below can be described as leisure activities. On the other hand, many people would describe them as work.
What are the people called who earn their living from these activities?

KEY VOCABULARY

Example: riding – *jockey*

- playing music
- photography
- fishing
- mending motorbikes
- making clothes
- cooking
- driving
- sailing
- gardening
- dancing
- DIY (Do-it-yourself)

Do-it-yourself

Nowadays, an increasing number of school-leavers are having great difficulty in finding a job. There are many reasons for this; one is that industry is getting more efficient and simply needs fewer people to make the same number of products; another is that the whole pattern of work is changing. For example, more and more people are starting small businesses, often offering services to householders or producing high-quality hand-made goods. It takes imagination, organisation, determination and hard work, but it can pay off.

• In **Sheffield**, Mike Hindmarsh (19), did it . . .

'In my later school years, I was quite certain I wanted to work for myself. I did all right at school, but left with no qualifications except Maths 'O' Level. The skills I had weren't brilliant – no particular knowledge about anything except music. At school, I helped to get a group together, organise concerts, design the sets and mix the sound. But I was never good enough to earn my living that way. But I *have* got a lot of imagination and determination. When I finally left school, I put my mind to what I could do for myself. Then I thought, since a lot of people are now into DIY, one way of earning money might be by servicing DIY equipment. For the moment I've narrowed that down to tool sharpening. I specialise in giving fast, reliable service. It's the organisation that counts most. I'm a one man show, so I have to advertise, man the phone and keep track of the financial side myself. The tool sharpening is only one aspect. But now I'm managing to break even and I keep my eyes open for any ways of expanding the business.'

• In **Cambridge**, QPL Motorcycle Couriers – Quentin (22), Toby (21) and Lynne (21) did it . . .

Quentin told us: 'We'd all had jobs, but been made redundant and spent some time out of work. I wanted to be a pop star, which meant going to London regularly. I decided that wasn't possible, I'd never make it, but I'd noticed a lot of motorcycle couriers in London, so I thought I'd try and get a job with a company locally. There wasn't one. I still had £100 of redundancy money and my bike. My girlfriend Lynne was good at accounts, so we set up with another friend Paul as the third partner. We started by advertising and that was terrible at first – the only thing that worked was putting a suit on and going round offering our services, and an advert in the Yellow Pages. When Paul left, Toby joined us but we kept the name QPL because we were starting to get known. Now we do a daily run to London and go anywhere in Great Britain. We use up to 20 riders and we buy ourselves a new bike every year. We've learned a tremendous lot about management and organisation and are now pretty confident about the future'.

• In **London**, Chrissie Roberts (24) Carpet Designer and Manufacturer, did it . . .

'I did screen printing at college and worked freelance for two years. But it didn't work out very well. Then I saw a programme about a Training Workshop on TV. I went there to do screen printing but finished up in the carpet department. I found that my designs were very suitable for the process of making carpets. I learned how use the machine and do everything myself. I suppose I also learned how to take responsibility for my own work and to be disciplined about it. I thought why don't I do this on my own? There seemed to be a gap in the market – I could offer really high quality carpets made to the customer's own specifications. So now I'm setting up a workshop and am out looking for orders.'

Note:
'O' Level: Ordinary Level examination, usually taken in 1–8 subjects at the age of 16.
motorcycle couriers: special messengers for parcels, letters, etc.
Yellow Pages: yellow telephone directory of services.
screen printing: process for printing on textiles, glass, metal, etc., as well as paper.

a) 1 Why does industry need fewer people to make the same number of products?
2 How does Mike earn his living at the moment?
3 What does he say is the most important thing in his business?
4 Why did Quentin decide to start a motorcycle courier company?
5 How did QPL manage to attract work?
6 Why did they call the company QPL?
7 How did Chrissie learn to make carpets?
8 Why is she setting up a workshop?

b) Find words or phrases in the text which mean:

requires
produce good results
thought about
do the accounts

make neither a profit nor a loss
look out
dismissed because no longer needed
unemployed
started a business
fairly
independently/for no fixed employer
wasn't very successful

c) Explain what the underlined words refer to.

1 It takes imagination . . .
2 . . . I've narrowed that down . . .
3 There wasn't one.
4 But it didn't work out very well.
5 I went there to do screen printing . . .
6 . . . why don't I do this on my own?

LANGUAGE PRACTICE

1 According to Mike, Quentin, and Chrissie, you need certain professional skills and personal qualities to run your own business. Read through the text again, and discuss which skills and qualities are particularly important.

Example: *You've got to have a lot of imagination.*

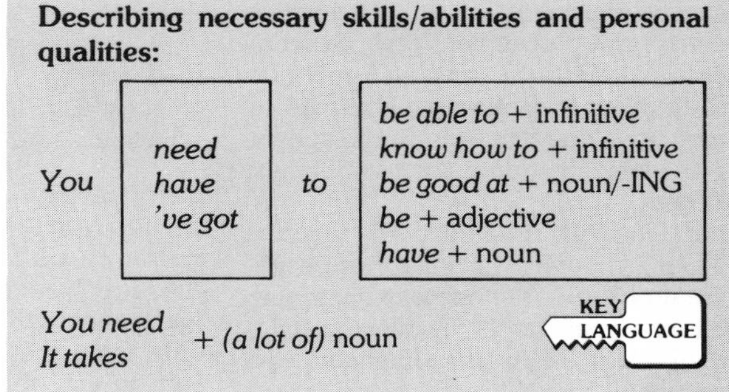

Describing necessary skills/abilities and personal qualities:

You	*need* *have* *'ve got*	*to*	*be able to* + infinitive *know how to* + infinitive *be good at* + noun/-ING *be* + adjective *have* + noun

You need
It takes + *(a lot of)* noun

2 a) Listen to these five people talking about their work. In each case, decide what their occupations are, and make notes on the following:
1 Necessary professional skills
2 Important personal qualities

b) Use your notes to describe the five occupations in terms of professional skills and personal qualities.

3 a) Think about the job you would most like, and complete the questionnaire opposite. Discuss your answers with another student. Can he/she guess what your ideal job is?

b) Write a short paragraph about yourself in terms of your ideal job.
Begin: *I would most like to . . . . because . . .*

Careers Guidance Questionnaire

YES ✓ **NO** ✗ **NOT SURE** ?

1 *Practical requirements*

Would you rather

work in an office?	
work outdoors?	
work with other people?	
work on your own?	
do paperwork?	
do practical work?	

Would you mind

working long hours?	
working in the evenings?	
working at weekends?	
doing shift work?	
getting up early?	
training for several years?	
travelling a lot?	

2 *What are your skills/abilities?*

Are you good at

using tools?	
designing things?	
adding up figures?	
talking to people?	
looking after others?	

Can you

think clearly?	

express yourself well:

when speaking?	
in writing?	
work in a team?	

3 *How do you see yourself?*

Are you

practical?	
efficient?	
strong?	
punctual?	
accurate?	
fair?	
gentle?	
organised?	
cheerful?	
friendly?	
charming?	
independent?	
capable?	
tough?	
responsible?	
disciplined?	
reliable?	
willing to learn?	

Do you have

good eyesight?	
a good memory?	
a sense of humour?	
(a lot of) imagination?	
determination?	
patience?	
skill?	
talent?	
energy?	
confidence?	
common sense?	

4 Discuss the practical requirements and the skills and qualities necessary for each of the occupations below. Use words and phrases from the questionnaire. Then write short paragraphs about three of the occupations.

accountant
actor
architect
carpenter
doctor
farmer
footballer
journalist
lawyer
librarian
musician
nurse
policeman
teacher

KEY VOCABULARY

Example: *If you're an accountant, you have to work in an office and do a lot of paperwork. You need to be good at adding up figures, and you have to be able to think clearly. You need to be accurate and organised, and it sometimes takes a lot of patience.*

5 Fill in the missing noun or adjective. Use your dictionary if necessary.

KEY VOCABULARY

NOUN	ADJECTIVE
	charming
common sense	
confidence	
determination	
	disciplined
	efficient
energy	
	friendly
	gentle

NOUN	ADJECTIVE
imagination	
	independent
	organised
patience	
	responsible
skill	
	strong
talent	

DISCUSSION

Which of the following aspects of work do you think is the most important?

job satisfaction
a good salary
good conditions of work
responsibility
job security
opportunities for creative work
prospects of promotion

Do you think a dustman should be paid more than a lawyer?

Do you think work is good for the individual?
Do you think it is good for society?

Do you like working?

Work banishes those three great evils: boredom, vice and poverty. (*Voltaire 1694–1728*).

Which of us . . . is to do the hard and dirty work for the rest – and for what pay? Who is to do the pleasant and clean work, and for what pay? (*John Ruskin 1819–1900*).

B APPLYING FOR A JOB

READING

Emma Hall has sent her CV and a covering letter of application in reply to this advertisement.

Arts Officer

The Leisure Services Council requires an experienced professional to work in a team responsible for concerts, theatre, children's entertainment, youth visits abroad, and community associations in a large city. The successful applicant will take over a well-established Arts Section and will organise projects and manage considerable financial resources. He or she will probably be a graduate with arts administration experience. Fluency in French or German will be an added advantage.

Please write to:

Personnel Officer, Leisure Services Council, Gower Street, London WC1G 3HH

CURRICULUM VITAE

Name: Emma Katherine HALL
Address: 205 Thompson Ave, Manchester, M60 4TH.
Tel: 236 1920 (Home)
236 2590 (Work)
Age: 29
Date of Birth: 12 February 1953
Marital Status: Single

Education: St Peter's Comprehensive School, Leeds 1965 – 1971
University of Bristol 1971 – 1974

Qualifications: GCE 'O' Level (8 subjects) 1969
GCE 'A' Level (English, French, Sociology) 1971
BA in English and Drama 1974
RSA Certificate in the Teaching of English as a Second or Foreign Language 1975

Experience: English Teacher College Internationale, Paris 1975 – 1976
Assistant Arts Officer Liverpool Arts Centre 1976 – 1979
(At present) Theatre Administrator Interspace Theatre, Manchester From 1979

Practical skills:
Languages: French (fluent), Spanish (good)
Secretarial: Able to type 40 w p m
Driving licence
I have recently learned how to program a microcomputer.

Interests: Cinema, music, swimming, hang-gliding.

Referees: Robert Davey MP, c/o The House of Commons, Westminster, London, SW1.

Mark Hayton (Manager), Interspace Theatre Co Ltd, 109, Chepstow St, Manchester.

Jane Woodruff, Dept of Community Education, Liverpool Arts Centre, Fortune Sq., Liverpool.

205 Thompson Ave,
Manchester M60 4TH

17 June 1983

Personnel Officer,
Leisure Services Council,
Gower Street,
London WC1G 3HH

Dear Sir,

I am writing to apply for the post of Arts Officer as advertised in the Daily Gazette of 16 June 1983.

As you will see from the enclosed curriculum vitae, I started working as an English teacher in Paris, where I learned to speak French fluently. I then spent three years at the Liverpool Arts Centre. Since 1979, I have been working for Interspace Theatre, and I have had the opportunity to organise workshops, concerts and children's events, as well as regular productions of plays. I am used to working in a team, and I have also been responsible for important financial decisions.

I have now worked in the field of arts administration for seven years and I have thoroughly enjoyed it. Unfortunately, Interspace Theatre is to be closed down as a result of redevelopment, but I should very much like to continue working in this field.

If you consider that my qualifications are suitable, I should be able to attend an interview at any time. I look forward to hearing from you.

Yours faithfully,

Emma Hall

UNIT FIVE

a) Choose the best alternative to the following words or phrases in the advertisement.

KEY VOCABULARY

1 REQUIRES
A takes B asks C demands D needs

2 RESPONSIBLE FOR
A on account of B in charge of
C dependent on D due to

3 ASSOCIATIONS
A connections B relations C groups
D meetings

4 MANAGE
A charge B control C arrange D succeed

5 FINANCIAL RESOURCES
A wealth B budgets C costs D funds

Now choose the best answer.

6 The job advertisement says that fluent French or German is
A necessary.
B profitable.
C desirable.
D extra.

7 Emma is a graduate in
A English, French and Sociology.
B English and Drama.
C the teaching of English.
D French.

8 She has been working as
A a teacher.
B an artist.
C an actress.
D an administrator.

9 She says that she
A used to work in a team.
B is good at working in a team.
C is employed to work in a team.
D is accustomed to working in a team.

10 She expects to be
A made redundant.
B resigned.
C closed down.
D retired.

b) There are several abbreviations in Emma's CV. What do the following stand for?

KEY VOCABULARY

CV	wpm
Ave	MP
Tel	c/o
GCE	Co
'A' level	Ltd
BA	St
Dept	Sq

LANGUAGE PRACTICE

Ask another student questions about his/her education, qualifications, experience, practical skills, and interests.

KEY LANGUAGE

Talking about the past:

Present perfect (indefinite past)	Have you (ever) worked in a shop?
(recent past)	I've just left school.
(unfinished past with *for/since*)	I've (already) worked there for four years/since 1979.
Present perfect continuous (for incomplete activity continuing into the present)	How long have you been working there?
Past simple (definite past)	How long did you stay there? I worked there for three years.
with *ago*	I started the job four months ago.

GUIDED WRITING ACTIVITY

a) Write a CV for yourself, using the headings in Emma's CV.

b) Think about your experience and qualifications, and decide what job you would be best qualified to do. Then write an advertisement for that job.

c) Write a letter of application in reply to your job advertisement, using Emma's letter as a model. Notice how Emma expands the information in her CV where she feels that her experience would be particularly useful in the job she is applying for. She organises her paragraph content as follows.

Paragraph 1: Opening with reference to the advertisement.
Paragraph 2: Information.
Paragraph 3: Reasons for application.
Paragraph 4: Conclusion.

Writing formal letters: KEY LANGUAGE

Look carefully at Emma's letter of application.

1 Notice the **position** of
   Emma's address.
   the date.
   the name and address of the person she is writing to.
   the beginning of each paragraph.
   'Dear Sir,' the ending and the signature.

2 Notice the **punctuation.**
   Remember that contractions are *not* used in formal letters.
   Example: *I am writing . . .*

3 Notice the **beginning** and **ending.**
   If you do not know the name of the person you are writing to:
   Begin: 'Dear Sir,' (or 'Dear Sir or Madam,')
   End: 'Yours faithfully,'

   If you know the person's name:
   Begin: (e.g.) 'Dear Miss Hall,' (or 'Dear Ms Hall,')
   End: 'Yours sincerely,'

Remember: *Never* write your name at the top of the letter.
Always write as clearly and simply as possible.
If your signature is difficult to read, you should print your name clearly beneath it.

C SPECULATING ABOUT THE FUTURE

READING

An industrial robot

Working it out

A REVOLUTION IS UNDER WAY. The technology of computer science is having a dramatic effect on our lives, and the most immediate consequence of this technology is its impact on employment. Robots and computer-controlled machines have already joined the work force in highly industrialised countries, such as the USA, West Germany, and Japan. They have taken over routine jobs on the car assembly line, and in Volkswagen, for instance, three robots can replace ten men working on a two-shift system. One giant American company has shown that it is now possible to replace half its 37,000 assembly workers with machines. Robots carry out tedious tasks with a high degree of reliability for an hourly 'wage' of about \$5 (the average cost of maintaining them). The average human worker on a car assembly line, in contrast, earns about \$18 an hour.

An automated office

Bill is an assembly worker

Automation? Well, it depends, doesn't it? I wouldn't mind if I had a shorter working week. In fact, I'd be delighted. More time with the family, the chance to take up sport again, maybe do some sailing. And I've always wanted to learn a foreign language, Russian, perhaps, or Chinese. But don't get me wrong – I don't mind working. And I'd be frightened if I lost my job. I've got a family to look after and I'm still paying the mortgage on our house. I run a car as well, and I couldn't do without that. It all costs money, and I don't know what I'd do if I couldn't earn anything. I'd have to give it all up, I suppose.

There is obviously a lot to be said for releasing people from work that is often noisy, dirty, and even dangerous, and many workers can be retrained for more pleasant and interesting work. Nevertheless, competition is forcing employers to cut back the labour force. As one managing director put it, 'Are you going to reduce your work force by 25% by putting in robots, or by 100% by going out of business?' As a result of automation, workers are being sacked, and many will be permanently unemployed.

While workers directly employed in manufacturing will certainly suffer, it is likely that the impact of automation on the information industry will be even greater. In Britain, about 40% of the working population is engaged in dealing with information: making telephone calls, writing reports, filing invoices and orders, for example. Employees in this sector, including secretaries, typists, clerks, managers and accountants, can be replaced by microelectronic information processsors. It may not be long before white-collar desk-workers join factory-workers in the increasing numbers of unemployed.

Prince Philip has commented, 'A few years ago, everybody was saying that we must have more leisure. Now that everybody has got so much leisure – it may be involuntary, but they have got it – they are complaining they are unemployed.' Not surprisingly, this rather tactless remark aroused angry reactions from the trade unions in Britain. People who are out of work lose their self-confidence and sense of dignity. People who have no income cannot afford to enjoy their leisure.

So what does the future hold, if the computer is taking jobs away from humans? A radical social change is necessary if we are to survive the automation revolution. If large groups in society are dissatisfied and restless, an increase in rioting and violent crime is inevitable. It is up to the politicians to come to terms with the problem. An obvious solution is a shorter working week. Less time at work would mean more time available to take up new leisure activities, and more opportunities for further education. An increased demand for leisure facilities would lead to an expansion of the service industries (like catering, travel agencies, entertainment and sport) and more job vacancies. In theory, even the unemployed should have a reasonable income. After all, thanks to the new technology, it will be economic to pay people *not* to work!

LANGUAGE PRACTICE

1 **a)** Look at the words and phrases in the box. They are used to indicate particular examples of a general idea. Find the indicators in the text, and in each case, underline the *example(s) indicated* and the *idea that is exemplified.*

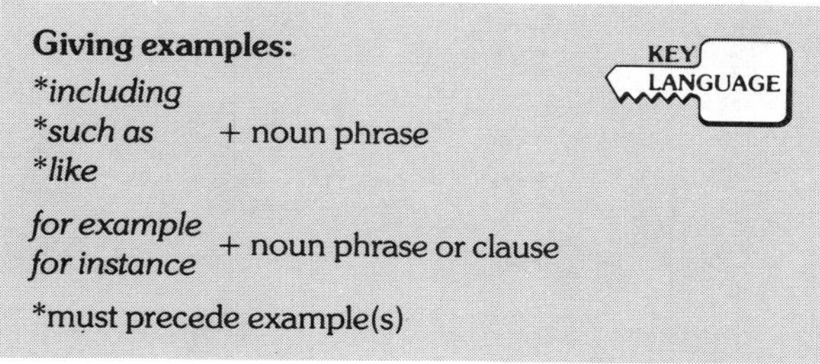

Giving examples:

KEY LANGUAGE

**including*
**such as* + noun phrase
**like*

for example
for instance + noun phrase or clause

*must precede example(s)

b) Expand the following sentences with suitable examples.

1 There are a variety of outdoor occupations.
2 Cars are produced in several countries.
3 Many people have to work at night.
4 Japan is famous for producing microelectronic goods.
5 Robots are taking over routine tasks in factories.

---

2 Read the following sentences, and decide what type of word is missing.
Choose the missing word from the list below.

KEY VOCABULARY

earn	gain	
economic	industry	
economical	job	salaries
employee	retired	staff
employer	sacked	task
career	factory	wages

1 Anna has decided to take up medicine as a _______.
2 I don't mind what I _______, as long as the work is interesting.
3 Bill is an assembly worker in a car _______.
4 Television producers usually have high _______.
5 It makes _______ sense to use robots on the assembly line.
6 The cashier was _______ for stealing from the till.
7 It's a large hotel with a _______ of several hundred.
8 Each _______ will receive a 10% pay increase.

---

3 Look at Bill's views on automation.
What would he do if he had a shorter working week? What would happen to him if he lost his job?

Talking about the hypothetical future:

KEY LANGUAGE

If + past simple, . . . *would(n't)* / *could(n't)* / *might(n't)* + infinitive

If I had a shorter working week, I wouldn't mind.
I'd be frightened if I lost my job.

INTERPRETATION ACTIVITY

Using information from the text, write two paragraphs describing the possible advantages and disadvantages of automation.

First paragraph: *Automation could have many social advantages. . . .*

Second paragraph: *On the other hand, there may be serious disadvantages. . . .*

D DISCUSSING A COURSE OF ACTION

LISTENING ACTIVITY

a) Listen to the news item about the *Daily Gazette*. After the news item, you will hear short interviews with four people who are involved in the newspaper. For each person interviewed, make notes on the following:

name
occupation/position
point of view

b) Listen to the tape again, and write down the answers to the following questions.

How many print-workers does the *Daily Gazette* employ at present?
How many print-workers does the *Daily Gazette* plan to lay off?
How much money will the proposed cutbacks save?
What is the print-worker's basic wage?
What is his average pay with overtime?

c) Can you work out how much money would be saved in one year if the printers didn't do overtime?

READING ALOUD

a) Listen to the interview with Sir Arthur Richardson, and follow the tapescript below. As you listen, mark those words which are stressed.

RICHARDSON: Well, basically, the *Gazette* is losing money. Our circulation is quite steady, but rising costs will put us out of business unless we economise. The new technology has given us a chance to do just that. Obviously, I don't like having to take away people's jobs. But I have considered the matter very carefully, and there's just no alternative if we are to save the paper. It would be an absolute tragedy if the *Gazette* had to close.

ANGIE: But surely new printing equipment will be extremely expensive.

RICHARDSON: Yes, of course it will. But, in the long term, it will pay off. It will certainly be cheaper and more efficient to use computer technology than to employ print-workers.

b) Sir Arthur stresses several words that are usually unstressed. Find some examples of unusual stress. Why do you think he does this? What effect does it have?

c) Now practise reading the text aloud in pairs. Change roles when you have finished.

DISCUSSION

The print-workers are likely to go on strike. Why?
Think of other reasons why workers go on strike.
Do you think workers should have the right to strike?
What are the people in this photograph doing?
Why are they doing this? What are they carrying?
Do you think this kind of action is ever effective?

I wrote a long composition

ROLE PLAY

a) Journalists and print-workers from the *Daily Gazette* agree to meet round the table to discuss the chairman's proposal. You have made notes on the various points of view expressed in the radio interviews. You are one of the journalists or print-workers at the meeting. Say where you think the responsibility lies for the *Gazette's* problems, and discuss what course of action should be taken.

KEY LANGUAGE

Blaming and accusing:

It's (his) fault that + clause
(He's) responsible for + noun/-ING
I blame (him) for + noun/-ING

Denying responsibility (1):

It's not (his) fault that + clause
(He's) not responsible for + noun/-ING
You can't blame (him) for + noun/-ING

Suggesting a course of action:

I suggest we . . .
I (don't) think we should . . .
We'd better (not) . . .
Wouldn't it be sensible to . . . ?
What about . . . ?
Shall we . . . ?
We could . . .

Accepting suggestions:

That's a good / an excellent / not a bad idea. / suggestion.

That's certainly worth thinking about. / considering.

Rejecting suggestions:

That's easier said than done.
That's all very well, but . . .
You don't seem to realise that . . .

b) **New information:** Now listen to a further news item.

c) The print-workers agree to meet the management of the *Daily Gazette* in a final attempt to reach a compromise solution in order to avoid the strike and closure of the newspaper. You are one of the print-workers or management representatives at the meeting. Continue the role play and try to come to a satisfactory agreement.

EXAM PRACTICE

PAPER 1: READING COMPREHENSION

Section A *(Suggestions for the exam – see Unit 1)*

In this section you must choose the word or phrase which best completes each sentence. For each question, 1 to 25, *indicate on your answer sheet* the letter A, B, C or D against the number of the question.

1 It _______ a lot of patience to be a nurse.
A uses B takes C spends D costs

2 I must write things down because I have a terrible _______.
A memory B mind C thought D sense

3 You're late again – please try to be _______ in future.
A accurate B efficient C punctual D reliable

4 Are you used _______ on your own?
A to work B to working C at work D with working

5 He's been teaching music for years, but he hasn't any _______.
A examinations B experience C experiences D qualifications

6 Do you _______ to use a computer?
A know B able C understand D know how

7 He has been out of work _______ a long time.
A during B since C for D through

8 The initials PS _______ *postscript*.
A make up B fill in C stand for D mean to

9 She ought to _______ singing with a voice like that.
A take on B take up C take to D undertake

10 Grace Kelly had a brief but highly successful _______ as an actress.
A career B occupation C work D profession

11 Write the name and address of your present _______ in block capitals.
A boss B chef C chief D employer

12 It's not my _______ that the money was stolen.
A mistake B crime C guilt D fault

13 They formed a partnership and _______ an engineering company.
A made up B set up C brought up D joined up

14 Some of the _______ were over-qualified for the job.
A appointments B applications C applicants D contracts

15 He earns a reasonable _______ as a builder.
A money B pay C wages D living

16 I'd like to do _______ work in the afternoons.
A part-time B overtime B full time C daytime

17 He was given the _______ to work abroad.
A possibility B opportunity C occasion D advantage

18 Some rock-stars live on the _______ from their record sales.
A pension B salary C benefit D income

19 He isn't _______ run the business alone.
A capable of B able to C good at D used to

20 The company pays expenses _______ accommodation and travel.
A such as B so as C such like D so on

21 Will you _______ the children while I'm out?
A pay attention to B care about C look out D look after

22 He's very amusing, and I like his _______ of humour.
A sense B feeling C mind D meaning

23 The company director _______ the workers for the low output.
A disapproved B complained C blamed D accused

24 She has the _______ to be a great dancer.
A possibility B ability C prospect D quality

25 The company _______ half its work force.
A unemployed B turned down C dismissed D retired

PAPER 2: COMPOSITION

(Suggestions for the exam – see Unit 3)

Your answers must follow exactly the instructions given, and must be of between 120 and 180 words each.

1 A British company is planning to make a film near your town and requires an English-speaking guide for three months. Write a letter to the film company applying for the job. You should make the beginning and ending like those of an ordinary letter, but the address is not to be counted in the number of words.

2 A popular colleague is leaving your company to work abroad. Write the speech you would make at the office farewell party.

3 You have been asked to supply a reference for one of your previous employees. Write the reference describing his/her professional skills and personal qualities, and recommending him/her for the job in question.

4 Job satisfaction or a good salary? Explain which in your opinion is more important, giving your reasons.

PAPER 3: USE OF ENGLISH

Section A, Question 2 *(Suggestions for the exam – see Unit 3)*

Finish each of the following sentences in such a way that it means exactly the same as the sentence printed before it.

Example: *The book was so interesting.*
Answer: *It was such* **an interesting book.**

a) She learnt to drive four years ago.
She has ....

b) It takes a lot of energy to be a teacher.
A teacher ....

c) He doesn't like his job, so he isn't happy.
If ....

d) I suggest we talk to the director.
What about ....

e) The factory closed down as a result of so many strikes.
Because there ....

f) The office is quite near the station.
The office isn't ....

g) We must go or we'll be late.
If ....

h) You'll miss the train if you don't hurry.
Unless ....

i) He left early because he wanted to avoid the rush-hour.
He left early in ....

j) I last heard from him in July.
I haven't ....

Section A, Question 3 *(Suggestions for the exam – see Unit 3)*

Complete the following sentences with an appropriate phrase made from TAKE.

Example: The plane **took off** a few minutes late.

a) Robert is like his father, but Jenny ______ her mother.

b) What are you going to ______ as a career?

c) Tom has ______ working late at the office.

d) The workers want to ______ the factory.

e) I haven't signed those letters yet, so don't ______

Section B, Question 5 *(Suggestions for the exam – see Unit 4)*

You are the secretary of David Evans, the Personnel Officer for the Leisure Services Council, Gower Street, London WC1G 3HH. He is at a meeting today and has left you some instructions on his desk. Using the information given below, write the letter according to Mr Evans' instructions. Your answer should be of between 120 and 180 words.

June 24 **MEMO** Friday

Would you write a letter in reply to Emma Hall's application for the post of Arts Officer, asking her to come for an interview at a suitable time next Friday – 45 mins should be long enough. Ask her to phone if she can't make it. Suggest best train from Manchester & explain that we're only 15 mins walk from Euston. Travel expenses will be paid.
Thanks – David.

205 Thompson Ave,
Manchester M60 4TH

17 June 1983

for the post of Arts Officer as
zette of 16 June 1983.
e enclosed curriculum vitae,
ve I
ee
have
e had
nd
plays.
been

istration
tunately,

e

sider that my qualifications are suitable,
to attend an interview at any time.
hearing from you,
Yours faithfully,
Emma Hall

rincipal Services:

Veekdays

		Manchester Piccadilly	London Euston
A	✗	**06.15a**	**09.02**
B	✗	**07.00**	**09.37**
	✗	**07.40**	**10.24**
A	✗	**08.10**	**10.50**
A	✗	**09.15**	**12.09**
E	⊕	**09.40**	**12.25**
A	✗	**10.15**	**12.59**
B	✗	**11.15**	**14.00**
E	⊕	10.45a	14.10
A	✗	**12.15**	**15.01**
	☕	11.45a	15.15
A	✗	**13.15**	**16.00**
B	✗	13.45a	16.56
C	✗	**14.15**	**17.07**
		14.23y	17.58
SX	✗	**15.15**	**18.06**
SO	⊕	**15.15**	**18.06**
SX		**15.45**	**18.25**
A	✗	**16.13**	**18.53**
A	✗	**17.12**	**19.56**
B	✗	**18.15**	**21.00**
	⊕	18.45a	21.48
	⊕	**19.15**	**22.01**
B	✗	19.45a	22.37

Notes
- a Change at Crewe
- y Change at Birmingham New Street
- A ✗ Mondays to Fridays. ⊕ Saturdays
- B ✗ Mondays to Fridays. ☕ Saturdays
- C ✗ Mondays to Fridays only
- E ⊕ Mondays to Fridays only
- SO Saturdays only
- SX Saturdays expected

FRIDAY JULY 1

9:30-10:30 am	Finance meeting
11 - 11.15 am	Daily Gazette reporter - give information on projects
11.45-12.30 am	Discuss new youth club project with local organiser
12.30 pm	Lunch with Vanessa
2.15 pm	Phone Athens to confirm travel arrangements
4-5pm	See manager of Angel Theatre about next year's grant

UNIT 6

HAPPY DAYS?

A TALKING ABOUT INTELLECTUAL QUALITIES AND PLACES OF EDUCATION

TALKING POINT

Look at these two photographs. Does/did your school look more like the one on the left, or the one on the right?

Which do you think is the better environment for education?

READING

The school that I'd like

IN DECEMBER 1967, The Observer newspaper organised a competition for secondary school children (age 11–18) to write an essay on **'The school that I'd like.'** In most of the entries, the children's ideal school was not at all like their present one. Here is a selection of their views.

The school I'd like would be one whose primary aim was to teach me how to live, and make me a responsible member of society. *Christa, 16*

At the moment we seem to be working merely for the sake of examinations, whereas we should work to satisfy our curiosities. *Patricia, 15*

The discipline and life of the school would be based on freedom for the pupil. No uniforms and a minimum of control would be vital, and the pupils, male and female, would be treated as adults and allowed to see if they can live together in a community like intelligent people. *Christopher, 16*

Essentially school must be part of family life, and for this reason, day schools should be the usual form of school. For how will a teenager, if unable at this stage of his life to combine school and home life, be able to cope with the frustrations and difficulties of life later? *Mary, 14*

. . . tables would replace desks, which are small and an enemy of knees. *Judith, 15*

The pupils would talk freely about religion, politics, music, sport or whatever else they would wish to discuss. They would quietly (or loudly) debate, read and laugh. *Judith, 13*

The pupils should be given more chance to speak and the teacher should be given a chance to listen. *Susan, 13*

The school I would like is one where there are young teachers because I find that most teachers who have been teaching for a long time try to model schools on what it was like in their own schooldays when it was not as enjoyable as today. *Mark, 11*

The school would be a large spacious building with underfloor central heating so that people who enjoyed going without their shoes could do so, if they wished, in comfort. *Angela, 15*

I myself would like more English and less arithmetic. English is so much more imaginative. The only imagination I use in arithmetic is when I guess the answers. *Melissa, 11*

If school-goers were treated as responsible people, many rules could be abolished. *Janet, 16*

I would like my school to be called St Monica's and if possible to be situated in the Austrian Alps. *Colette, 13*

The object is to promote creative ability in the individual, and not simply to present facts. In the future, the school will try to present material so that the student will become deeply involved and interested in his work; for the student who enjoys his work is always the one who makes good progress and understands his work as opposed to simply learning it. *K (boy), 17*

Schools usually have one thing in common – they are institutions of today run on the principles of yesterday. *M (girl), 15*

a) Find words or phrases in the text which mean:

main	pupils
only	regulations
essential	got rid of
type	aim
period	encourage
deal with	instead of
opportunity	theories

KEY VOCABULARY

b) Explain what the underlined words refer to.

1 The school I'd like would be one whose primary aim . . .

2 . . . part of family life, and for this reason, day-schools . . .

3 For how will a teenager, if unable at this stage of his life . . .

4 . . . their own schooldays when it was not as enjoyable . . .

5 . . . could do so if they wished . . .

c) Do/did you have similar views about school? Talk about your experiences at school.

LANGUAGE PRACTICE

1 a) If the schoolchildren had their way, what would school be like? Talk about their opinions on the following points:

aims of schooling
the school environment
discipline
choice of subjects
teachers and teaching methods
the role of the child's family
exams

b) What do you suppose are the schoolchildren's opinions of their present school?
Use the headings in **a**).

KEY LANGUAGE

Talking about an imaginary situation:

(If they *had* their way), the school *would* be a large spacious building.
tables *would* replace desks.

Note: It is possible to leave out *if* + clause when the situation has been mentioned previously or is understood.

2 a) In your opinion, what must a school offer in order to provide a good education for a child? Choose the five most important points from the list below.

KEY VOCABULARY

b) Discuss your choice with another student.

c) Write a short paragraph about what you think a school should offer and give your reasons.

Begin: *I think it's very important for a school to have . . . because . . .*

Pleasant surroundings	☐	Sports facilities	☐
Wide range of subjects	☐	Strict discipline	☐
Close contact with parents	☐	Good exam results	☐
Non-examination subjects	☐	Library facilities	☐
Opportunities for pupils to take responsibility in running the school	☐	Language laboratories	☐
		Friendly teaching staff	☐
Opportunities to do arts subjects e.g. Painting, Music, Drama	☐	Facilities for fast and slow learners	☐
		Homework	☐
Good careers information	☐	Short holidays	☐
Small classes	☐		
Educational visits outside school	☐	Opportunities to do practical subjects e.g. Computer Studies, Typing, Home Economics	☐
Contacts with local industry and commerce	☐		

3 In Britain, reports are written by the teachers about the pupils' progress, usually twice or three times a year, and the pupils take the report home to their parents. Look at Duncan Webber's report.

a) Find words in the school report which mean the opposite of the words below.

KEY VOCABULARY

boring	lazy	
stupid	easy	dull
uninterested	reluctant	clumsy

BEECHCROFT SCHOOL

Name: *Duncan Webber* Term: *Autumn* Form: *4B*

Number in form: *29* Place in form: *10th* Average age: *14.4* Attendance: *–*

Mark		
72	English	*Very able. His essays are very interesting But at times he is a little too enthusiastic*
52	Geography	*A little careless in his work, although seems to be quite intelligent*
60	History	*Keen and hard-working.*
69	Languages	*His written French is quite fluent. However he finds the oral work quite difficult.*
45	Mathematics	*He needs to concentrate on his algebra which is not satisfactory. He does not seem to enjoy his maths.*
70	Physics	*Willing but has some difficulties.*
35	Chemistry	*Not a successful term. Must do better if he hopes to do his 'O' level.*
50	Biology	*He is quite bright but has not done his best.*
68	Art and Craft	*Shows an imaginative and critical approach to history of art as well as practical work.*
–	Music	*Careless at times.*
—	Sport	*A skilful football player, and very impressive on the basketball court.*

General Progress and conduct: *Duncan is a clever boy but he is not very ambitious about his future. He has clearly made progress in certain subjects, but does not seem willing to make an effort in those subjects which interest him less. He must work harder if he is to be successful in his 'O' levels next year.*

Form Master: *[signature]* Headmaster: *[signature]*

Next term begins: *Tues 11 Jan* Next term ends: *Thurs 19 April.*

b) Make nouns out of the following adjectives:

KEY VOCABULARY

able	successful
enthusiastic	imaginative
intelligent	critical
fluent	ambitious

c) What subjects do/did you study at school? Which ones do/did you like most? Which ones do/did you like least? If you have left school, did you find any subject particularly useful in your career?

4 In Britain, children have to attend school from the age of 5 to 16. Before this, they may go to *nursery school*. At the age of 5, they go to *primary school* and at 11 they go to *secondary school* which is either a state school (usually *comprehensive*), or an independent school where the parents must pay the fees.

At the age of 14 or 15, the pupils have some very important decisions to make about their future. Look at the chart below which shows the choices open to them.

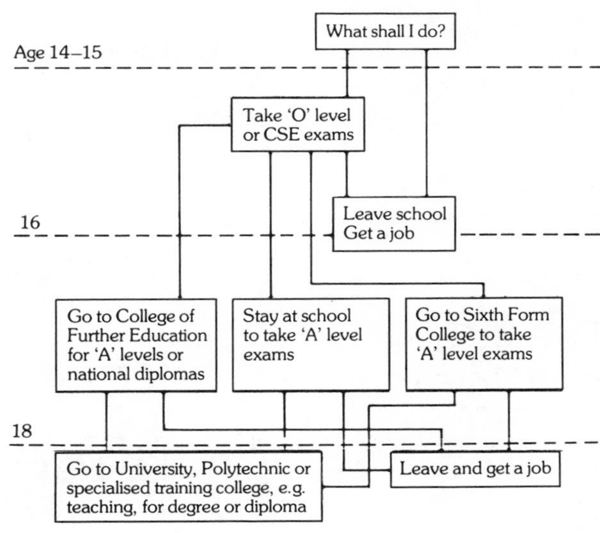

NOTE: CSE = Certificate of Secondary Education, a less academic exam taken at 16.

a) Write a short paragraph explaining these alternatives.

Begin: *At the age of 16, pupils can either take their exams or leave school. If they want to continue their education, they can either . . .*

b) Draw a chart showing the educational system in your country.

5 Listen to these five teenagers talking about their plans for the future.

a) In each case, decide how old the speakers are, and make notes about their plans.

b) Write sentences about what each pupil is hoping to do and what choices are open to him or her.

c) What do you think these pupils are like at school? What subjects are they good or bad at? Use the adjectives in 3 to describe them.

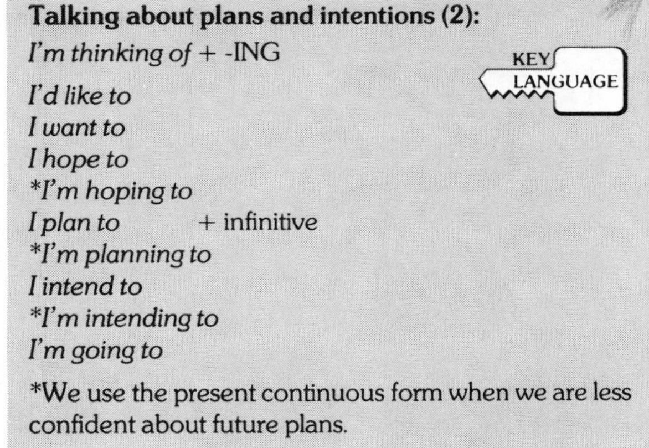

Talking about plans and intentions (2):

KEY LANGUAGE

I'm thinking of + -ING

I'd like to
I want to
I hope to
**I'm hoping to*
I plan to + infinitive
**I'm planning to*
I intend to
**I'm intending to*
I'm going to

*We use the present continuous form when we are less confident about future plans.

DISCUSSION

Do you think that children have to make important decisions about their future before they are old enough?
Should parents take an active role in the education of their children or is it entirely the responsibility of the school?

In the school system of your country, is success in exams important? Should it be more or less so?
Does school education give a good preparation for adult life?

B REPORTING PAST EVENTS

READING

Operation Drake

EARNING is not confined to the classroom or the university lecture hall. Research is continually being carried out to discover more about the world we live in. One of the most ambitious research projects ever undertaken was *Operation Drake*, a scientific expedition which followed the route taken round the world by the explorer Sir Francis Drake in the sixteenth century. The object of the expedition was to find out more about the plants, the wildlife, the people, the environment and the history of the places it visited. But *Operation Drake* was unique because it involved over four hundred young people between the ages of seventeen and twenty-four, of both sexes and from twenty-seven nations. These 'Young Explorers' assisted the scientists at every phase of the expedition, and their contribution to the project was extremely valuable. Above all, *Operation Drake* gave them the opportunity to live and work in environments and amongst cultures very different from their own, and so allowed them to learn more about themselves and their attitudes towards others.

The sailing boat *Eye of the Wind* was the base of the expedition. It set sail from Plymouth on November 8th, 1978 on its two-year voyage of exploration and discovery. When it arrived in Panama on January 1st, 1979, the research team carried out a number of projects, including crossing to the Pacific coast on foot, and studying the animal and plant life in the tropical rain forests. Then the *Eye of the Wind* sailed across the Pacific Ocean to Fiji. No sooner had it arrived there than the islands were hit by a hurricane, and the Young Explorers spent four months helping to rebuild the houses destroyed by the winds. After leaving Fiji, they sailed to Papua New Guinea, where one of their tasks was to study the health of the population in remote areas, and to advise the government on the planning of health facilities. During their stay in the country, they explored the Strickland River to make a collection of animals and plants. But before doing this, they had to walk through the jungle for fifteen days, and climb 1,000 metres.

On January 22nd, 1980, the expedition reached Indonesia, where they made a survey of the forest areas to study the possibility of setting up a nature reserve. At the same time, another team was diving on the coral reef surrounding the neighbouring islands. The next stop was Kenya. As soon as they arrived, they began work on a survey of the ruins of an old trading town. They were also asked to mark the boundaries of a game reserve. After it had left Kenya, the *Eye of the Wind* made its way through the Suez Canal, and the Young Explorers did research into the effects of pollution on marine life while sailing through the Mediterranean Sea. Finally the expedition returned home to Plymouth on December 9th, 1980.

At times, conditions were extremely difficult, and some projects had to be modified or abandoned. But despite this, *Operation Drake* was an outstanding success. The information gathered was useful not only to the researchers. Tapes of interviews were flown back from the most distant expedition camps to Capital Radio in London. These were broadcast to some 220 schools which received a newsletter each week, as well as charts and photographs of the expedition's progress and findings. In this way, many young people who would probably never have the opportunities offered to the Young Explorers could take part in the project and learn about subjects that they might never have thought about.

a) Choose the best alternative to the following words or phrases in the text.

KEY VOCABULARY

1 CONFINED TO
A controlled by B limited to C found in D surrounded by

2 UNIQUE
A single B individual C typical D exceptional

3 PHASE
A stage B season C day D place

4 TASKS
A jobs B teams C works D difficulties

5 SURVEY
A plan B view C study D estimate

6 FINDINGS
A opinions B discoveries C measurements D experiences

Now choose the best answer.

7 The expedition offered unique opportunities to
A teenagers.
B both sexes.
C scientists.
D young people.

8 The expedition arrived in Fiji
A before the hurricane.
B during the hurricane.
C after the hurricane.
D as soon as the hurricane.

9 They explored the Strickland River
A while they were carrying out a project for the government.
B before collecting animals and plants.
C before walking through the jungle for fifteen days.
D as soon as they reached Papua New Guinea.

10 *Operation Drake*
A was fairly successful.
B made valuable research findings.
C wasn't useful to researchers.
D had to be abandoned.

b) How do you think the Young Explorers were chosen to take part in *Operation Drake?* Make a list of the qualities and skills needed for such an expedition.

LANGUAGE PRACTICE

Look at these notes made by a member of the *Operation Drake* team. Make sentences using the words that follow each note.

Example – Jan 1st: *After arriving in Panama, we crossed to the Pacific coast on foot.*

Date	Notes	Words to use
1979 Jan 1st	Arrive Panama On foot to Pacific coast	AFTER + -ING
	Leave Panama Sail to Fiji	AFTER + clause
March	Arrive Fiji Islands hit by hurricane	AS SOON AS + clause
	Help to rebuild houses Leave Fiji	BEFORE + -ING
August	Arrive Papua New Guinea Study health conditions	WHEN + clause
	During stay in Papua New Guinea explore Strickland River	WHILE + -ING
1980 June	Arrive Kenya Survey of ruins	NO SOONER . . . THAN + clause
	Mark boundaries of game reserve Leave Kenya	BEFORE + clause
Sept.	Sail through Mediterranean Research into pollution	WHILE + clause
Dec 9th	Arrive Plymouth	IT WASN'T UNTIL . . . THAT + clause

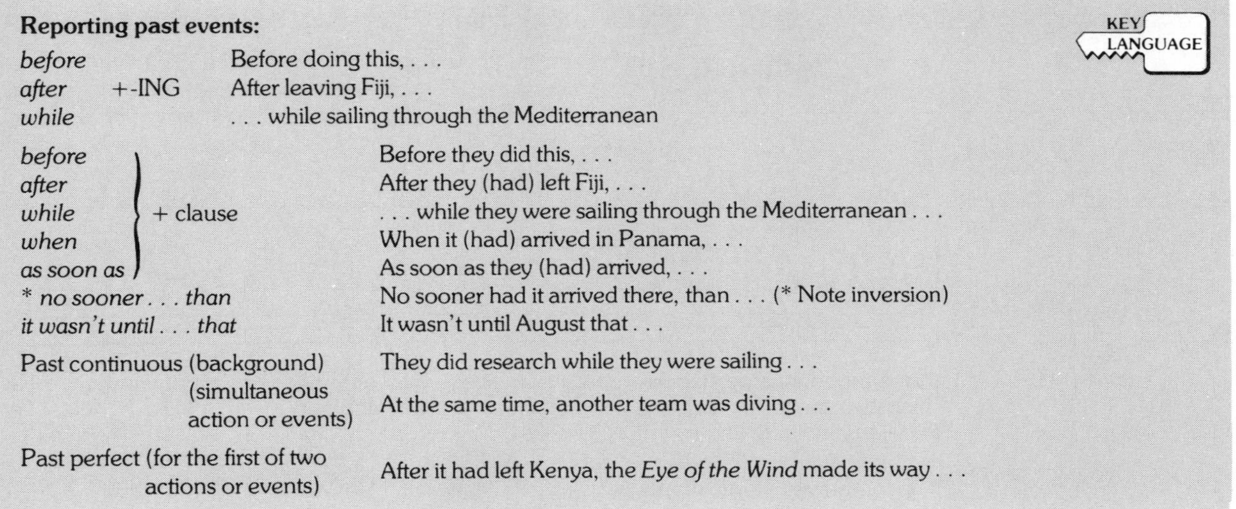

KEY LANGUAGE

Reporting past events:

before		Before doing this, . . .
after	+ -ING	After leaving Fiji, . . .
while		. . . while sailing through the Mediterranean
before		Before they did this, . . .
after		After they (had) left Fiji, . . .
while	+ clause	. . . while they were sailing through the Mediterranean . . .
when		When it (had) arrived in Panama, . . .
as soon as		As soon as they (had) arrived, . . .
* *no sooner . . . than*		No sooner had it arrived there, than . . . (* Note inversion)
it wasn't until . . . that		It wasn't until August that . . .
Past continuous (background)		They did research while they were sailing . . .
(simultaneous action or events)		At the same time, another team was diving . . .
Past perfect (for the first of two actions or events)		After it had left Kenya, the *Eye of the Wind* made its way . . .

GUIDED WRITING ACTIVITY

Operation Drake was one of the biggest expeditions of its kind, but it was not the first. Perhaps the most important voyage of discovery was made between 1831 and 1836 by the famous naturalist, Charles Darwin. His findings during this journey formed the basis of his book, *The Origin of Species.* Look at the map of the route he took in his ship, the *Beagle.*

Write an account of Darwin's journey round the world, based on the information on the map.

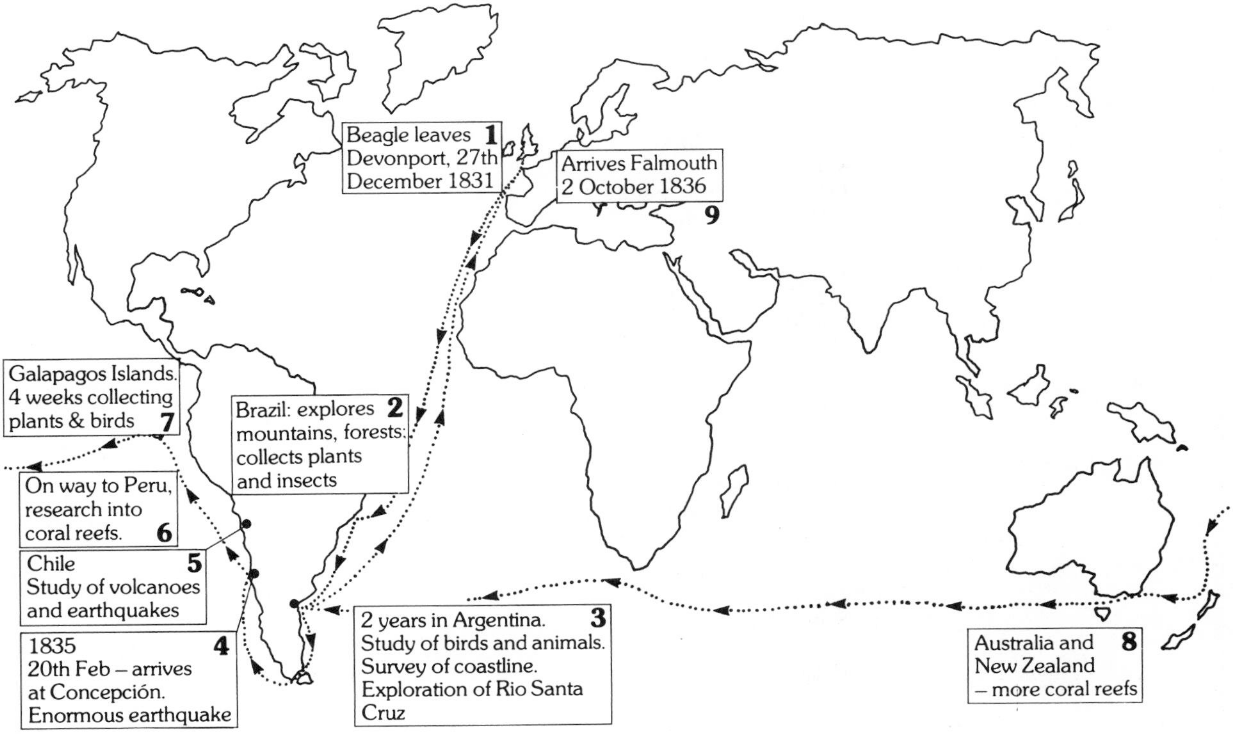

Beagle leaves Devonport, 27th December 1831 **1**

Brazil: explores mountains, forests; collects plants and insects **2**

2 years in Argentina. Study of birds and animals. Survey of coastline. Exploration of Rio Santa Cruz **3**

1835 20th Feb – arrives at Concepción. Enormous earthquake **4**

Chile Study of volcanoes and earthquakes **5**

On way to Peru, research into coral reefs. **6**

Galapagos Islands. 4 weeks collecting plants & birds **7**

Australia and New Zealand – more coral reefs **8**

Arrives Falmouth 2 October 1836 **9**

C TALKING ABOUT STUDY SKILLS

READING

HOW TO PASS YOUR EXAMS!

Preparing for exams involves more than just trying to remember a series of facts at the last minute. It means careful study and efficient revision right from the start of your course. Try this questionnaire and see if you're ready.

1 When you study, do you:
a) try and find a quiet well-lit room?
b) read while lying on your bed or taking a bath?
c) play the latest rock record?

2 Do you study:
a) if possible, during the morning with regular breaks every two or three hours?
b) for twenty minutes, then get up and make some coffee, phone a friend, another twenty minutes, more coffee . . . ?
c) mostly at night?

3 When you learn something, how long do you remember it?
a) I don't know, about a month, I suppose.
b) Once I've learnt something, I can remember it – that's just common sense!
c) Probably less than twenty-four hours, so I must make an effort to revise.

4 If you come across a word you don't understand, do you:
a) ignore it?
b) look it up in the dictionary immediately?
c) read on and try to work out the meaning from the context?

5 How often do you go over your notes?
a) Every day.
b) Every month.
c) The night before the exam.

6 When you're in class, do you:
a) read the newspaper?
b) talk as much as possible?
c) join in as much as possible and ask questions when you don't understand?

7 When you're given homework, do you:
a) hand it in on time?
b) hand it in late?
c) think of an excuse (e.g. the dog ate it) and not hand it in at all?

8 If you get bad marks, do you:
a) check how the others did, to see if they got bad marks as well?
b) ask the teacher to give you better marks?
c) leave the room in a temper?

9 When the teacher corrects your work, do you:
a) try and understand the mistakes you made?
b) put it in your bag and forget about it?
c) put it in your bag and promise to look at it later?

10 Can you reproduce what was taught in class by looking at your notes?
a) Yes.
b) Yes, if I can read my handwriting.
c) No, because I don't take any.

11 Do you ever take notes in diagram form?
a) No, I just write down what the teacher says.
b) Yes, I think it's clearer when I revise.
c) What's a diagram?

12 At the end of your class, do you:
a) ask your friend for his notes?
b) fold up your newspaper and go and have a coffee?
c) think over what you've just learnt?

13 How much do you know about the exams you're taking?
a) Well, I know there are five papers.
b) I'm still waiting for the teacher to tell me.
c) I've looked at some of the past papers.

14 When you start revising for exams, do you:
a) panic a few weeks before and work all day and night?
b) not worry at all and put it off until the night before?
c) work out a timetable which allows you plenty of time?

15 What material do you use for your revision?
a) The course book, because the authors know it all.
b) Notes, course book, further reference books, e.g. dictionary, grammar.
c) Lists of words.

16 The evening before an exam, do you:
a) work all night?
b) do something other than revision and go to bed early?
c) take your mind off the exam by staying out late?

17 In the exam, do you:
a) read the whole paper carefully and answer those questions you can do quickly?
b) work steadily through the paper without reading it through?
c) read the whole paper and then move closer to your neighbour so you can copy his answers?

18 If the exam paper says, 'DO NOT WRITE IN THIS MARGIN', what do you do?
a) I don't write in the margin.
b) I *try* not to write in the margin.
c) I put candle wax in the margin, so the examiner can't write in it.

How to score

1	a)5	b)2	c)0	**10**	a)5	b)2	c)0
2	a)5	b)0	c)1	**11**	a)2	b)5	c)0
3	a)2	b)0	c)5	**12**	a)2	b)0	c)5
4	a)0	b)2	c)5	**13**	a)1	b)0	c)5
5	a)5	b)3	c)0	**14**	a)2	b)0	c)5
6	a)0	b)0	c)5	**15**	a)1	b)5	c)1
7	a)5	b)2	c)0	**16**	a)1	b)5	c)0
8	a)5	b)0	c)0	**17**	a)5	b)2	c) Oh dear!
9	a)5	b)0	c)1	**18**	a)5	b)1	c) Are you sure you want to pass?

Now add up your total score.

61–90 points: Well done, you are preparing yourself for the exams very efficiently but don't be too satisfied with yourself. Make sure you keep up the good work with regular revision and by reading as much as possible. And don't forget to do some practice papers under exam conditions – and that means timing yourself!

31–60 points: You'll have to make more effort if you want to do well. Be a little more positive in class and do make sure you've made a revision timetable which you can stick to. Cut down on those discothèques and parties; studying can be fun as well!

0–30 points: Oh dear, you've got a lot of work to do if you're going to catch up! But there's still time if you get down to work immediately. Try and think very carefully about everything you do in class. Write your notes down on small cards and read them while you're cleaning your teeth or waiting for the bus. There's no time to lose!

LANGUAGE PRACTICE

1 **a)** What do the following compound verbs in the questionnaire mean?

come across	hand in
look up	write down
read on	think over
work out	put off
go over	keep up
join in	catch up

b) Idle Alfred got no points at all when he did the questionnaire above. Find out how little work he did for his exams by completing the following teacher's report with the words below:

through	up for
back	down
by	of
for	up
behind	up to

At the beginning of the course, he went ______ with 'flu and missed several classes. Because of this, he fell ______ with his work and never managed to make ______ it. He was not a very enthusiastic student in class and could never think ______ anything to say when he was asked the simplest of questions. He annoyed his friends by refusing to give ______ the books they had lent him. He hardly ever took any notes and when he did, he never bothered to look ______ them to prepare himself for the next day's lesson. Towards the end of the course, he gave ______ working in the library during his spare time at school and used to spend all day in the coffee bar. He thought he could get ______ without doing any revision at all. He refused to face ______ the fact that he simply wasn't ready to sit ______ the exam.

2 **a)** You're Idle Alfred on the morning before the exams. You're just beginning to get a bit worried!

Examples: *I wish I hadn't gone down with 'flu at the beginning of the course.*
It's a pity I went down with 'flu at the beginning of the course.

b) Do you have any regrets about your time at school?

Expressing regret about the past:

I wish / *If only* + past perfect

What a pity / *It's a pity* + past simple

INTERPRETATION ACTIVITY

Write a paragraph about what you should do to prepare yourself properly for your exams.

D TALKING ABOUT FURTHER EDUCATION

DISCUSSION

Does your country offer courses for adults?
Apart from English, what courses does your school/college offer?
Have you ever attended any courses other than your language class?
If so, why did you attend? Did you find it/them useful?

READING

In Britain there are centres all over the country where adults can continue their education or make up for opportunities missed at school. Look at the Greencroft programme of courses opposite. Which of these courses would interest you?

Greencroft Centre for Adult Education

Principal: Dr G. Edwards

Literature

The Foreign Novel Dr A. Brooks
Wednesday 7p.m.–9p.m. Autumn term.

The development of the novel outside England in the nineteenth century was extremely important. The course will study examples taken from French, German, Russian and American novels.

Enjoying Twentieth Century English Literature Mrs V. Ward
Tuesday 7.30p.m.–9.30 p.m. Spring Term.

Literature always reflects the time and society in which it was written. English literature of the twentieth century has been no exception and there have also been major changes in the form of the novel. The course will review the whole period and take a closer look at the work of Graham Greene, D.H. Lawrence and Virginia Woolf.

Languages Head of Department: Mrs L. Peters.

Courses in French, German, Spanish, Italian, Russian and Mandarin Chinese are proposed for all levels. Students with a good knowledge of their language can sit for the 'A' level exam. For further information contact the Head of Department.

Cookery Mrs Y. Forbes

Thursday 6.30p.m.–9p.m. Autumn term.

An introduction to the basic techniques used in cooking dishes from all over the world. Some experience is necessary.

Natural Sciences

Wildlife of Asia and Africa Dr J. Jones
Tuesday, Friday 7p.m.–9p.m. All year.

A series of illustrated talks about the plants and animals of Asia and Africa by Dr Jones, who has spent a large part of his life in the two continents. A general instruction in the principles of ecology and conservation will complete the course.

Man and his Environment Miss J. Ewell
Tuesday 7p.m.–9p.m. Spring term.

This course includes a general description of the plants and animals to be found all over the world and the threat that the presence of man poses to their continued existence. It will look at the dangers of pollution and the importance of conservation.

Business Studies

Management Studies Mr D.G. Rawlings
Tuesday, Friday 7p.m.–9.p.m. All year.

This course is part of a two-year diploma programme which will cover the basic skills necessary for managers of today, with special reference to marketing, accountancy and sales techniques. It will also look at how the state of the world economy affects the public and private sectors of business.

Computer Studies Mr H. Wall
Friday 7p.m.–9p.m. All year.

An introductory course to computer technology and how it can be used effectively in your professional life. It will include advice on how to choose a computer that suits your needs and how to program it. It will also look at the future and where the technological revolution will take us.

Music Head of Department: Dr J. Green

A number of different courses are available for students wishing to take 'A' level or the diploma, as well as those who want to develop their skills in playing a variety of instruments, e.g. piano, guitar, strings, wind and percussion. Students must have their own instruments. For further information about times, etc. contact the Head of Department.

Jazz Appreciation Mr K. Lentwall
Tuesday 7p.m.–9p.m. All year.

A look at jazz from its traditional roots of Louis Armstrong to the modern styles of Miles Davis and Keith Jarrett.

Politics

Political Change in Britain Mr John Seward
Monday, Thursday 7p.m.–9p.m. Summer term.

This course will study political movements in Britain during the twentieth century and in particular the political changes that social and economic factors have brought about since 1945. It will look closely at such topical issues as government policy, the power of the Trade Unions and the rise of the Social Democratic Party.

Basic Car Maintenance Mr I. Murray

Monday 7p.m.–9p.m. All year.

This course will give an introduction to car mechanics, show you how to cut down on garage bills and prolong the life of your car by careful servicing.

LISTENING ACTIVITY

1 **a)** Listen to these people talking about why they want to take a course at an adult education centre and take notes.

b) On a number of occasions in their lives they were all obliged to change their plans. Write sentences about their original intentions and why it wasn't possible to realise them.

c) Which courses in the Greencroft programme do you think would be most useful to them?

Talking about unfulfilled actions and plans: KEY LANGUAGE

I would(n't) have + past participle, *if* + past perfect

I'd have gone to university if I hadn't gone to France.

I was *hoping* / *planning* / *intending* / *going* *to* + infinitive, *but* + past simple

I was intending to go to university, but I went to France.

2 Listen to this radio interview with the principal of an adult education centre, and make notes on the following:

types of student
qualifications offered at the end of the course
qualifications necessary to attend the course
length of course
homework
fees

READING ALOUD

a) Listen to part of the interview again and follow the tapescript below. As you listen, mark the stressed words and the intonation.

INTERVIEWER: What about the length of the courses?

PRINCIPAL: They usually last from September to May or June. But it depends on the type of course. Often, if you're not taking an exam, you can enrol for just a term to see if you like it or not.

INTERVIEWER: Is there any homework?

PRINCIPAL: Of course, 'A' level and diploma courses require some extra work at home and you must make sure that you'll have the time to do this before you begin. It's surprising how difficult it is to study seriously if you finished school several years ago. For other courses there's no homework unless you want to do some.

b) Now practise reading the conversation aloud in pairs. Change roles when you have finished.

ROLE PLAY

1 Choose one of the people in the first listening text. Explain your situation and your intentions to your partner. Ask for advice on a suitable course to attend and for any other information you may need. Use the headings above to help you.

2 **a)** In groups, think of subjects which each of you could prepare a short talk on. It might be your hobby, like cookery, or a sport, or something to do with your job. Prepare a programme of these subjects with a short description and other details. Use the Greencroft programme as a model.

b) Visit other groups and look at their programmes. Ask for details about the course which interests you.

c) Prepare a five-minute talk on the subject you have chosen.

d) In groups, give your talk or listen to other people talking about their subjects.

Asking for information: KEY LANGUAGE

Can you / *Could you* / *I wonder if you could* } *tell me . . .*

Do you know if . . . ?

A EXAM PRACTICE

PAPER 1: READING COMPREHENSION

Section B *(Suggestions for the exam – see Unit 3)*

In this section you will find after the text a number of questions or unfinished statements about the text, each with four suggested answers or ways of finishing. You must choose the one you think fits best. For each question, *indicate on your answer sheet* the letter A, B, C or D against the number of the question.

The masters went upstairs.
'That's your little mob in there,' said Grimes; 'you let them out at eleven.'
'But what am I to teach them?' said Paul in sudden panic.
'Oh, I shouldn't try to *teach* them anything, not just yet, anyway. Just keep them quiet.'
'Now that's a thing I've never learned to do,' sighed Mr Prendergast.
Paul watched him walk into his classroom at the end of the passage, where a burst of applause greeted his arrival. Dumb with terror, he went into his own classroom.
Ten boys sat before him, their arms folded, their eyes bright with expectation.
'Good morning, sir,' said the one nearest him.
'Good morning,' said Paul.
'Good morning, sir,' said the next.
'Good morning,' said Paul.
'Good morning, sir,' said the next.
'Oh, shut up,' said Paul.
At this the boy took out a handkerchief and began to cry quietly.
'Oh sir,' came a chorus of reproach, 'you've hurt his feelings. He's very sensitive; it's his Welsh blood, you know: it makes people very emotional. Say 'Good morning' to him, sir, or he won't be happy all day. After all, it is a good morning, isn't it, sir?'
'Silence!' shouted Paul above the noise, and for a few moments things were quieter.
'Please, sir,' said a small voice – Paul turned and saw a serious-looking youth holding up his hand – 'please, sir, perhaps he's been smoking cigars and doesn't feel well.'
'Silence!' said Paul again.
The ten boys stopped talking and sat perfectly still, staring at him. He felt himself getting hot and red under their gaze.
'I suppose the first thing I ought to do is to get your names clear. What is your name?' he asked, turning to the first boy.
'Tangent, sir.'
'And yours?'
'Tangent, sir,' said the next boy. Paul's heart sank.
'But you can't both be called Tangent!'
'No, sir, *I'm* Tangent. He's just trying to be funny.'
'I like that. *Me* trying to be funny! Please sir, I'm Tangent sir; really I am.'
'If it comes to that,' said Clutterbuck from the back of the room, 'there is only one Tangent here, and that is me.'
Paul felt desperate.

1 According to Grimes, Paul's main task was to
A finish the class at eleven o'clock.
B teach the pupils as little as possible.
C make the pupils behave.
D learn the boys' names.

2 Paul was very frightened because
A it was his first class.
B he had lost his voice.
C he didn't like teaching.
D he didn't like boys.

3 We know that the boys
A managed to annoy Paul.
B were pleased to see Paul.
C were upset by Paul.
D were scared of Paul.

4 According to the passage,
A the boys smoked cigars in class.
B the boys thought people from Wales were very sensitive.
C the boys were singing.
D each pupil had to say 'Good morning' to the teacher.

5 We know that
A Paul had trouble with his heart.
B Paul was in a bad temper.
C it was a very hot day.
D Paul had difficulty in controlling this class.

6 It appears that
A at least three boys were called Tangent.
B the boys were all related to each other.
C Paul wouldn't allow two boys to have the same name.
D the boys were trying to confuse Paul.

PAPER 2: COMPOSITION

(Suggestions for the exam – see Unit 3)

Your answers must follow exactly the instructions given and must be of between 120 and 180 words each.

1 You have been in charge of a two-week educational tour of several countries for schoolchildren. Describe where you went, what you did and any other events which occurred during the trip.

2 Describe your first day at school.

3 'School does not prepare you for adult life.' Discuss.

4 You have to do a retraining course in order to get a better job. Write a letter to an institute asking for information about the type, the length and the price of the courses that the school offers, and explain why you want to do a course.

PAPER 3: USE OF ENGLISH

Section A, Question 1 *(Suggestions for the exam – see Unit 1)*

Fill each of the numbered blanks in the following passage. Use only *one* word in each space.

The Open University ________ (1) created in 1969 to provide university education ________ (2) anyone aged 21 or over who wanted ________ (3), whatever his or her background, status or previous educational qualifications. It uses teaching methods ________ (4) are quite unlike anything to ________ (5) found in other universities, but awards degrees that are recognised as equal ________ (6) those of any other.

By way of correspondence, television and radio, the Open University teaches its students ________ (7) the comfort and privacy of their own homes. Given this revolutionary teaching method, it's not surprising that, fourteen years ________ (8), there were many who said the Open University ________ (9) never succeed. They claimed that adults without previous academic ________ (10) simply would not be ________ (11) to study at university level. Today, those critics have ________ (12) proved wrong.

So far, about 43,000 students of the Open University ________ (13) graduated with BA degrees – worth just as much ________ (14) those from any ________ (15) university in the country. This year, ________ (16) than 80,000 men and women will be studying Open University courses ________ (17) home, in their own time. And next year you ________ (18) be among them, working towards a BA degree. Or advancing your knowledge to advance your career. Or just studying because you want to.

Next year, you could be ________ (19) that second chance you've ________ (20) wanted – if you really want it, of course.

Section A, Question 2 *(Suggestions for the exam – see Unit 3)*

Finish each of the following sentences in such a way that it means exactly the same as the sentence printed before it.

Example: What about us going to evening classes this year?
Answer: Why *don't we go to evening classes this year?*

a) He was planning to go to teacher training college, but his father died.
If . . . .

b) What a pity he didn't spend more time revising.
If only . . . .

c) He started work as soon as the term had finished.
No sooner . . . .

d) Could you give me some information, please?
I wonder . . . .

e) I should have learnt French at school!
I wish . . . .

f) She doesn't do her homework, so she doesn't get good marks.
If . . . .

g) During my time at university I made a lot of friends.
While . . . .

h) Special qualifications are not necessary.
You . . . .

i) I spent seven years at secondary school and then I went to university.
After . . . .

j) The exam took place a week after the end of term.
The course . . . .

Section A, Question 3 *(Suggestions for the exam – see Unit 3)*

Complete the following sentences with *one* appropriate word connected with learning.

Example: I have a music . *lesson* . . at five o'clock tonight.

a) The professor is giving his weekly . . . . in the main hall.

b) She's taking a . . . . in car maintenance at the Adult Education Centre.

c) The teacher usually set them a couple of grammar . . . . for homework.

d) The students were carrying out a number of different . . . . in the chemistry laboratory.

e) At the end of the week, he gives his pupils a . . . . to check what they've learnt.

PAPER 5: INTERVIEW

Part (i)
(Suggestions for the exam – see Unit 4)

1 Where do you think this is?
2 What is the boy doing?
3 What the advantages of this kind of learning?
4 Have you ever used a computer? Where?
5 Would you like to have used computers at school?

Related Topics.

The role of the teacher.
The aims of school education.
Schools in the future.

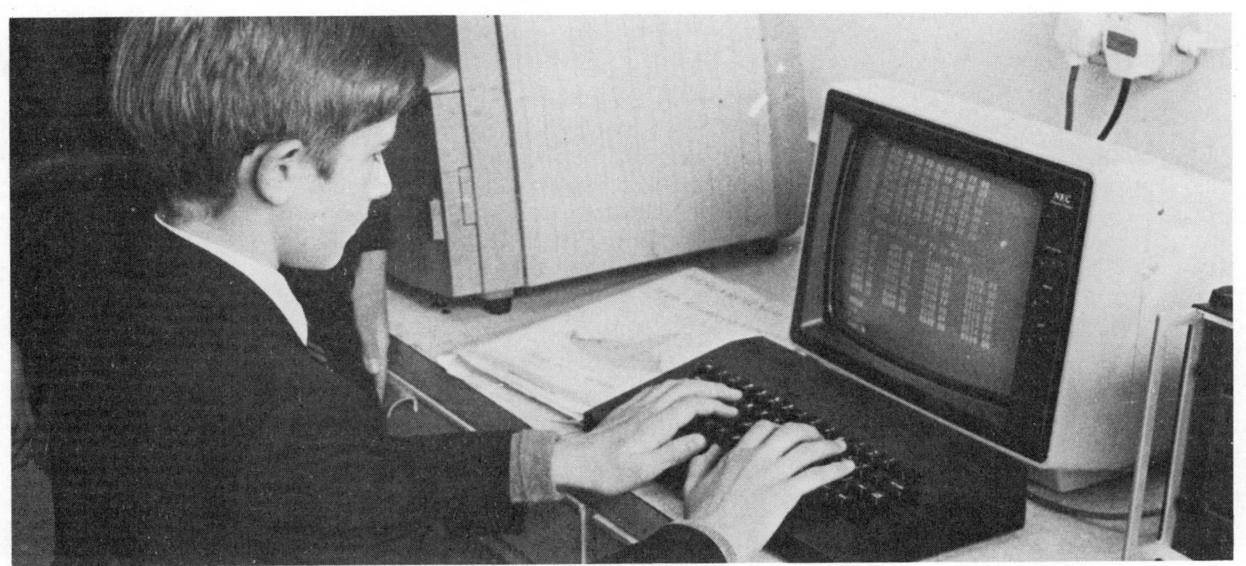

Part (ii) *(Suggestions for the exam – see Unit 4)*

Look through the following text for a few moments.

The books for study will be decided by the class itself. Traditionally I try to ensure variety and balance, so we choose plays and poetry as well as novels, and we choose from different historical periods. It's up to you to join in as much as possible. In my experience, the more students take part in the course, the more they enjoy it.

What do you think the situation is?
Who do you think is speaking? To whom?

Now read the passage aloud.

Part (iii) *(Suggestions for the exam – see Unit 1)*
You are at the information desk in a library and you are enquiring about membership.

Ask about: Borrowing books.
How long you can keep them.
How many you can borrow.
Opening hours, etc.

UNIT 7

MAKING ENDS MEET

A COMPARING AND CONTRASTING

TALKING POINT

This graph shows the expenditure of the average British family.

a) To which category in the graph do the following items belong?

books	hotel bills
boots	petrol
cigarettes	rent
dry-cleaning	tea
electricity	tights
fares	washing machines

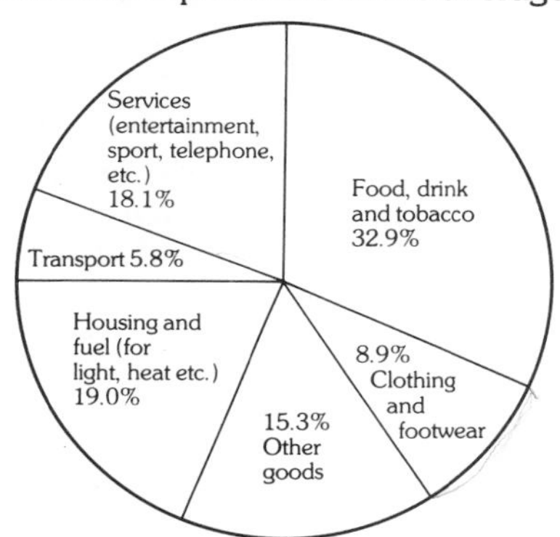

b) The average British family spends about one-fifth of its income on services. What proportion of its income does it spend on:

food, drink and tobacco?
clothing and footwear?
housing and fuel?

c) Make an approximate estimate of your weekly expenditure using the six categories from the graph. What proportion of your income do you spend on each category? Compare your results with another student. How does your expenditure compare with that of the average British family?

READING

Rich Man, Poor Man

People in different areas of the world can have quite different standards of living. To see just how wide these differences can be, let us look at the situations of three men. One lives in a very poor country, another in a moderately rich one, while the third lives in a very rich nation.

Sivapatham

Sivapatham, aged thirty-eight, is married with three sons and three daughters. The family live in a sub-divided hut in the Chettithottam area of Madras City, in India. Made entirely from coconut leaves and timber, the hut is in a poor state of repair. It has no toilet facilities, no water supply and no electricity, but this is not unusual in Madras, where many thousands of homes are in a similar state.

Sivapatham has been a leather worker since the age of ten, yet his wages remain pitifully small. As a result the family eat sparingly. Cold

Huts in Madras City

rice is eaten for breakfast, tea is taken in the late afternoon, and in the evening the family have a warm meal (rice with vegetables and perhaps a fish sauce). The household have hardly any furniture, although they do have two aluminium pots. Clothing means cotton shirts and shorts, with sarees and frocks for the females. Although Sivapatham has somehow learned to write his signature, he and his family are illiterate. His knowledge of the world is limited to the city where he has spent his whole life. Equally limited are his ambitions. He worries about surviving from day to day and about the health of his family. Knowing that he is poor and will never be anything else, he is also well aware that his neighbours on all sides share exactly the same standard of living.

George Murray

George is forty-four and lives with his wife and three daughters in a small semi-detached house in Renfrew, near Glasgow. His home was built in 1972, is centrally heated and comfortably furnished. Mr Murray works as a vehicle mechanic, while his wife and eldest daughter are employed in offices. The combined family income is quite enough to let them eat well.

Semi-detached house in Scotland

Whereas a member of Sivapatham's household might have a daily calorie intake of 1850, the Murrays would average 3000 calories. In addition, each member of the Murray family has a separate wardrobe, full of clothes.

The family have a small, four-year-old car, and an ancient caravan which Mr Murray has fitted up for holiday use. While none of the family has travelled much, they have all been as far as southern England, and the eldest daughter has even been on a summer visit to relatives in New York.

Bob Gauldie

Due soon to retire from his joinery business, Bob Gauldie has, since 1948, occupied a large timber bungalow on Paling Avenue in the industrial city of Hamilton, Ontario. He and his wife live alone, since their two sons are now married. Bob learned his trade as a carpenter in Scotland. Since emigrating to Canada over thirty years ago, he has worked as a subcontractor on numerous building projects in southern Ontario. Although harsh winters have often

Timber bungalow in Canada

meant reduced earnings, Bob can look back on a profitable working life. His house and large garden are kept in fine condition, and he and his family have never been short of food or clothing. Since 1960, Bob and his wife have revisited Scotland every other year. They also pay frequent visits to Lake Muskoka, where Bob has built his own summer cabin. Over the years, the Gauldies have travelled widely across southern Canada and the northern part of the USA visiting other Scots friends. Every few weeks, they drive 400 km to see relatives in Detroit. In a large, air-conditioned vehicle, long journeys are easy, say the Gauldies. Bob regrets that his education finished when he was fourteen, but he is proud that both his sons have graduated from university. One is a professor at McMaster University, while the other teaches in high school at Orillia.

These three men, Sivapatham, George Murray and Bob Gauldie, have something in common. Each has his own skill and each is the hard-working head of a family. But they lead different lives, and these differences are linked to the economic standing of India, Scotland and Canada.

a) 1 Which man is the oldest?
2 Which is the largest family?
3 Whose home is the most modern?
4 What do Sivapatham and his sons wear?
5 What are his limited ambitions?
6 Which of the Murrays contribute to the family income?
7 How often did the Gaudies go to Scotland between 1960 and 1975?
8 When did Bob Gauldie leave school?

b) Find words or phrases in the text which mean:

KEY VOCABULARY

wood	unable to read or write
bad	total
uncommon	very old
family	carpentry
almost no	one-storey house
dresses	many

LANGUAGE PRACTICE

1 Write down the adjectives which are formed from the following nouns. Then check your list of adjectives against the text.

difference	industry
width	profit
poverty	length
warmth	pride
day	economics

2 **a)** Fill in the missing adjective or adverb. Use your dictionary if necessary.

KEY VOCABULARY

b) What rules can you deduce from your list about the formation of adverbs from adjectives ending in:
a consonant or *e* (except *able*)?
able?
a vowel + l?
y?
Which adverb is the exception?

ADJECTIVE	ADVERB	ADJECTIVE	ADVERB
	centrally		pitifully
	comfortably	profitable	
easy		proud	
	entirely	separate	
	equally		sparingly
	exactly	unusual	
frequent			well
	moderately		widely

3 'These three men ... have something in common.'
What do all three men have in common?
What do George and Bob have in common?

Talking about numbers:

KEY LANGUAGE

Each *man* / *of the men* / *of them* *has* a skill.

Both / *All* *(of) the men* / *of them* *have* a skill.

They *each* / *both* / *all* *have* a skill.

Note: *both* = 2
all = more than 2

4

a) Make comparisons and talk about the contrast between the three families in relation to:

ages	income
size of families	food
kind of houses	clothing
furniture, etc.	education
occupations	travel

b) Write sentences comparing the three families and their standards of living.

KEY LANGUAGE

Making comparisons (3):

He *isn't as old* / *doesn't earn as much* / *hasn't travelled as widely* *as* . . .

He *is older* / *earns more/less* / *has travelled more/less widely* *than* . . .

He *is the oldest.* / *earns the most/least.* / *has travelled the most/least widely.*

Expressing contrast (2):

While/Whereas Bob has two children, George has three.

Bob has two children, *while/whereas* George has three.

Bob has two children. George, *on the other hand*, has three.

5

a) Arrange the following household contents under three headings:

Furniture, Household appliances, Soft furnishings.

KEY VOCABULARY

bedding	cushions	tables
beds	dishwasher	tablecloths
bookshelves	freezer	telephone
carpets	refrigerator (fridge)	television
chairs		vacuum cleaner
cooker	rugs	wardrobes
curtains	sideboard	washing machine

A Japanese interior

b) Which of the above items would you probably find in:

Sivapatham's hut?
the Murray's house?
the Gauldie's bungalow?

c) For each room in your house or flat, make a list of the main contents. What additions are there to the list above? Use your dictionary if necessary.

d) Some of these household contents depend on our culture. For example, many Japanese homes have no chairs. Which items in the list above are not included in your list? Are there any items in your house which would be unusual in other countries?

6 Look at the diagrams showing the diets of a typical city-dwelling American and an Indian workman.

In one day, a city-dwelling American eats:

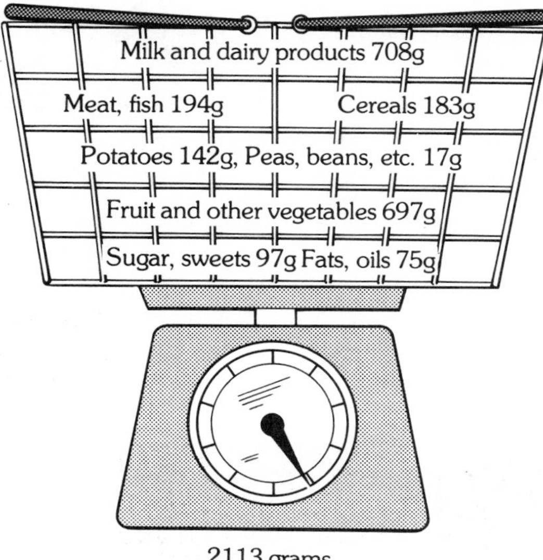

2113 grams

In one day, a workman in India eats:

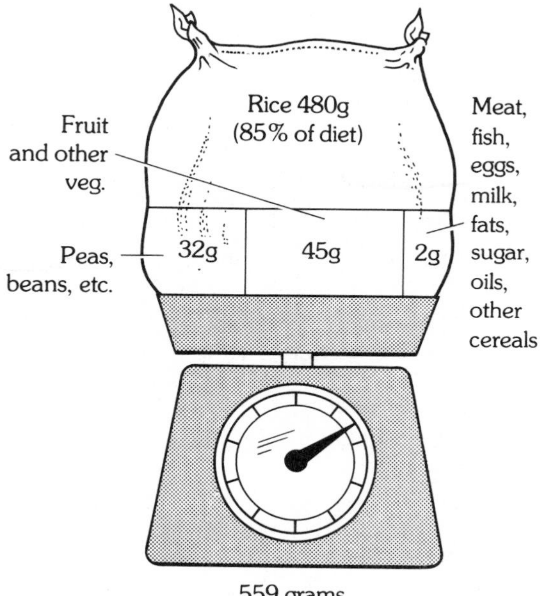

559 grams

a) Talk about the quantities of different types of food in each diet.

Examples: *The American eats a lot of vegetables. The Indian workman drinks very little milk, and he doesn't eat much fruit.*

b) What are the differences between the two diets?

Examples: *The American eats many/far more potatoes than the Indian workman. The Indian workman eats much/far less meat than the American.*

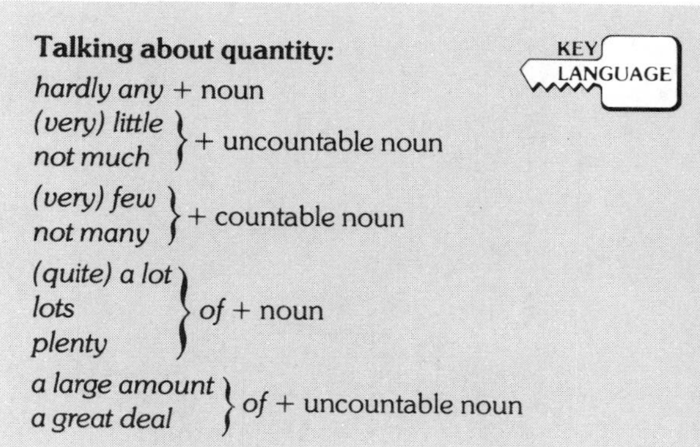

Talking about quantity:

KEY LANGUAGE

hardly any + noun

(very) little / *not much* } + uncountable noun

(very) few / *not many* } + countable noun

(quite) a lot / *lots* / *plenty* } *of* + noun

a large amount / *a great deal* } *of* + uncountable noun

7 **a)** Group the words below under the following headings:

Cereals, *Dairy products*, *Fruit*, *Meat*, and *Vegetables*.

apple
bacon
banana
blackberry
bean
beef
bread
butter
cabbage
carrot

cheese
chicken
corn
cream
egg
flour
grape
lamb
maize
milk

onion
orange
pea
pear
potato
rabbit
rice
sausage
wheat
yoghurt

b) Some nouns may be either countable or uncountable, depending on the meaning. In what situations would you say the following?

1 'Could I have a cabbage?'
2 'Could I have some cabbage?'

What is the difference in meaning between the following statements?

1 I like chickens.
2 I like chicken.

c) Which of the nouns in **a**) above can be both countable and uncountable?

DISCUSSION

What are the three basic necessities for survival?
As societies become more civilised, people work for things beyond the basic necessities. These things are, in theory, luxuries. But is a telephone a luxury to a doctor, or a sick person living at home? Is a typewriter a luxury to an author? Discuss which goods you regard as necessities, and which you think are luxuries.

B DISCUSSING ADVANTAGES AND DISADVANTAGES

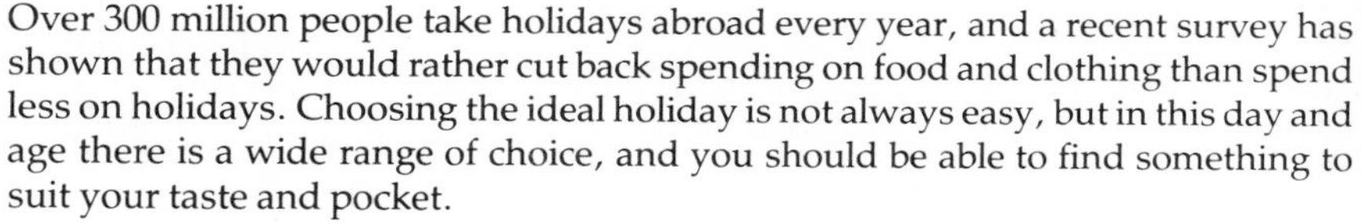

READING

Holiday Choice

Over 300 million people take holidays abroad every year, and a recent survey has shown that they would rather cut back spending on food and clothing than spend less on holidays. Choosing the ideal holiday is not always easy, but in this day and age there is a wide range of choice, and you should be able to find something to suit your taste and pocket.

Some people like planning their holiday independently, while others prefer to book a package. It depends on where you're going, how much money you have, and whether you're travelling alone, or with friends or family.

The obvious advantage of a package holiday is that it's simple to organise. You book the holiday through a travel agent, and transport, insurance and accommodation are all arranged for you. All you have to do is pay the bill. If you take an independent holiday, on the other hand, you can spend a lot of time and a small fortune checking complicated timetables, chasing cheap flights, and trying to make hotel bookings in a language you can't even speak. What is more, package holidays are often incredibly cheap. For the price of a suit, you can have a fortnight in a foreign resort, including accommodation, meals, and air travel. A similar independent holiday, however, can work out much more expensive.

Yet the advantages of planning your holiday yourself are considerable. You are free to choose exactly where and when you want to go, how you want to travel, and how long you want to stay. You can avoid the large resorts, whereas holidaymakers on package tours are often trapped among crowds of other tourists. You can eat the food of the region at reasonable prices in local restaurants, while they are served with 'international' dishes and chips with everything. Besides, although package holidays are usually extremely good value for money, they are not always cheaper. If you're willing to take a little trouble, you may be able to save money by fixing up a foreign holiday yourself.

Moreover, although most people return from package holidays reasonably satisfied, this is not always the case. Take, for instance, the nightmare experience of a Frenchman who went on a package to Colombia. The hotel in the small Caribbean port was overbooked. The holidaymaker was wandering round the streets, looking for a bed and breakfast place, when he was arrested for vagrancy. He was taken to court, where he told the magistrate that it was the hotel's fault. The magistrate was the hotel-owner's brother, and he charged the tourist with making false accusations and sent him to prison for eight days. By the time of his release, his return flight had left. He had insufficient funds to buy a return ticket, so he went to the Post Office to send a telegram to his home in Montpellier, asking for money. He was re-arrested before he could send it. This time he was charged with illegal immigration. It was explained that, having missed his return flight, he could no longer be classified as a tourist. He now needed a work permit, and he didn't have one. He was fined $500 for this offence, and a further $500 when he again blamed the hotel for overbooking. His luggage was confiscated because he couldn't pay the fines. Down to the clothes he stood up in, he hitch-hiked to Bogota where the consulate finally arranged to send him home.

All things considered, I would prefer to plan my holiday independently. In my view, it's safer to 'do it yourself'!

a) Choose the best alternative to the following words in the passage.

KEY VOCABULARY

1 YET
A Besides B However C Although
D Up till now

2 CONSIDERABLE
A thoughtful B many C sensible
D respectable

3 REASONABLE
A moderate B low C practical D bargain

4 FUNDS
A pay B information C money D change

5 CONFISCATED
A stolen B taken away C searched D fined

Now choose the best answer.

6 You should be able to have a holiday
A where you can eat the food you like.
B where you can wear the clothes you like.
C with people of your own age.
D that you can afford.

7 If you take an independent holiday, you may
A be lucky to find a hotel.
B not be able to speak a foreign language.
C spend a lot of money making arrangements.
D have to run after planes.

8 The Frenchman was first arrested for
A stealing something.
B having no work permit.
C making false accusations.
D wandering round the streets.

9 He hitch-hiked to Bogota
A in his pyjamas.
B because he was depressed.
C with nothing but the clothes he was wearing.
D to get some money.

10 His problems all arose because
A he didn't have enough money.
B his hotel was full.
C he hadn't had any breakfast.
D he missed his return flight.

b) Find the following words and phrases in the text. Decide whether their meaning *in the context* is positive or negative, and make two lists.

Examples:	**Positive**	**Negative**
	wide	*complicated*

wide
simple
a small fortune
complicated
chasing
considerable
large resorts
crowds
food of the region
local
international
chips

LANGUAGE PRACTICE

The following words and phrases are used to link ideas. Some are used to express *contrast*, while others are used for *reinforcement*, to make an *additional point*. Find examples of each word or phrase in the text, and notice how they are used. Then complete the lists in the box.

but	whereas
on the other hand	while
what is more	besides
however	although
yet	moreover

KEY LANGUAGE

Expressing contrast (3):
but

Making additional points:
what is more

GUIDED WRITING ACTIVITY

a) Read the text again, and make notes on the advantages and disadvantages discussed for each type of holiday. Then complete the table below.

Examples:

Package holidays		**Independent holidays**	
FOR	AGAINST	FOR	AGAINST
simple to organise		*freedom of choice*	

b) Look at the notes below on staying in a hotel and camping.

Staying in a hotel		**Camping**	
FOR	AGAINST	FOR	AGAINST
relaxing – beds made, meals served, everything done for you comfortable	set mealtimes children often unpopular comparatively expensive	free to come and go when you like can eat when you want fun for children very cheap	can spend half your holiday buying and preparing food, etc. may wake up soaking wet because tent is leaking

Write a composition discussing the advantages and disadvantages of staying in a hotel and camping. Use paragraphs 2, 3, 4 and 6 of the Holiday Choice text as a model.

Paragraph 1: Introduction
Paragraph 2: Advantages of A over B
Paragraph 3: Advantages of B over A
Paragraph 4: Conclusion

Summing up (2):

KEY LANGUAGE

On balance, . . .
All things considered, . . .

In my view/opinion, . . .
Personally speaking, . . .
As far as I'm concerned, . . .

c) Write a composition discussing the relative advantages and disadvantages of one of the following:

Living in the town – Living in the country
Sharing a flat – Living alone
Television – Cinema
Flying – Travelling by car/train/boat

C TALKING ABOUT CONSUMER RIGHTS

READING

There are many laws to protect the customer in Britain. If you are not satisfied with a purchase, you may be able to get your money back. But you must have a good reason to complain. Look carefully at the *Consumer-Wise* chart below.

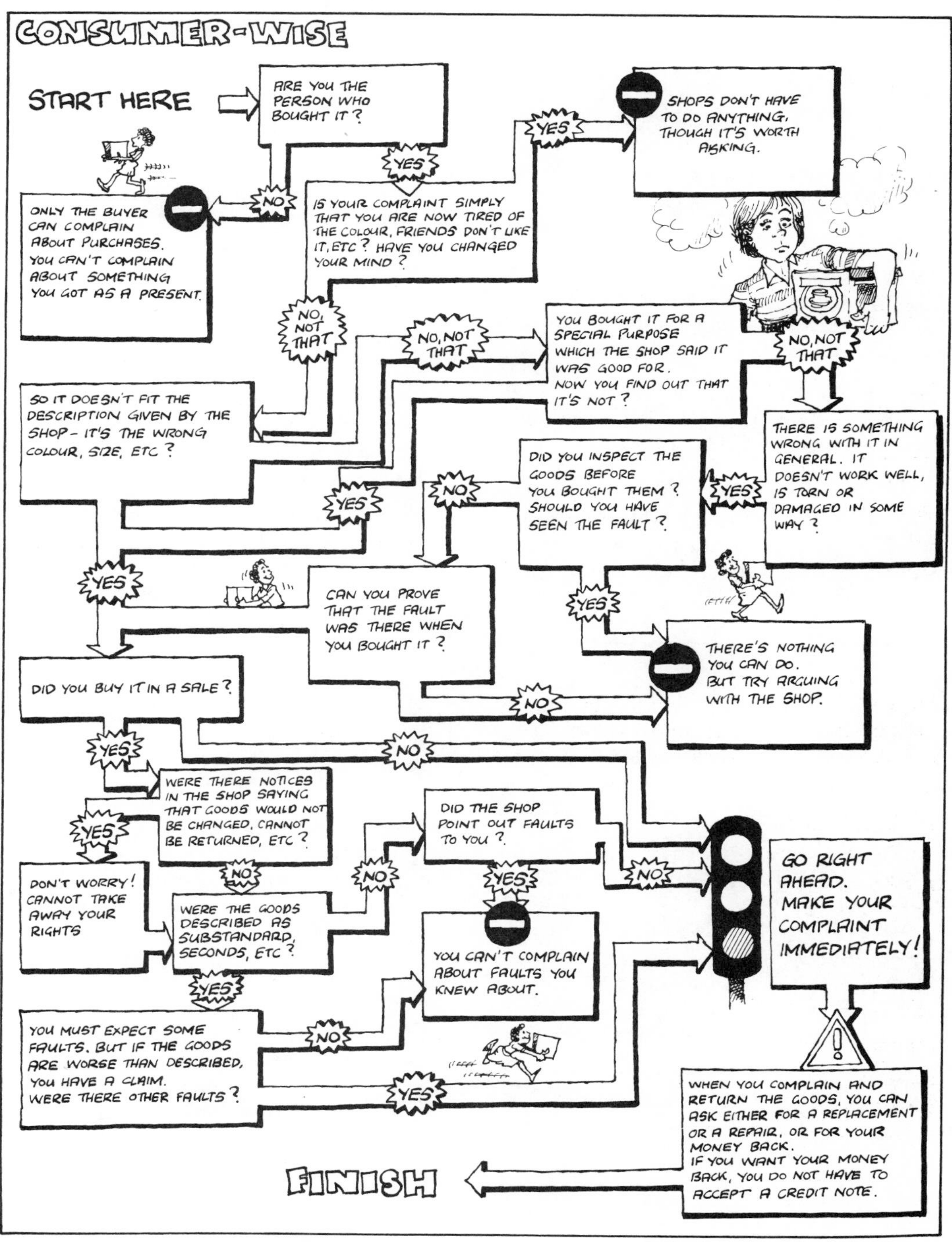

INTERPRETATION ACTIVITY

Work out the answers to the following questions, using the information in the chart. In each case, give the reasons for your judgement.

Expressing criticism:

General rule

should(n't)
ought(n't) to + infinitive

A coffee-maker ought to work properly.

About the past

should(n't)
ought(n't) to *have* + past participle

He shouldn't have said it was leather.

1 You buy a coffee-maker marked 'substandard' in a sale. It does not work at all. Can you insist on your money back?

2 You buy a book for a friend. Unfortunately, he already has a copy, and he takes it back to the shop. The assistant refuses to change it. Is the assistant right?

3 You buy a shirt which is reduced in a sale. When you get home and unfold it, you find a mark on it which will not wash out. Have you the right to complain?

4 You give your sister a ring which is slightly scratched. She returns it to you and you take it back to the shop. The shopkeeper refuses to refund your money. Is he within his rights?

5 You buy an expensive handbag which the shop assistant said was made of leather. A few days later, it splits, and you realise it is made of plastic. Can you claim your money back?

6 You buy a disposable cigarette lighter. It runs out of fuel the following day. You take it back and ask for a replacement. Are you likely to get one?

7 You buy some tablets for a headache. It says on the label that they work very quickly, but you take the recommended dose and nothing happens at all. You return the tablets and ask for an alternative. Are you within your rights?

8 You buy a radio at a bargain price. When you get home, you find that it does not work. A notice in the shop says. 'No money refunded under any circumstances'. Is the notice effective?

LANGUAGE PRACTICE

1 Role play: Choose one of the situations in the previous exercise, and work in pairs to prepare the dialogue that takes place between the customer and the shopkeeper/assistant. Perform the dialogue for the rest of the class.

CUSTOMER: Explain when and where you bought the goods and reason for complaint. If necessary, try to persuade shopkeeper/assistant to give replacement/money back.

SHOPKEEPER/ASSISTANT: Apologise and offer a replacement/repair/money back OR
Apologise but refuse to accept the customer's claim and explain why.

KEY LANGUAGE

Making complaints:
You/It said it was . . . , but it . . .
It's too . . .
It's not . . . enough

Apologising:
I'm (so/very) sorry.
I **am** *sorry.*
I **do** *apologise.*

Accepting responsibility:
You're quite right.
It's not your fault.

Denying responsibility (2):
I'm sorry, but / *I'm afraid* — *there's nothing we/I can do.* / *I/we can't offer you . . .* / *it's not our/my fault.*

2 If you were in a town with no supermarkets or department stores, where would you buy the following goods? Choose from the list on the right.

a packet of envelopes
a pair of boots
a packet of biscuits
a bottle of tablets
a loaf of bread
a joint of meat
stamps
apples
a train set
a magazine
a dictionary
a bucket

baker
barber
bookshop
butcher
chemist
greengrocer
grocer
hardware store
laundry
library
newsagent
post office
shoe shop
station
stationer
surgery
sweetshop
toyshop

3 Fill in the blanks in the following sentences with a suitable compound formed from the word in capitals.

KEY VOCABULARY

Example: HAND The Italians make beautiful leather shoes and *handbags*.

1 HAND
His ______ is difficult to read.
The theatre company printed ______ to advertise the play.

2 SHOP
The two boys were arrested for ______.
Sarah found a temporary job as a ______ in a department store.

3 NEWS
Many people have ______ delivered in Britain.
The ______ is open on Sunday mornings.

4 HARD
He's not very bright, but he's extremely ______.
You can buy glasses, crockery and saucepans in the ______ store.

5 HAIR
He'd look quite smart if he had a ______.
I'm training to be a ______.

6 HEAD
The newspaper ______ said 'BUS FARES TO RISE'.
I've got a sore throat and a ______.

7 HOUSE
It's a good idea to insure ______ contents.
Modern appliances help to cut down the ______.

8 BOOK
She bought some wood to make ______.
I found a volume of his poems in a second-hand ______.

INTERPRETATION ACTIVITY

a) Summarise the information in the Consumer-Wise chart by completing the lists below.

You have a claim if the goods you have bought:

1 don't fit the description given by the shop.
2
3

You have no right to complain if:

1 you damaged the goods yourself.
2
3
4
5

b) Are there similar laws to protect the consumer in your country? Find out what your consumer rights are, and make a summary of them as above.

D TALKING ABOUT DAMAGE AND GETTING IT REPAIRED

DISCUSSION

A housing association has raised funds to buy a large property.

a) Study the photograph and describe the house. What do you think is required in the way of 'modernisation'?

b) What do the abbreviations in the advertisement stand for?

PROPERTY FOR SALE
Impressive 18c house requiring modernisation. 25ft × 40ft lnge, lge dining rm, study/library, kit, hall, cellar, 10 beds, 3 baths, sep w.c., dble gge, lge gdn. Approx 50 mins cent. London.
Offers over £100,000.
Tel. Walker Bros. 01 223 7283

LISTENING ACTIVITY

A member of the housing association goes round the house with a builder to look at its condition and talk about necessary repairs and modernisation. Listen to their conversation, and make notes about the points that need attention.

KEY VOCABULARY

Example: *tiles – missing*

READING ALOUD

a) Listen to part of the conversation again, and follow the tapescript below. As you listen, mark the intonation when the voice rises or falls. Pay particular attention to the question tags.

BOB: I must say, you've got a splendid hall, haven't you?
JUDY: Yes, it's huge, isn't it? Here's the lounge.
BOB: Hmm. This has seen better days, hasn't it? But the beams seem to be in good condition . . . and the plaster looks OK. It could do with a coat of paint, though.
JUDY: Yes, it could, couldn't it? Actually, the whole house needs completely redecorating. And it's a pity about the broken windows.
BOB: Yes, you should get those fixed immediately . . . you don't want the rain coming in, do you? It's like a refrigerator in here. By the way, you're going to put in central heating, aren't you?
JUDY: Yes, I think we'll have to . . . it's the only way of keeping a place like this warm.

b) Now practise reading the conversation aloud in pairs. Change roles when you have finished.

ROLE PLAY

You are one of the members of the housing association. Using your notes, discuss what work needs to be done on the property, and decide which areas need attention most urgently. You may be able to do the work yourselves, but you will probably need outside help for some of it. Decide which particular kinds of skilled professionals you will need to hire.

Expressing obligation and necessity (2): KEY LANGUAGE

It needs / wants + -ING — The roof needs repairing.

It needs to / should / ought to + passive infinitive — The roof should be repaired.

We must / should / ought to get / have it + past participle

We must get someone to + infinitive

EXAM PRACTICE

PAPER 1: READING COMPREHENSION

Section A *(Suggestions for the exam – see Unit 1)*

In this section you must choose the word or phrase which best completes each sentence. For each question, 1 to 25, *indicate on your answer sheet* the letter A, B, C or D against the number of the question.

1 I couldn't decide between the two records, so I bought ______ of them.
A each B both C either D all

2 The government is ______ a lot of money on education.
A spending B paying C giving D using

3 The house is old and it's in bad ______.
A condition B state C damage
D situation

4 ______ Richard is a businessman, his brother is a rock singer.
A However B Yet C Whereas D Despite

5 I don't know the ______ price, but it costs about £50.
A accurate B true C proper D exact

6 He's very poor, and he has ______ possessions.
A any B little C a little D few

7 If we want to buy a house, we'll have to ______ our spending.
A care for B cut back C let down
D miss out

8 I took the shoes back to the shop, but the manager ______ to change them.
A denied B disliked C refused
D disagreed

9 The walls are damp because the drain-pipe is ______.
A flowing B running C leaking
D dropping

10 She earns ______ more money than her husband.
A money B much C some D lot

11 The only ______ of the flat is that it's a bit too small.
A mistake B pity C complaint
D disadvantage

12 You really ought to ______ your shoes repaired.
A make B do C get D take

13 My address is 44 Gayton Road, and I live in the ______.
A cellar B ground floor C foundations
D basement

14 The receptionist ______ us that the hotel was full.
A told B explained C apologised D said

15 Please would you pass ______ salt?
A a B the C some D any

16 This second-hand cooker is extremely good ______.
A price B value C worth D cost

17 In my ______, the best way to travel is by train.
A mind B opinion C concern D advice

18 The thief was ______ and taken to the police station.
A prevented B avoided C delayed
D arrested

19 Make sure you ______ us a visit when you're in town again.
A pay B have C give D do

20 Thank you for taking the ______ to phone me.
A trouble B effort C care D difficulty

21 I liked the coat when I bought it, but now I've ______ my mind.
A altered B changed C reversed
D decided

22 We don't take cheques, so you'll have to pay in ______.
A money B cash C change D coins

23 My washing machine has ______, so I'm going to the launderette.
A gone out B broken down C run down
D worn out

24 All the single rooms are the ______ size.
A same B similar C equal D like

25 These jeans will ______ when you wash them.
A decrease B reduce C shrink D lessen

PAPER 3: USE OF ENGLISH

Section A, Question 2 *(Suggestions for the exam – see Unit 3)*

Finish each of the following sentences in such a way that it means exactly the same as the sentence printed before it.

Example: Finding a flat isn't easy.

Answer: It isn't *easy to find a flat*. . . . . . .

a) They ought to mend the roof.
The roof . . . .

b) We flew to Athens, and then we took the ferry to Crete.
After . . . .

c) They didn't follow the map, so they got lost.
If . . . .

d) He was wrong to say the ring was gold.
He shouldn't . . . .

e) Someone is painting our house.
We . . . .

f) The old man had few friends.
The old man didn't . . . .

g) The coat was so expensive that I didn't buy it.
The coat was too . . . .

h) He's likely to stay in the Grand Hotel.
He'll . . . .

i) It's time your car was cleaned.
Your car . . . .

j) Moscow is further south than Edinburgh.
Edinburgh isn't . . . .

Section A, Question 3 *(Suggestions for the exam – see Unit 3)*

Complete the following sentences with *one* appropriate word for a form of payment.

Example: The man left the restaurant without paying the *bill*.

a) How much is the air ______ from London to Hong Kong?

b) The more you earn, the more income ______ you have to pay.

c) I had to pay a ______ for parking my car outside the police station.

d) The bus-drivers are demanding a 10% increase in ______.

e) When you register for the exam, you must pay a ______ of £10.

Section A, Question 4

Suggestions for the exam
In the exam, you may be asked to complete a dialogue like the one below. Read the **whole** *dialogue through carefully before you write anything. Notice the punctuation, and decide which sentences are questions. Finally, make sure that the sentences in your completed dialogue follow each other* **naturally** *and* **logically.** *You should allow about 15 minutes for this exercise.*

Instructions

Complete the dialogue with suitable phrases or sentences.

TRAVEL AGENT: Good morning. Can (1) . . . .?
ROBERT: Yes, I'd (2) . . . . a holiday.
TRAVEL AGENT: I see, sir. Where (3) . . . .?
ROBERT: I'm not sure. (4) . . . .?
TRAVEL AGENT: Well, it rather depends (5) . . . .
ROBERT: I can't afford more than £300.
TRAVEL AGENT: Well, (6) . . . . to Spain?
ROBERT: No, (7) . . . . last year.
TRAVEL AGENT: Then (8) . . . . Sweden?
ROBERT: I'd rather (9) . . . .
TRAVEL AGENT: In that case, (10) . . . . one of the Greek islands. Two weeks in Crete would only cost you £280.
ROBERT: (11) . . . . wonderful!
TRAVEL AGENT: Yes, I'm sure you'll (12) . . . .

PAPER 4: LISTENING COMPREHENSION

(Suggestions for the exam – see Unit 1)

Fill in the information you hear on the form below. Some of it has been filled in for you.

SURVEY ON STANDARDS OF LIVING

Tick (✓) box or write information where necessary.

Name (optional): ____________

Address: ____________

(optional) ____________

SURREY

Male ☐ Female ☐

Single ☐ Married ☑

Age

18–25 ☐ 26–35 ☐ 36–49 ☐ 50–59 ☐ 60+ ☐

Children (Write boy/girl + age)

Girl Age ____

____ Age ____

____ Age ____

Occupation: Personnel Manager

Previous jobs: ____________

(within last ____________

five years) ____________

Travelling time to work

Under 15 minutes ☐

15–30 minutes ☐

30 minutes – 1 hour ☐

Over 1 hour ☐

Home

House ☐ Owner ☐

Flat ☐ Tenant ☐

Other ☐ Other ☐

(e.g. rent free)

Rooms

Number of bedrooms ____

Living-room YES ☐ NO ☐

If yes, is the dining-room separate? YES ☐ NO ☐

Are the following shared with another household?

	YES	NO
Kitchen	☐	☐
Bathroom	☐	☐
Toilet	☐	☐

Household appliances

List items: television

____

____

____

____

Means of transport

Number of Cars 1 __ years old

Motor bikes __ __ years old

Mopeds __ __ years old

(under 50cc)

Entertainment/Leisure activities

How often?

Once/twice a month ☐

Once/twice a week ☐

More than once a week ☐

Never ☐

Type of entertainment/activity:

Pub ☐

Restaurant ☐

Hobbies ☐

Sport ☐

Cinema ☐

Friends ☐

Other ☐

Holidays

How often?

Every year YES ☐ NO ☐

If yes, how often in year?

Once ☐

Twice ☐

More than twice ☐

Usually spent abroad? YES ☐ NO ☐

LAW AND ORDER

A TALKING ABOUT RULES AND REGULATIONS

TALKING POINT

Which of the following people do you consider to be committing a serious crime?

A driver who knocks down a pedestrian and doesn't stop.
An underpaid office worker who steals money from the firm's cash box.
A shoplifter who has enough money to pay for the stolen goods.
A football fan who starts a fight with fans from the opposing team.
A person stopped at the customs for possessing a small amount of drugs.
Someone who gives away his country's secrets to a foreign power.
A person who buys goods knowing that they are stolen.
A gang who attack an old lady in the street and steal her purse.
A person who kills a burglar in his own house.
Someone who drives the get-away car in an armed robbery.

Under what circumstances might people who commit these crimes not be entirely responsible for their actions?

READING

News in Brief

WOMEN WIN EQUAL RIGHTS FIGHT

TWO WOMEN today won the right to be served in Garrett's restaurant in Piccadilly after a High Court judge's decision ruled that the restaurant's policy of only serving male customers was an offence against the Equal Opportunities Act. Their lawyer said: 'The restaurant claimed they had a legal right to refuse to serve whoever they wished. My clients' case was to challenge this men-only rule, because it was not only against women, but more important, against the law.'

NUCLEAR PROTEST MARCH – 20 ARRESTS

AT LEAST 5,000 people marched through central London yesterday in protest against the government's decision to build a nuclear power station near Balford Beeches on the south coast. The demonstration began at Hyde Park with a mass meeting and then moved to Downing Street to hand in a petition with over 20,000 signatures to the Prime Minister. Police arrested a number of people on a charge of obstruction when they sat down in the middle of Whitehall and blocked the traffic. After spending the night in jail, they will appear in court this morning.

OLD TOWN HALL TO GO

BERKHAM TOWN Council are still going ahead with their plans to demolish the Old Town Hall in Kenning Street despite objections from conservationists. Said Councillor Jim Payne, Mayor of Berkham, 'We haven't used the Old Town Hall for about five years now, and although we recognise that it's a lovely building, we think we can use the site for a new community hall and swimming baths.' Protestors claim that it will probably be used for offices. They are now trying to get a protection order placed on the building.

MPS BID TO SAVE HOSPITAL

AFTER THE Minister of Health's decision to close Mincham Womens' Hospital in Sherbourne Street because of lack of funds, politicians all over the country have received letters complaining about the move. Said one MP 'Although I can quite understand that the Minister was faced with a difficult decision, I must ask him to reconsider. I have received over a hundred letters and visits from groups of women who have been able to make good use of the excellent service that the hospital has provided. No taxpayer will see this move as being justified and I shall be organising a committee to resist the closure.'

TEA LADY WINS COSTS

A TEA lady who refused to use the teapot supplied to her by her company and was dismissed, has been awarded £5,000 costs for unfair dismissal by an Industrial Tribunal today. She claimed that the weight of her tea pot, which, when full, contained five litres of tea had caused her to injure her back and arms. When she made a request to be supplied with a smaller teapot, it was refused by the management and she was asked to leave her job.

UNIT EIGHT

a) 1 Why did the two women go to court?
2 What do you think the Equal Opportunities Act is?
3 Why had 20,000 people signed a petition?
4 Why were twenty protesters arrested?
5 Why is the Old Town Hall to be demolished?
6 What are the protesters hoping to do to save the building?
7 Why is the hospital to close?
8 Who is responsible for the decision to close it?
9 How did the tea lady injure herself?
10 How did she try to resolve the problem?

b) Find words or phrases in the news items which mean:

question	pull down	sacked
regulation	protests	hurt
walked	take advantage of	
prison	oppose	

KEY VOCABULARY

c) Explain what the underlined words refer to.
1 Their lawyers said . . .
2 . . . they will appear in court . . .
3 Protesters claim that it will probably . . .
4 No taxpayer will see this move as . . .
5 . . . it was refused by the management.

d) In each of the news items, people had decided to challenge a situation. Do you think they were right to do so?

LANGUAGE PRACTICE

1 a) People do not necessarily agree with the law. Listen to four people who think the law has treated them unfairly. In each case, take notes on the following:

person's occupation
offence/crime
place
punishment

b) Choose one of these people. Tell another student what has happened, and express your annoyance.

Expressing annoyance:

KEY LANGUAGE

How dare they . . . ?
They've got no right to . . .
The thing that really annoys me is . . .
They can't just . . .
Why can't/couldn't they . . . ?
Why did they have to . . . ?

c) Do you think the law is right to punish such people? If not, what do you think would be the most sensible action for them to take?:

Organise a pressure group?
Send letters to MPs and government ministers concerned?
Organise a campaign in the press and on radio and television?
Hire a lawyer and take the dispute to court?
Write to the local authorities?

2 a) Where would you see these signs?

All visitors should report to reception

NO WAITING

NO ENTRY

IN CASE OF FIRE BREAK GLASS

DO NOT LEAN OUT OF THE WINDOW

NO SMOKING

HELMETS MUST BE WORN

KEEP OUT

DO NOT touch the fruit

b) What kinds of signs would you expect to see in the following places?

on a station platform	on a beach
on the banks of a river	in a lift
in a library	in a theatre
in an art gallery	at a bus stop
at a pedestrian crossing	in a hospital

c) Most rules are either to protect our personal safety or to respect the wishes of others. What are the functions of the signs in **a**) and **b**) above?

d) Choose one of the places in **a**) or **b**). Your partner should try to guess where you are by asking permission to do things.

Example: *(A is in a theatre)*

B: Do you mind if I smoke?
A: I'm sorry, it's not allowed.
B: Is it all right if I sit down?
A: Yes, go ahead.
B: Would you object if I read?
A: No, but you won't see the show if you do.
B: Can I take photographs?
A: . . . .

KEY LANGUAGE

Expressing permission (1):
Asking permission:

Can/May/Could I . . . ?
Would it be possible to . . . ?
Is it all right if I . . . ?
Do you mind/object if I . . . ? + present simple
Would it be all right if I . . . ?
Would you mind/object if I . . . ? + past simple
Have you any objection to my + -ING . . . ?

Giving permission

You can/may if you want/like.
Yes, of course.
Certainly.
By all means.
Go ahead.
Not all all. (when request uses *mind/object*)

Refusing permission

No, you can't/may not.
I'm sorry, it's not allowed.
I'm afraid it's forbidden to . . .
I'd rather you didn't.
I'd prefer you not to.

3

a) Many regulations are mere formalities, but we still have to obey them. Listen to this conversation giving advice to a man travelling to the United States.
Take notes on the following:

travel documents
customs regulations
insurance
health requirements
drinking laws
motoring laws

b) Write a summary of the principal regulations concerning visitors to the United States.

Example: *You must have a valid passport, and you need a visa.*

c) What are the principal regulations and laws which a visitor to your country should know about? Work in groups to prepare an information sheet using the headings in 3**a**).

KEY LANGUAGE

Expressing obligation and necessity (3):

You *must* / *need to* / *have (got) to* + infinitive
You *need* + noun

Expressing absence of obligation and necessity;

You *don't need to* / *needn't* / *don't have to* + infinitive

Expressing prohibition:

You *mustn't* / *can't* / *may not* + infinitive
You're not allowed to / *It's forbidden to* + infinitive

Expressing permission (2):

You're allowed to / *They let you* / *You can/may* + infinitive reversing the car = go back / lost his footing = lost his balance

4 Read the following sentences, and decide what type of word is missing. Then choose the missing word from the list below.

KEY VOCABULARY

citizen	illegal	tax
immigrant	election	security
investigate	prison	vote
democratic	political	proof
court	allowance	duty
suspected	permission	demonstration

1 The USA has a large _______ population which came from Europe.

2 The judge sentenced her to two years in _______ for robbery.

3 After the government was defeated, a general _______ was held.

4 The bearer of this pass has the management's _______ to enter the building.

5 Because of recent attempts on the lives of government officials, _______ will be tightened.

6 It is _______ to carry guns without a licence in Britain.

7 The police _______ him of attempted murder, but since they had no proof, no accusation was made.

8 In protest against the new Trades Union laws, a _______ will be held in Trafalgar Square on Sunday.

9 He was annoyed because he had to pay a lot of _______ at the customs.

10 In the USA, there are two main _______ parties.

DISCUSSION

Do you think the law protects you enough?
Do you think it overprotects you?
Is the individual ever justified in taking the law into his own hands?

Do you think there are some laws which are now out of date?

B REPORTING PAST EVENTS

READING

7, Golden Hill,
Maidenhead,
Berkshire,

12th September 1983

Dear Jack,

I thought I'd drop you a line to thank you once again for a lovely holiday. We feel very relaxed after such a restful break.

However, we had a slight problem on our way home, just after saying good-bye to you all. We were just on the edge of town when Fiona remembered that she needed to buy some aspirin. We caught sight of a chemists by the junction leading to the motorway - Brent Corner, I think it's called. Fiona got the aspirin but as we were reversing the car out to leave, an old man, who'd been sitting on a bench in front of the chemist's, got up, lost his footing and fell over. We stopped, of course, and helped him up. We asked him if he'd hurt himself and he replied that he was all right. We noticed that he'd cut his forehead. As soon as he took a few steps, he was very unsteady, so we said we'd take him to hospital. After three hours the doctor arrived, asked how it had happened, gave the old man a check-up and said he wasn't injured but that they'd keep him there for the night, just to be sure. It was getting late so we told a nurse to get in touch with us if there were any problems and left.

But yesterday, while I was at work, Fiona got a phone call from the old man's son-in-law. He explained that the old man was still in hospital and not at all well. He said that he thought the old man had been knocked down by a car and what's worse, that his wallet was missing. Fiona asked him if he was suggesting that I'd actually knocked the old man down. He replied that he wasn't making any accusations at the moment, but that it was an offence not to have given an official statement to the police. He said they might take us to court.

Of course, we immediately rang the hospital and the doctor said he couldn't be sure but the old man might have been hit by a slow-moving car. I know I didn't run him down, but we've got no evidence. So I was wondering if you could go over to the shops, and ask if there were any witnesses. Try the chemist's in particular. Let me know what you find. I'd really be grateful if you could help.

Give our love to Mary and the children.

Best wishes,

Gerry

Choose the best alternative to the following words from the text.

KEY VOCABULARY

1 JUNCTION
A crossroads B bend
C traffic lights D road

2 REVERSING
A driving forwards B driving backwards
C accelerating D slowing down

3 CHECK-UP
A investigation B inquiry C search
D examination

4 INJURED
A damaged B hurt C ill D sick

5 STATEMENT
A check-list B information C confession
D report

6 EVIDENCE
A proof B facts C sign D reasons

Now choose the best answer.

7 The accident occurred
A as soon as they left town.
B not long after leaving their friends.
C when they had just left the motorway.
D just before they arrived home.

8 When they helped the old man to his feet, he
A fell over.
B sat down.
C was very weak.
D was hurt.

9 At the hospital, the doctor
A was three hours late.
B decided the old man should stay overnight.
C was sure that the old man wasn't hurt.
D took three hours to do the check-up.

10 Fiona received a phone call from
A one of the old man's relatives.
B the old man's lawyer.
C the old man's adopted son.
D the police.

11 He said that
A the police were offended.
B the old man might have been run down.
C Gerry had hit the old man himself.
D the old man's wallet had been stolen.

12 Gerry wants Jack to
A take the son-in-law to court.
B search the shops.
C find Brent Corner.
D look for people who saw what happened.

LANGUAGE PRACTICE

What was actually said in the following sentences?

Example: The doctor said he couldn't be sure, but . . .
'I can't be sure, but . . .'

1 We asked him if he'd hurt himself . . .

2 . . . he replied that he was all right.

3 . . . (the doctor) asked how it had happened . . .

4 . . . (the doctor) said he wasn't injured . . .

5 . . . (the doctor) said they'd keep him there for the night . . .

6 . . . we told a nurse to get in touch with us if there were any problems . . .

7 He explained that the old man was still in hospital . . .

8 He said he thought the old man had been knocked down by a car . . .

9 Fiona asked him if he was suggesting that I'd actually knocked the old man down.

10 He replied that he wasn't making any accusations . . .

KEY LANGUAGE

Reporting what has been said (1):

Direct speech	**Indirect speech**
'She's my wife,' he said.	He said (that) she *was his* wife.
'I'm going out,' she said.	She said (that) *she was going* out.
'She's locked the door,' he said.	He said (that) she'*d locked* the door.
'I caught a cold last week,' he said.	He said (that) *he'd caught* a cold *the week before.*
'We'll do it tomorrow,' she said.	She said (that) they'*d do* it *the following day.*

Note: The contraction *'d* means either *had* or *would.*

today	that day
yesterday	the day before
tomorrow	the following day/the next day
this week/month, etc.	that week/month, etc.
last week/month, etc.	the week/month etc. before
next week/month, etc.	the following week/month, etc.

LISTENING ACTIVITY

Gerry's friend Jack went along to the shops and made some enquiries.

a) Listen to the conversation he had with one of the assistants and place the following sentences in the right order.

Example: *1* = **F**

A She told him to speak to one of the assistants.

B He asked her if the car had hit the old man.

C She told him to ask at the baker's.

D He asked her what had happened that afternoon.

E He said he would.

F He asked her if she'd been working there the Friday before.

G She told him that the old man had collapsed after getting up from the bench.

H She replied that it hadn't.

b) Listen to the conversation again, and write down what was actually said in each of the sentences above.

LANGUAGE PRACTICE

a) Look at the notes Jack made when he spoke to the baker's assistant. In pairs, act out the conversation they had, using the notes.

b) Now write the conversation in indirect speech.

Reporting what has been said (2): KEY LANGUAGE

Statements

say
explain (*to* + noun/pronoun) + (*that*) clause

He explained (to them) that he was ill.

tell + noun/pronoun + (*that*) clause

He told me (that) he was going out.

reply + (*that*) clause

She replied that she hadn't seen him.

Questions

ask (noun/pronoun) + *who/what/why/how* etc. / *if* + clause

He asked (her) what had happened.
She asked (him) if he was over 18.

Commands

ask
tell + noun/pronoun + *to* + infinitive

He told me to close the door.

Baker's

Betty: – working there Friday p.m.
– didn't see what happened outside.
– remembers old man – often comes in.
– came in on Friday.
– asks me why.
Fri. 2.30p.m. (?) – old man came in for a loaf.
took out wallet, dropped £1 note.
looking v. pale – not feeling v. well.
told him to go and sit down outside for a few minutes.
5.30p.m. – closing shop, found old mans wallet behind door.
Kept it in case he returned, hasn't come back.
– old man's address in wallet!
2, Franklin Terrace
East Street

GUIDED WRITING ACTIVITY

a) Jack decided to go to the old man's address to find out more about him. Listen to the conversation he had with one of the neighbours, and take notes.

b) Jack has now been to the chemist's, the baker's and to the old man's neighbour. He replies to Gerry's letter, explaining what he has been able to find out.

Look at the beginning and ending, and complete Jack's letter to Gerry.

91 Chalk Street,
London N.19
17 September 1983

Dear Gerry,
Many thanks for your letter. It was lovely to see you and Fiona again, and we thoroughly enjoyed having you.
I'm sorry you had problems on the way home. I've been doing some detective work for you, as you asked, and I've got some interesting information for you. First of all I went to the chemist's where one of the assistants told me she'd seen the old man.

So you needn't worry about a thing! If the son-in-law rings back, just tell him that you've got some witnesses to prove your story.
Best wishes,
Jack

C DESCRIBING THE ROLE OF THE POLICE

READING

A Day in the Life . . .

Most people think that the police spend their time fighting crime. *In fact they spend much more time on other activities, like* traffic control, services to the community *and* keeping public order *at events where there are large crowds. Look at this account of a typical day at a police station.*

It was the beginning of another day at the Broadlees Road police station. Twenty police officers sat in a small room receiving their instructions for the day. Special tasks included crowd control at the local football stadium, which would take up a large number of officers. There'd also been a series of attacks on people in the street in broad daylight, and public opinion was demanding a more visible police presence.

The first call of the day came from a lady who'd just noticed a couple of youths climbing into the local school through the window. It was Saturday and the school was closed, so PCs Gray and Shaw were sent to investigate. News of an accident on the main road leading into the city centre arrived; a lorry had run into a car, two people were injured and a cargo of fruit had been spread all over the road. A traffic jam had already begun to build up. Assistance was needed to redirect the traffic and let the ambulance get through.

A woman came in to report that she'd lost her cat. Sergeant Yates took a description as he kindly explained that there wasn't much they could do to help. PC Davis came in with two boys, one of whom was carrying a knife, caught stealing in a sweet shop. Neither could be over twelve years old. PC Gray reported that the 'youths' at the school were council maintenance workers repairing the central heating system; the pipes were too long to go in through the door. An abandoned car had been reported in Mafeking Street and PC Gray was sent over to take a look. The accident on the main road was by this time causing a queue over a mile long in both directions. Sergeant Brown and PC Wills were taking statements from witnesses of the crash. PC Davis left for the youth centre to give a course of instruction in riding motor bikes safely.

The parents of the two boys caught shoplifting came in and told Sergeant Ellis that they were in fact nine and ten years old. PC Gray asked for a check on the abandoned car and was told that it had been stolen over 200 miles away about a fortnight ago. A call from a local pub informed Sergeant Yates that supporters of the rival football team had started to gather there before the match. The barman was concerned that there would be an outbreak of violence when the supporters of the home team came in. A special van with ten officers was sent over to keep an eye on the situation. An explosion was reported at an old factory site and fire had broken out. No one seemed to be hurt but someone had to find out what had happened. A man was brought in after being stopped by WPC Jones for not wearing a seat belt. It turned out that the car's lights and brakes weren't in working order, the tyres were bald and the exhaust pipe was too noisy; he'd also had a bit too much to drink. Sergeant Yates calmly listened to him complaining that the police should be out on the streets catching criminals and not annoying people like him, and then put him in a cell.

The lady who'd lost her cat came back to say she'd found it but asked if she'd left her handbag when she'd been in before. Sergeant Yates told her that she hadn't and spent ten minutes asking her where she might have left it. At the pub, the police went in and turned out all those who were too young to be drinking there. About twenty gave in without a fight and left. Sergeant Wilkins learned that the traffic lights in Acton Place were out of order, and sent PC Turner over there to direct the traffic. PC Turner was not pleased.

Fighting had already broken out at the football match and ten youths had been arrested. A group of demonstrators gathering for a march in Eaton Square had 'forgotten' to inform the police of the march. PC Arnold and WPC Charles were told to ask them to go home. The lady came back; she'd found her handbag at home. The factory fire had spread and the local radio station was asked to broadcast a police message warning people to keep clear of the area. Traffic was now flowing freely along the main road after the accident. The demonstrators refused to go home and Arnold and Charles called for help. As soon as the football match was over, Sergeant Wilkins sent some men over to Eaton Square. A man had been attacked in the High Street and had his wallet stolen. All he'd heard was someone running up behind him and then he'd been hit over the head.

The fans of the defeated football team were not too happy about the result and a large group of them were making for the town centre. There was a fair on in the local park that night, and six officers were sent along to patrol. The lady who'd lost her handbag and her cat came in to complain about a noisy party in her street. A new team of officers arrived to take over from those who had been on duty all day. It was going to be a busy night.

LANGUAGE PRACTICE

1 **a)** Role play: Choose one of the situations in the text in which someone asks the police for help. Explain your problem to your partner, who is a police officer and will tell you what the police can do to help.

b) Role play: Think of another situation where the police would be helpful. In pairs, prepare the dialogue which takes place between you and the police officer.

KEY LANGUAGE

Expressing fear and anxiety (1):

I'm afraid/frightened/worried/scared + (*that*) clause
I don't like it at all.
Whatever can have happened to + noun?
I do hope . . .
Supposing / *What if* (*something happens/has happened*)?

Giving reassurance:

Calm down.
Don't worry.
I'm sure it'll be all right.
There's nothing to be alarmed/worried about.

Thanking (2):

Thanks *a lot.* / *very much (indeed).*
Thank you so/very much (*for* + noun/-ING)
How can I thank you?
I can't thank you enough.
I can't tell you how grateful I am.
I'm (really) very grateful to you.
You've been very kind/helpful.

2 Complete the following sentences by choosing the missing word from the list below.

KEY VOCABULARY

spare	fine	alarm
inspect	innocent	crime
accelerate	van	illegal
offence	detective	run over
steering	overtake	ticket
guns	gear	brand new
headlamp	vehicle	second-hand
lawyer	release	punishment

1 In Britain you have to be seventeen before you can drive a motor ________.

2 They couldn't prove anything so they had to ________ the suspect.

3 It is an ________ to drive a car without a licence.

4 You have to carry a ________ wheel in the car in case you have a puncture.

5 He tried to ________ the lorry while it was waiting at a pedestrian crossing.

6 Under British law, a man is ________ until he is proved guilty.

7 In Britain, police don't usually carry ________.

8 After the murder was reported, a ________ went round to look for clues.

9 Most shops have ________ bells which start ringing when there's a break-in.

10 If the police stop you for speeding you have to pay a ________.

3 **a)** How many parts of the car can you name? Choose from the list below.

KEY VOCABULARY

sidelights	indicator	seat
headlights	windscreen	tyre
bonnet	boot	steering wheel
number plate	wing	wipers

b) It's illegal to drive a car that's unsafe. Which of these things would the police check if they stopped you?

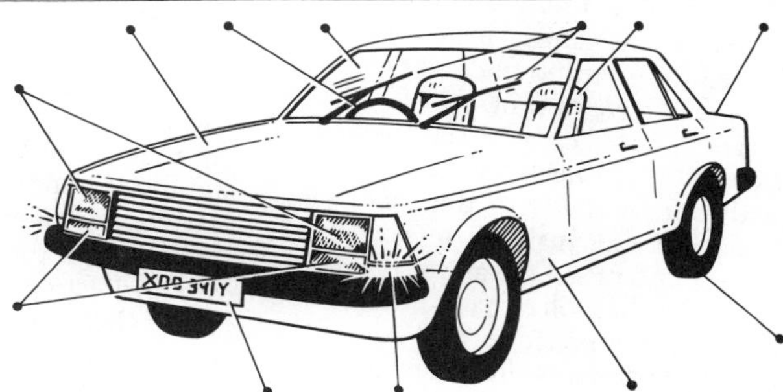

INTERPRETATION ACTIVITY

Read the text again. Write about forty words in answer to each of the questions below.

1 Which type of police work takes up the largest number of men? Why?

2 What kind of services to the community do the police perform?

3 Which type of work do you think is the least interesting for the police officer? Why?

4 Which type of activity has the greatest influence on public opinion? Why?

DISCUSSION

In Britain, the four types of police work are all dealt with by the same police force. How is the police force organised in your country?

What is the role of the police in your country? What do they have to do?

D MAKING DEDUCTIONS

READING

Mona Lisa stolen – Crime of the Century

THE 'MONA LISA' (La Gioconda), the world's most famous painting, has been stolen from the Louvre in Paris. This astonishing news was announced yesterday at 5.30 p.m. by Mr Bénédite, a director of the world-famous museum.

The theft was discovered by art student Louis Béroud when he went to the museum on Tuesday morning to continue his painting of the 'Salon Carré', where the Mona Lisa usually hangs. But to his surprise, when he arrived, there were only four hooks where the Mona Lisa was usually to be found. He was told by a guard that it had probably been taken to the photographic studios. But Béroud was impatient to finish his work, and bribed the guard to find out how long he would have to wait.

The guard came back with the extraordinary news that the painting had not been seen that morning. Suddenly he realised it had been stolen, and raised the alarm.

So far the police have no clues. A puzzled Mr Bénédite told reporters, 'The museum was closed on Sunday at 4 p.m. On Mondays the public are not allowed in so that essential cleaning and repair work can be carried out. A lot of works of art are moved around by the staff, some of whom are brought in just to do this on Mondays. But they are all checked before entering and leaving and there are regular patrols by guards during the day. We've found the frame and the glass case protecting the picture. It must have taken the thief some time to remove them. We feel sure that whoever did it made careful plans; it wasn't just a sudden decision'.

Mona Lisa

Asked why anyone should want to steal the Mona Lisa, he replied, 'We really don't know. It's too well-known to be sold to another gallery, although there are some private collectors rich enough to buy it just for the pleasure of owning such a famous painting. But they could never show it to anyone other than trusted friends. There's also a chance that whoever did it will demand a sum of money for its safe return. If they do, we'll have to make sure they don't try and give us a copy and not the real Mona Lisa! Maybe you people can help. I'm sure there are plenty of journalists who'd steal it just to get a good story!'

'Or to show how bad security is at the Louvre!' said a journalist. Bénédite refused to make any comment.

The editors of this newspaper deny this outrageous suggestion. The directors of the Louvre are equally capable of organising such a crime just to get some publicity for their museum! To show our concern, we are offering a reward of 25,000 francs to anyone who can give information which will lead to the safe return of this priceless national treasure.

LISTENING ACTIVITY

a) Listen to the report on the theft of the Mona Lisa. Take notes on the points which give clues as to how the painting was stolen.

b) Why would anyone steal the Mona Lisa? How did they do it? Discuss with another student the possible motives behind the theft, and how the painting was stolen. Use information from the newspaper article and the notes you have made.

Example: *They might have stolen it to sell to a private collector.*

c) **New information:** Now listen to the explanation of how the painting was stolen, and make notes.

d) How do the facts compare with your theories? Did you guess how the Mona Lisa was stolen?

KEY LANGUAGE

Making deductions (3):

Possibility

It / *They* *may* / *could have* + past participle / *might*

There's a chance that . . .
It's possible that . . .

Probability

It was probably . . .

It's / *They're* *(not) likely to have* + past participle

Certainty

It / *They* *must* / *can't* *have* + past participle

ROLE PLAY

a) Out of hundreds of people questioned by the police, there were a number of suspects, all of them answering the description given by the plumber. Here are just four of them:

A *Michel REY*, 32, French. Waiter in bar opposite the Louvre. Used to work as a guard at the museum until he was sacked in July for stealing money from his colleagues. Began work at midday on Monday.

B *Vincenzo PERUGIA*, 35, Italian. Carpenter working for a private firm. Had worked with a different company in April making a special frame to protect the Mona Lisa. Arrived at work half an hour late on Monday, at 8.30 a.m.

C *Benoît GALLET*, 30, French. Art dealer specialising in Italian paintings. Works as a guide once a week, giving tours of the galleries at the Louvre. Says he was out of town until Tuesday morning.

D *Jacques BIRON*, 37, French. Restores paintings at the Louvre. Has made some brilliant copies of famous works of art. Was arrested once for trying to sell one as genuine. Served six months in prison.

Groups A, B, C, D
In your group, prepare some details about one of the suspects (Group A – Suspect A, etc.) Be ready to answer questions from the police about your life and what you were doing on Monday 22 August. Make sure you all have the same information.

Group E
You are police detectives. Prepare a list of questions you would like to ask the four suspects.

b) Form new groups with one person from each of the old groups. The detective interviews the four suspects.

c) At the end of the interview, the detectives compare notes. Which suspects have made the most mistakes in their answers?

d) The detectives present their conclusions to the whole class. Who do you think stole the Mona Lisa?

LISTENING ACTIVITY

a) Listen to the next part of the story, and take notes.

b) Why do you think the thief waited two years before trying to sell the painting? Was there someone else involved in the affair? Was this person meant to sell the painting?
Why do you think the copies of the Mona Lisa are mentioned by the narrator?

c) **New information:** Now listen to the end of the story.

d) Why did Perugia wait two years before trying to sell the painting?
What did de Valfierno do with the copies?
Why didn't he sell the real Mona Lisa?
What happened when the painting was returned to the Louvre?
What happened to the people involved in the crime of the century?
When did all this take place?

e) Write an account of the 'crime of the century'.

READING ALOUD

a) Read the following part of the tapescript. Mark those words which you expect to be stressed with a dot. Remember that it is always the most important words in a phrase or sentence which are stressed. Then listen to the person talking again, and check whether you were right.

But who? And why? The police were sure that he was telling lies, but they were no nearer to finding out the truth. They might've got closer if they'd remembered two facts. First, there are a number of copies of the Mona Lisa in the world. Part of the painting's fascination is whether the one in the Louvre is genuine or not. There are a number of brilliant artists even today who could make a very good copy. Everyone who owns one of these 'Mona Lisas' claims it's the real one. But how can they be sure?

b) Now read the text aloud.

DISCUSSION

What is so special about the Mona Lisa? Describe the painting and say whether you like it.
Why do you think the Mona Lisa is considered to be the most valuable painting in the world?
Why do you think paintings exchange hands at such enormous prices these days? Do you think the prices are reasonable?
What kind of paintings do you like? (classical – Renaissance – impressionist – surrealist – modern, etc.)
Who is your favourite artist?

EXAM PRACTICE

PAPER 1: READING COMPREHENSION

Section B *(Suggestions for the exam – see Unit 3)*

In this section you will find after the text a number of questions or unfinished statements about the text, each with four suggested answers or ways of finishing. You must choose the one which you think fits best. For each question, *indicate on your answer sheet* the letter A, B, C or D against the number of the question.

Why seat belts are necessary

More than 30,000 drivers and front seat passengers are killed or seriously injured each year. The impact on you of an accident can be very serious. At a speed of only 30 miles per hour it is the same as falling from a third-floor window. Wearing a seat belt saves lives; it reduces your chance of death or serious injury by more than half.

Who has to wear a seat belt?

Drivers or front seat passengers in most vehicles. If you are 14 or over it will be your responsibility to wear the belt. If you do not, you could be fined up to £50. It will not be up to the driver to make sure you wear your belt. But it will be the driver's responsibility to make sure that children under 14 do not ride in the front unless they are wearing a seat belt of some kind.

A very few vehicles have a middle front seat between the front passenger seat and the driver's seat, for example a bench seat. Your vehicle may be one of them. If just one passenger sits in front, he must wear a seat belt. But if two passengers sit in front, the person sitting in the middle will not have to wear a belt.

When you do not have to wear a seat belt

You do not have to wear a seat belt in certain circumstances, such as if you are reversing your vehicle, if you are making a local delivery or collection using a vehicle constructed or adapted for that purpose, or if you have a valid medical certificate which excuses you from wearing it. Make sure these circumstances apply to you before you decide not to wear your seat belt. Remember you may be taken to court for not doing so, and you may be fined if you cannot prove to the court that you have been excused from wearing it.

Medical exemptions

Certain people ought not to wear a seat belt because of their health. It may be more risky for them to wear a belt than to be in a road accident without one. But they will not have to wear a belt if they get a valid medical certificate from a doctor. If you think this applies to you, *go and talk to a doctor* as soon as possible. The doctor may reassure you that you can wear a seat belt. Or he may have to examine you before he can decide whether or not to give you a certificate. When you go and see him you should ask him *at the start* how much this would cost. Keep the certificate. If the police ask you why you are not wearing a seat belt, you should show them the certificate. If you cannot show it to them on the spot, you should take the certificate to a police station of your choice within five days.

1 This text is taken from
- A a medical magazine.
- B a police report on safety.
- C a legal document.
- D a government information leaflet.

2 Wearing a seat belt in a vehicle
- A reduces road accidents by more than half.
- B saves lives only at a speed of 30 miles per hour.
- C reduces the risk of death and injury to drivers and passengers.
- D saves the lives of more than 30,000 drivers and front seat passengers.

3 It is the driver's responsibility to
- A make the front seat passenger wear a seat belt.
- B make children under 14 wear a seat belt in the front.
- C stop children riding in the front seat.
- D wear a seat belt on all occasions.

4 According to the text, which of the following people does not have to wear a seat belt?
- A Someone who is backing into a parking space.
- B Someone who is picking up the children from the local school.
- C Someone who is delivering invitations to a party.
- D Someone who is under 14.

5 For some people, it may be better
- A to wear a seat belt for health reasons.
- B not to wear a seat belt for health reasons.
- C to get a valid medical certificate before wearing a seat belt.
- D to pay the fine rather than wear a seat belt.

6 If you are excused from wearing a seat belt on medical grounds,
- A you must take the certificate to the police station within five days.
- B you must show the certificate to the police on the spot.
- C the doctor will give you a certificate.
- D the doctor will have to examine you.

PAPER 2: COMPOSITION

(Suggestions for the exam – see Unit 2)

Your answers must follow exactly the instructions given and must be of between 120 and 180 words each.

1 Your house or flat has been burgled while you've been away on holiday. Describe the scene that meets your eyes when you return home, your reactions, and what you did.

2 An English friend is planning to tour your country by car. Write to him/her suggesting places worth visiting and suitable accommodation, and giving useful information on driving regulations, local customs, etc. You should make the beginning and ending like those of an ordinary letter, but the address is not to be counted in the number of words.

3 Describe the rules of a sport or game you know well.

4 'Prison is not a suitable punishment for crime.' Do you agree? What other methods of punishment would you suggest?

PAPER 3: USE OF ENGLISH

Section A, Question 3 *(Suggestions for the exam – see Unit 2)*

Complete the following sentences with the appropriate phrase made from LOOK.

Example: Slow down! You'll have an accident if you don't .*look out*. . . .

a) After a long search the police found the man they were . . . .

b) We will have to . . . . the possibility that he was killed.

c) She . . . . the number in the telephone directory.

d) You really should . . . . yourself with a cold like that!

e) He was a brilliant teacher, and everybody in the school . . . . him.

Section A, Question 4 *(Suggestions for the exam – see Unit 2)*

Make all the changes and additions necessary to produce, from the following eight sets of words and phrases, eight sentences which together make a complete letter. Note carefully from the example what kind of alterations need to be made. Write each sentence in the space provided.

Example: Thank you so much/letter; it be nice of you/write/us.

Answer: *Thank you so much for your letter; it was nice of you to write to us.*

Dear Mary,

I be sorry/I not reply/until now/but we/be very busy/since we move/our new house.

a) . . . .

We be very happy/now that we finish/the decorating.

b) . . . .

Jack enjoy/new job/but he have/get up/6 every morning/get to work.

c) . . . .

He tell me last week/he intend/stay/bed all weekend!

d) . . . .

I reply/his parents come/lunch/Sunday/and he be not very pleased!

e) . . . .

My parents love/new house/and they tell us/they come/stay/a few days next month.

f) . . . .

It be lovely/if you be able/find the time/come and visit us soon.

g) . . . .

You be able/see for yourself/how quickly/we adapt/our new life.

h) . . . .

Best wishes,

Jill

Section B, Question 5 *(Suggestions for the exam – see Unit 4)*

Using the information given in the following conversation, answer each of the four questions below. Use no more than 50 words for each paragraph.

(Doorbell)

POLICEWOMAN: Mr Jones?

MR JONES: Yes?

POLICEWOMAN: Good morning. I'm the local Crime Prevention Officer. You made an appointment a few days ago to see me.

MR JONES: Oh, yes, do come in.

POLICEWOMAN: Thank you. Well, you've got a very nice house. It'd be a pity to lose anything from it.

MR JONES: Yes, and we've had so many burglaries in this street. It's very worrying.

POLICEWOMAN: Well, there's always a risk that someone will try and break in, but there are a few simple precautions you can take. For example, when you go out for the evening do you leave any lights on? It makes the burglar think twice before he tries to get into a house if it looks as if it's occupied.

MR JONES: Oh yes, I always try and do that, and I make sure the curtains are pulled as well. But it's not always possible if I get home late . . .

POLICEWOMAN: You can always ask a neighbour to come in and do it for you. Or put a couple of lights on time switches.

MR JONES: Yes, I hadn't thought of that.

POLICEWOMAN: What about your windows? Have you got locks on them?

MR JONES: No, we haven't . . .

POLICEWOMAN: Well, it's very easy in a house like this just to slip the window-catch and climb in. I think that locks on all the windows is the first thing you need.

MR JONES: Yes, I'll see to that.

POLICEWOMAN: What about when you go away? Do you tell the newsagent and the milkman to stop their deliveries?

MR JONES: Yes, we always do that.

POLICEWOMAN: Good. Some people forget and then newspapers or bottles of milk start piling up on the front door step. It's obvious to the burglar that the house is empty. But do you also tell the police?

MR JONES: Oh, no, I don't like to trouble them with things like that.

POLICEWOMAN: Well, it's no trouble, Mr Jones, that's what we're there for. You could ask your neighbour to keep an eye on the house as well. And it sounds silly, but it's even worth asking him to cut the grass.

MR JONES: Oh yes, that's a good idea.

POLICEWOMAN: You can give him a spare key. Much better than leaving it on a bit of string in the letter box or under the mat. That's the first place a burglar will look.

MR JONES: Yes, of course.

POLICEWOMAN: Make sure you lock the garden shed as well. There might be some tools he could use to force his way in. And ladders. Keep them well locked up. Otherwise he'll use them to get up to that window upstairs that you forgot to close!

MR JONES: Yes, we have got a ladder in the garage.

POLICEWOMAN: Well, make sure it's locked up. Now, inside your house. Have you got photos of all your valuables? If the worst comes to the worst, it will at least help us to get them back. And take a note of all the serial numbers on your TV, radio, hi-fi, and so on.

MR JONES: Yes, I'll do that.

POLICEWOMAN: And how about your car? We have so many cars stolen each year just because the owner has left the ignition key inside. And it only takes a few seconds for the thief to drive away. Even when it's in the garage, you should always take the keys out and lock it.

MR JONES: Well, sometimes I leave it open for a few minutes while I'm in a shop . . .

POLICEWOMAN: You're asking for trouble if you leave the keys in the car. And make sure you hide any valuables you've left in the car. If a thief can't see if there's anything to steal, he might decide not to take the risk.

MR JONES: Yes, I've got all that.

POLICEWOMAN: Right, well, let's have a look round the house, if we may. There might be some things we've overlooked . . . ah, yes, now this window . . .

1 What will show a thief that a house is unoccupied during the evening? How can you protect your house?

2 What will show a thief that you're away on holiday? What should you do to stop him taking advantage of your absence?

3 How can you stop your car from being stolen?

4 What can you do to protect your personal possessions?

NEW HORIZONS

A GIVING DEFINITIONS AND PHYSICAL DESCRIPTIONS EXPLAINING SIMPLE OPERATIONS

TALKING POINT

Match each of the following major discoveries/inventions with the correct name(s) and date, and make sentences.

Example: *I think the television was invented by John Logie Baird in 1926.*

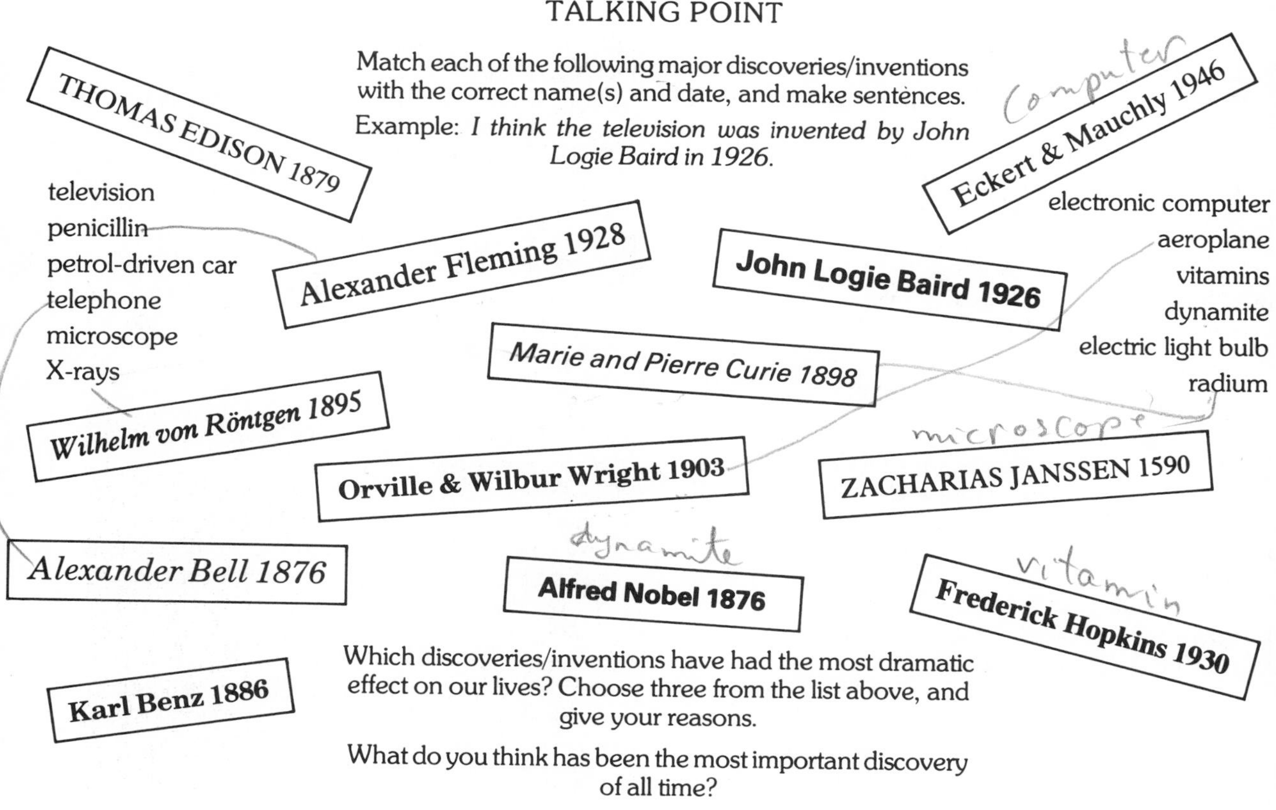

Which discoveries/inventions have had the most dramatic effect on our lives? Choose three from the list above, and give your reasons.

What do you think has been the most important discovery of all time?

READING

Read the text opposite and then answer the following questions.

a) 1 How does a hologram look different from a photograph?

2 Why was Professor Gabor unable to make a successful hologram in 1948?

3 In what way is a holographic plate specially treated?

4 Study the diagram showing the apparatus for making holograms, and label the following:
beam-splitter
reference beam
object beam
mirrors (2)

b) Explain what the underlined words refer to.

1 . . . but they also move . . .
2 . . . or walk past it.
3 . . . who later received the Nobel Prize . . .
4 . . . which produces a very powerful beam . . .
5 . . . that is sensitive to light.
6 . . . where it meets the reference beam . . .
7 . . . that is recorded on the plate . . .

HOLOGRAMS • HOLOGRAMS • HOLOGRAMS

WHAT IS A HOLOGRAM?

A hologram is a three-dimensional image produced by a laser on a specially treated glass plate or piece of film. When you look into a hologram, not only do objects on the plate appear 3D, but they also move in relation to one another as you move the plate or walk past it. The image looks so real that you might well think that you were looking at the actual object.

The theory of holography was first developed in 1948 by Professor Dennis Gabor, who later received the Nobel Prize in Physics. It took the invention of the laser (a device which produces a very powerful beam of light of *one* frequency) in 1960, though, before the theory could be put into practice and a successful hologram could be made. While considerable specialist knowledge is required to understand the science involved in holography, it is not difficult to understand the processes involved in making a hologram.

Hologram: The Meeting

HOW IS IT MADE?

A hologram is made by recording laser light on a holographic plate (a piece of glass coated with a substance that is sensitive to light). The laser beam is split, by means of a device called a *beam-splitter*, into two separate beams. One beam is reflected off the mirror onto the holographic plate; this is called the *reference beam.* The other beam is reflected off another mirror onto the object; this is called the *object beam.*

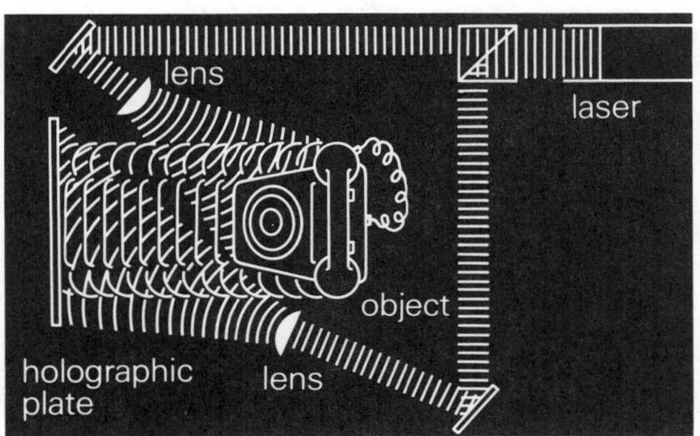

Laser light is reflected off the object onto the holographic plate, where it meets the reference beam and an 'interference pattern' is produced. It is this interference of the two beams that is recorded on the plate to produce a hologram.

LANGUAGE PRACTICE

1 Fill in the missing noun or verb.

KEY VOCABULARY

NOUN		interference	invention	knowledge	
VERB	appear				move

NOUN	reference				
VERB		reflect	think	treat	understand

2 a) *A laser is a device which produces a very powerful beam of light of one frequency.*

Find an example for each of the following definitions. Check your answers in the dictionary.

1 an instrument which measures time
2 a piece of metal that attracts iron
3 a tool for chopping wood
4 a piece of glass coated with a substance that reflects images
5 an apparatus used for weighing things
6 an instrument which magnifies things that are too small to be seen by the naked eye
7 a tool for opening tins
8 a substance used for washing hair

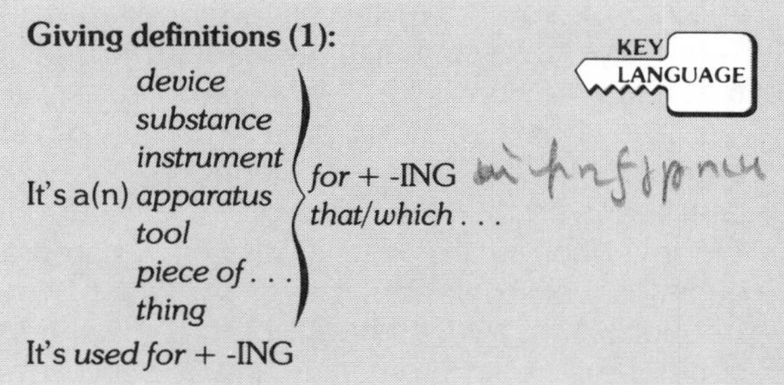

Giving definitions (1):

KEY LANGUAGE

It's a(n) *device* / *substance* / *instrument* / *apparatus* / *tool* / *piece of . . .* / *thing* — *for* + -ING / *that/which . . .*

It's *used for* + -ING

b) Give simple definitions for each of the following, using the sets of words below. Check your definitions in the dictionary.

KEY VOCABULARY

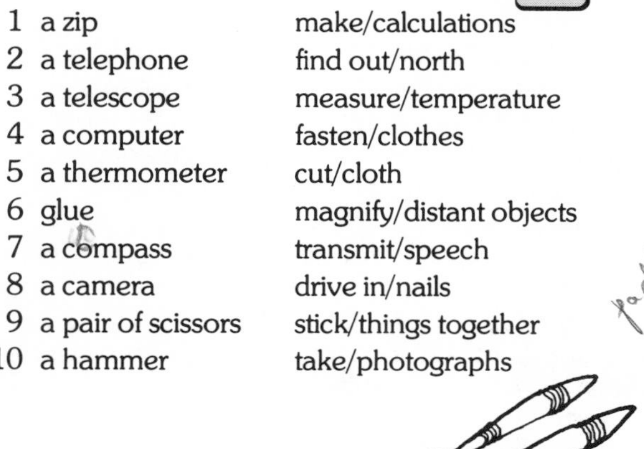

1 a zip	make/calculations
2 a telephone	find out/north
3 a telescope	measure/temperature
4 a computer	fasten/clothes
5 a thermometer	cut/cloth
6 glue	magnify/distant objects
7 a compass	transmit/speech
8 a camera	drive in/nails
9 a pair of scissors	stick/things together
10 a hammer	take/photographs

c) You may not know the names of these objects in English, but you can define them.
Choose one of the objects, and tell your partner what it's for. (Don't say what it's called, even if you know.)
On hearing your definition, your partner should be able to point to the correct object.

Example: *It's (a thing) for opening bottles (with).*

3 a) The following adjectives are used for giving precise descriptions of objects. Arrange the adjectives in three groups.

Examples:

Size, Weight and Texture	*Shape*	*Material*
enormous	circular	cardboard

cardboard	glass	metal	round	straight
circular	gold	narrow	short	thick
copper	hard	nylon	silver	thin
cotton	heart-shaped	oval	small	tiny
curved	heavy	paper	smooth	triangular
cylindrical	iron	plastic	soft	wide
enormous	large	pointed	square	wire
flat	light	rectangular	steel	wooden
flexible	long	rough	stiff	woollen

KEY VOCABULARY

b) You should have eighteen words under the heading *Size, Weight and Texture*. Find the nine pairs of opposites.

4 a) Listen to the descriptions of six objects. Guess what each object is, and complete the table below.

KEY LANGUAGE

ORDER OF ADJECTIVES PRECEDING NOUN				NOUN	PHRASE OR CLAUSE
Size/Weight/Texture	Shape	Colour	Material		Further Details
1					
2					
3					
4					
5					
6					

KEY LANGUAGE

b) Look at your notes under *Further Details.*

with a narrow neck = *and it has* a narrow neck
containing little sticks of wood = *which contains* little sticks of wood
made of cotton = *which is made* of cotton

Rewrite the following sentences using *with*, present participle (active) or past participle (passive).

1 A hologram is a three-dimensional image which is produced by a laser.
2 A pencil is a long thin object and it has a pointed end.
3 Water is a liquid which consists of hydrogen and oxygen.
4 I heard a loud noise which sounded like an explosion.
5 It's a wedding photograph, which is framed in silver.
6 I've lost a piece of paper and it has an important telephone number on it.
7 It's a beautiful leather handbag, which was made in Italy.
8 It's a black wallet, which contains about a hundred pounds.

c) Write a short description of a 'mystery' object, paying particular attention to adjective order. Then read out your description and see if the other students can guess what the object is. If they need help, explain what the object is for.

5 **a)** Look back at the diagram showing how a hologram is made.

How is the holographic image produced?
By (means of) a laser.

How is the laser beam split?

How is the reference beam reflected onto the holographic plate?

How is the laser light expanded?

b) Read the text, and then answer the questions below.

The *camera obscura* led directly to the invention of photography. A camera obscura can be made out of a cardboard box with a black inside. Make a hole in one end with a knitting needle. Make a big hole in the opposite end, and cover this hole with tracing paper. In bright sunshine you will see faint images on the tracing paper if you cover your head and the box with a cloth.

1 How can you make a camera obscura out of a cardboard box with a black inside?
By making ....
and by ....

2 How can you see faint images on the tracing paper in bright sunshine?
By ....

3 Underline the three phrases where *with* is used to express instrument.

Expressing means: KEY LANGUAGE

by (means of) + noun/-ING
. . . by means of a beam-splitter.
. . . by recording laser light.

Note: by means of is more formal than *by*, and is usually found in technical explanations.

Expressing instrument:

with + noun . . . with a knitting needle.

c) Look at the instructions below and explain how you:

call the operator
start the machine
open the packet
open the bottle of tablets
lock the door
sound the fire alarm
get coffee from the drinks machine
cook the pasta

1 FOR THE OPERATOR DIAL 100
2 PRESS RED BUTTON TO START MACHINE
3 TEAR ALONG DOTTED LINE
4 TO OPEN PRESS DOWN AND TURN
5 PUSH DOWN HANDLE TO LOCK
6 BREAK GLASS TO SOUND ALARM
7 TO OPERATE INSERT COINS THEN PRESS SELECTION BUTTON
8 BOIL GENTLY FOR SIX MINUTES

DISCUSSION

Do you think that scientific discoveries and technological developments have improved the quality of life? Think about TV, cars, the telephone, etc.

Enormous sums of money are spent on scientific and technological research (e.g. space research). Do you think the expense is justified?

Do you think scientific research is dangerous? For example, atomic research showed that nuclear power can offer a reliable source of useful energy. On the other hand, much nuclear waste is highly radioactive, and poses serious health hazards. Furthermore, the atomic bomb threatens the future of life on this planet.

B DESCRIBING A PROCESS

READING

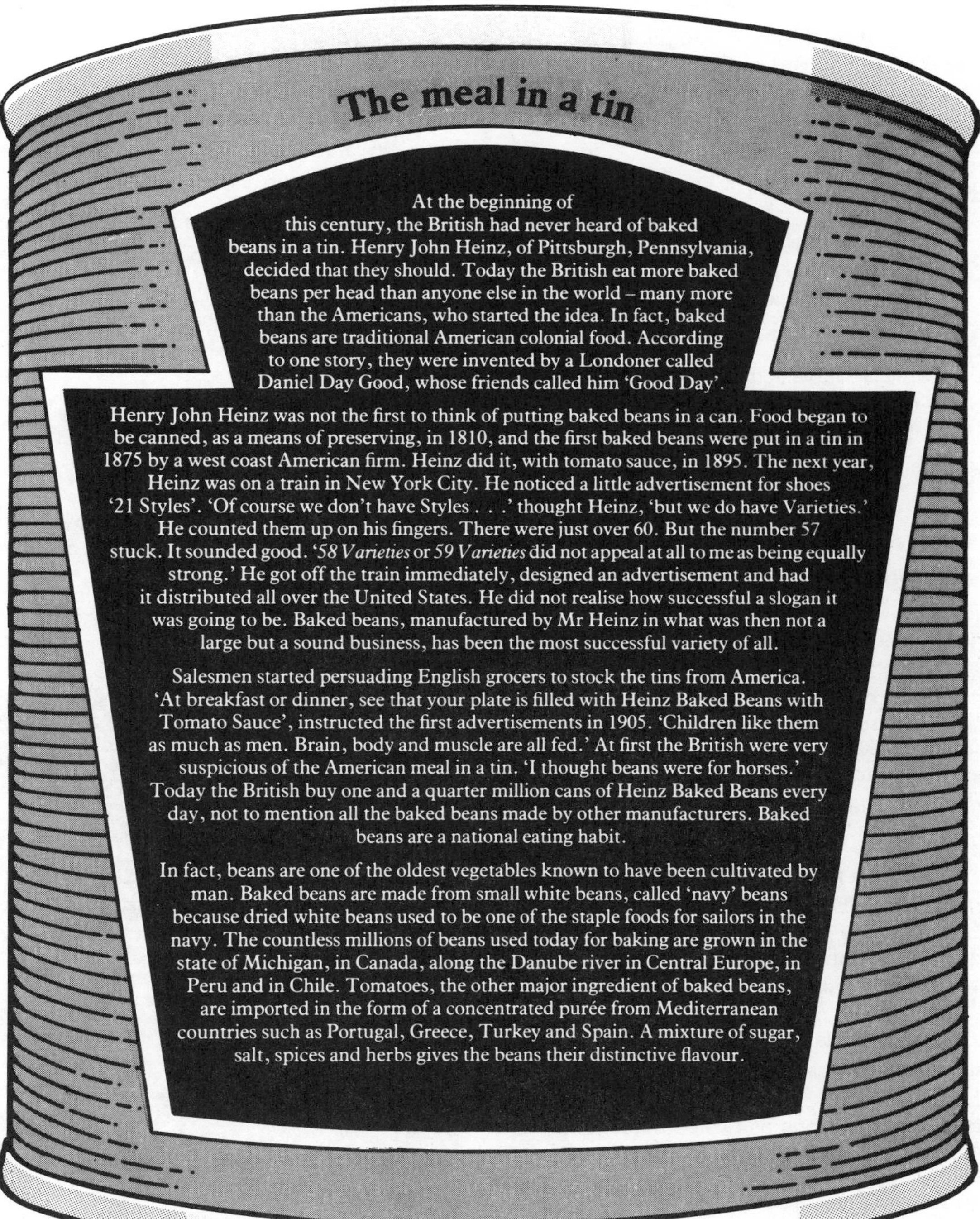

The meal in a tin

At the beginning of this century, the British had never heard of baked beans in a tin. Henry John Heinz, of Pittsburgh, Pennsylvania, decided that they should. Today the British eat more baked beans per head than anyone else in the world – many more than the Americans, who started the idea. In fact, baked beans are traditional American colonial food. According to one story, they were invented by a Londoner called Daniel Day Good, whose friends called him 'Good Day'.

Henry John Heinz was not the first to think of putting baked beans in a can. Food began to be canned, as a means of preserving, in 1810, and the first baked beans were put in a tin in 1875 by a west coast American firm. Heinz did it, with tomato sauce, in 1895. The next year, Heinz was on a train in New York City. He noticed a little advertisement for shoes '21 Styles'. 'Of course we don't have Styles . . .' thought Heinz, 'but we do have Varieties.' He counted them up on his fingers. There were just over 60. But the number 57 stuck. It sounded good. '*58 Varieties* or *59 Varieties* did not appeal at all to me as being equally strong.' He got off the train immediately, designed an advertisement and had it distributed all over the United States. He did not realise how successful a slogan it was going to be. Baked beans, manufactured by Mr Heinz in what was then not a large but a sound business, has been the most successful variety of all.

Salesmen started persuading English grocers to stock the tins from America. 'At breakfast or dinner, see that your plate is filled with Heinz Baked Beans with Tomato Sauce', instructed the first advertisements in 1905. 'Children like them as much as men. Brain, body and muscle are all fed.' At first the British were very suspicious of the American meal in a tin. 'I thought beans were for horses.' Today the British buy one and a quarter million cans of Heinz Baked Beans every day, not to mention all the baked beans made by other manufacturers. Baked beans are a national eating habit.

In fact, beans are one of the oldest vegetables known to have been cultivated by man. Baked beans are made from small white beans, called 'navy' beans because dried white beans used to be one of the staple foods for sailors in the navy. The countless millions of beans used today for baking are grown in the state of Michigan, in Canada, along the Danube river in Central Europe, in Peru and in Chile. Tomatoes, the other major ingredient of baked beans, are imported in the form of a concentrated purée from Mediterranean countries such as Portugal, Greece, Turkey and Spain. A mixture of sugar, salt, spices and herbs gives the beans their distinctive flavour.

Choose the best alternative to the following words in the text.

KEY VOCABULARY

1 HEAD
A leader B family C person D body

2 MEANS
A reason B method C intention
D condition

3 DISTRIBUTED
A arranged B divided up C sent out
D shared out

4 SLOGAN
A saying B password D comment
D catch-phrase

5 INSTRUCTED
A taught B told C explained D said

6 CULTIVATED
A grown B harvested C developed
D processed

Now choose the best answer.

7 Baked beans were invented
A by sailors.
B over a hundred years ago.
C by a Londoner.
D by an American company.

8 In 1896, Henry John Heinz
A produced sixty varieties of goods.
B was manufacturing radios.
C invented baked beans in tomato sauce.
D was running a successful business.

9 At the beginning of this century, the British
A did not like baked beans very much.
B fed baked beans to animals.
C were not used to baked beans.
D were not used to tinned food.

10 Today, the British
A buy 1¼ million cans of baked beans every day.
B eat baked beans regularly.
C eat more baked beans than anything else.
D do not ask for beans produced by other manufacturers.

LANGUAGE PRACTICE

Describe the process for manufacturing baked beans by putting the sentences below in the correct order, and putting the verbs into the present simple passive (*is/are* + past participle).

- In the more recent process, they (pass) in a current of hot water through a pipe about 1200 metres long.
- After that, the baked beans (carry) to a filling head and the correct quantity of beans (measure) into each can.
- Next the beans (blanch) in one of two ways.
- First of all, the beans (grade), (sort), and (clean).
- In the older process, the beans (soak) in cold water, sometimes for as long as twelve hours, and then (simmer) in hot water until soft but firm.
- The tomato sauce now (add), and finally the cans (seal) and (label).
- Then the blanched beans (bake).

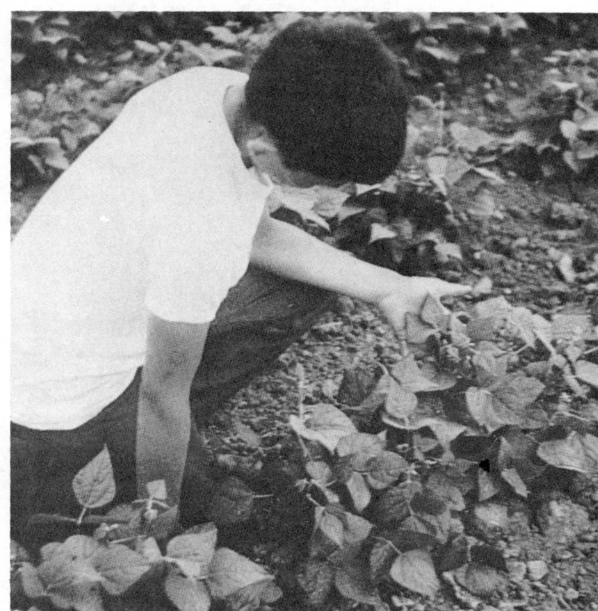

Young Bean Plants

GUIDED WRITING ACTIVITY

a) Listen to this description of the process for manufacturing Nescafé, and mark the following stages of the process at the correct points on the diagram below.

Packaging	Atomisation and drying
Grinding	Blending
Percolation	Roasting

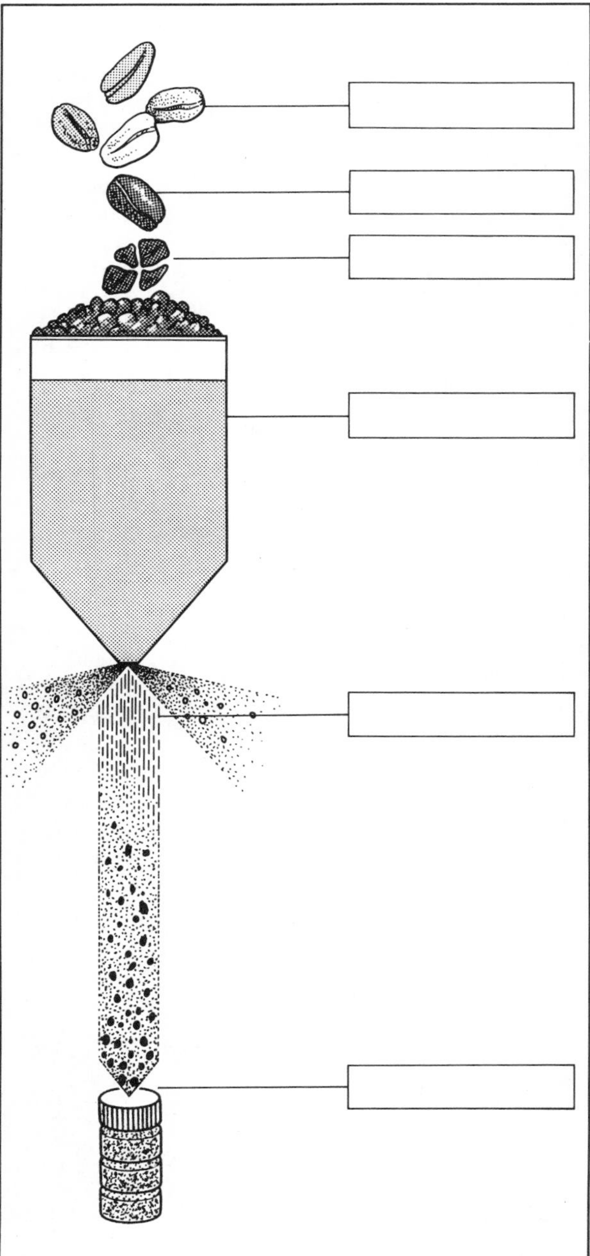

b) Listen to the description again, and make notes for each stage on the diagram.

c) Using the information you have gathered, write a short description of the process for manufacturing Nescafé. Connect your sentences with sequencers and use the present simple passive as in **Language practice** on page 142

d) Write a step-by-step description of how you make *fresh* coffee at home.

C GIVING DEFINITIONS

READING

Vitamins are vital

It was not until the beginning of the twentieth century that it was recognised that certain substances were essential in the diet to prevent, or cure, some diseases. These substances are now known as *vitamins*, and they are vital for growth, good health, and maintenance of the normal functions of the body. The Hungarian biochemist, Szent-Gyorgyi, who first isolated vitamin C (ascorbic acid), defined the vitamin as 'a substance which makes you ill if you don't eat it!'

A well-balanced diet should provide all the vitamins we normally require. Those of us who are fortunate enough to be able to buy sufficient food should not suffer from vitamin deficiency. However, for various reasons, some people do not maintain a balanced diet. People often lose their appetite because of illness. People living alone may not bother to eat proper meals, and people on a diet may not eat sufficient quantitites of necessary foods. Elderly people are at risk because they may be unable to shop and cook. Moreover, modern methods of preserving, freezing, and long-term storage of food, together with overcooking, can destroy many of the vitamins. Food served in restaurants and canteens has often lost much of its vitamin content because it has been kept hot, or even prepared the day before, so you may have problems if you eat out regularly.

Are *you* getting enough vitamins . . . ?

Vitamin	Common Source	Important functions	Problems caused by lack of vitamin
A	Dairy produce, vegetables, tomatoes, margarine, liver, fruit	Essential for normal growth and good eyesight. Helps prevent infection.	Night blindness, skin trouble, tendency towards colds, and throat and chest infections, poor growth.
B	Meat, milk, fish, whole cereals	Keeps nerves and muscles functioning efficiently. Helps new blood cell formation, and vital for clear, healthy skin.	Nervous disorders, poor appetite, sore tongue and mouth, cracked lips, stiffness in limbs, skin troubles, oversensitivity to sunlight.
C	Fresh fruit, green vegetables, potatoes, tomatoes	Necessary for healthy blood formation.	Sore bleeding gums, loosening of teeth, pains in joints, slow wound healing.
D	Egg-yolk, fish, fish-liver oils, sunshine	Helps the body convert and use calcium, which is essential for strong teeth and bones.	Soft bones, weak spine, bow legs.
E	Eggs, peanuts, wheatgerm, apples, lettuce	Believed to be necessary for healthy nerves and muscles, and a vital factor in blood cell formation.	Red blood cell deficiency.

LANGUAGE PRACTICE

1 **a)** Fill in the missing verb or noun. Check your complete list against the text.

VERB	NOUN
bleed	
	definition
form	
grow	
infect	
maintain	
	preservation
	prevention
	provision
tend	

b) Write down the nouns which correspond to the following adjectives. Check your list of nouns against the text.

blind, stiff, infectious, ill, healthy, nervous, painful

2 Form the opposite/negative of the words below by adding the prefix *dis-* or *un-*.

Examples: order – *disorder*
able – *unable*

advantage	dress	known
agree	easy	like
appear	fair	likely
approval	fortunate	necessary
certain	grace	pleased
comfort	healthy	satisfaction
comfortable	honest	willing

Which word can have both prefixes? Why?

3 **a)** The prefix *over-* often means *too much*. Find two examples in the text.

b) Fill in the missing words with suitable compounds formed with OVER + the correct form of the words below.

charge, do, eat, weigh, crowd, dose, sleep, work

KEY VOCABULARY

1 He never stops eating, so it's not surprising he's ________.
2 The restaurant was ________ and very noisy.
3 He's exhausted because he's been ________.
4 This bill is enormous – I think we've been ________.
5 She didn't have time for breakfast because she ________.
6 If you ________, you'll put on weight.
7 This steak has been cooked too long – it's ________.
8 An ________ of vitamin tablets can be very dangerous.

4 Label the parts of the body indicated with the words below.

KEY VOCABULARY

ankle	jaw
cheek	knee
chest	lips
chin	nail
elbow	neck
eyebrow	shoulder
eyelid	stomach
finger	thumb
fist	toe
heel	wrist

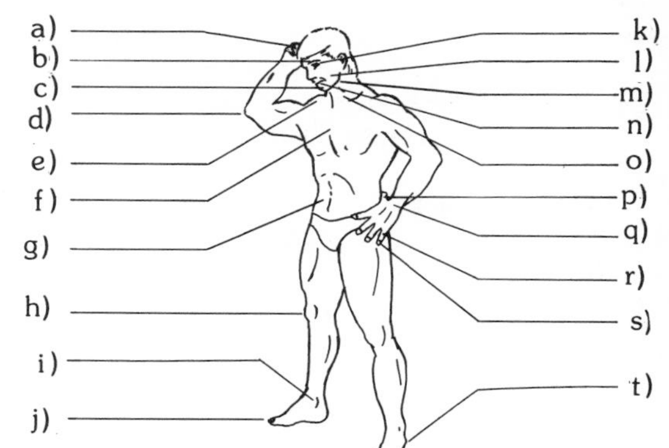

5 **a)** According to the text, certain people may be short of vitamins. What kinds of people are at risk?

Example: *People who are ill.*

b) Give examples of the foods which contain each vitamin.

Examples: *Foods that/which contain vitamin A include . . .*

Vitamin A is contained in various foods, such as . . .

c) Why are the following foods good for you?

meat	oranges
potatoes	eggs
cheese	wholemeal bread
carrots	cabbage

Example: meat

Because it contains vitamin B, which is good / necessary / essential / vital for . . .

KEY LANGUAGE

Giving definitions (2):

Defining relative clause introduced by *who* or *that/which*	People *who are ill* may be short of vitamins. Foods *that/which contain vitamin* A include . . .
Participle (-ING) clause	Foods *containing vitamin* A include . . .

Giving additional information:

Non-defining relative clause introduced by *who* or *which*	Meat contains vitamin B, *which is good for* . . .

Note: A non-defining relative clause is separated from the preceding noun by a comma, and cannot be introduced by *that.*

Compare: a) Meat contains vitamin B, *which is good for the nerves.*

b) Meat contains a vitamin *that /which is good for the nerves.*

In a), the relative clause *gives additional information* about vitamin B.

In b), the relative clause is necessary to *define* the vitamin.

INTERPRETATION ACTIVITY

a) What do you normally eat – for breakfast?
for lunch?
for supper/dinner?

Write down what your meals usually consist of, and compare your list with the vitamin table. Is your diet well-balanced?

b) Plan and write a well-balanced day's menu, using the vitamin table as a guide.

D TAKING PART IN A FORMAL DISCUSSION

LISTENING ACTIVITY

a) Listen to the radio programme and take notes on the arguments given FOR and AGAINST nuclear power.

b) In formal situations, people use certain phrases to:

introduce their questions

express their opinions

emphasise the points they are making

Listen to the radio programme again, and write down further examples under each heading in the box.

KEY LANGUAGE

Introducing questions:
I should like to ask . . .

Expressing opinions (3):
in our view . . .

Emphasising points:
I can assure you that . . .

READING ALOUD

a) Look at the following extract from the radio programme. Can you tell which words are stressed, and on which words the intonation rises or falls? Mark the stress and intonation on your tapescript. Then listen to the extract again, and check whether you were right.

SIR ROLAND: Well, there are several good reasons. Firstly, while we are indeed fortunate to have natural energy resources in the form of coal, gas and oil, these resources are limited. There's no doubt that supplies will run out. We must be sure that we can maintain energy supplies to meet the growing demands of the modern world. Secondly, if we can produce enough nuclear power to generate all the energy we need, we won't have to rely on importing fuel. We can be completely independent, which is obviously an advantage today given the rising prices on the oil market. And thirdly, nuclear power production is extremely efficient and clean. It causes far less pollution than energy production from burning coal, for example.

b) Now read the text aloud.

ROLE PLAY

Situation

Tremolo is a volcanic island in the North Atlantic Ocean. It's about half the size of Switzerland and has a population of two million. The climate is warm and sunny most of the year, which makes Tremolo a popular tourist resort. Indeed, tourism is the island's only industry, and all food and fuel supplies have to be imported. Consequently the cost of living is high, and the numbers of visitors to the island are rapidly falling. Furthermore, 25% of the work-force is unemployed.

The government is planning to develop a nuclear energy programme to provide the island with all the electricity it needs. The people of Tremolo have demanded a public enquiry to discuss the nuclear proposals.

The following groups are present at the public meeting:

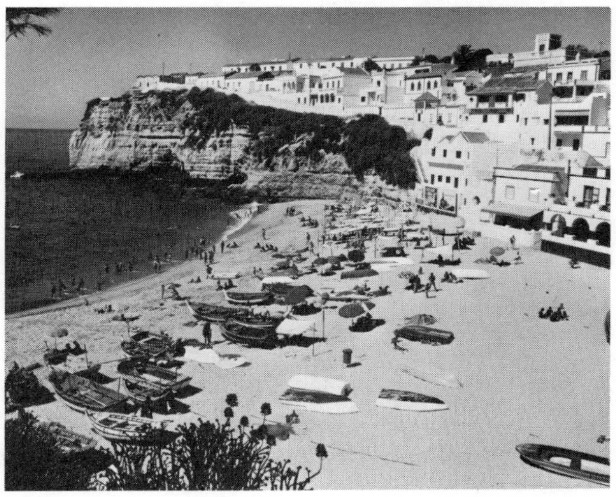

Government Ministers

You are convinced that nuclear power is the answer to Tremolo's economic problems. The programme will create several thousand jobs, and when Tremolo can produce sufficient power for all its needs, fuel prices will go down. This will lead to a fall in the cost of living, which in turn will encourage more tourists to visit the island.

'NO to Nuclear Energy' – NONE

You are totally opposed to nuclear power production. You believe that the risks to the lives of the islanders far outweigh the advantages of being economically independent in energy production. You also think that the cost of the programme will be extremely high, and that the government will have to raise taxes to pay for it.

Tremolo Tourist Authority – TTA

You are worried that tourists who might come to Tremolo will be put off by the nuclear power stations, and you are also concerned that the natural beauty of the island will be destroyed. On the other hand, you realise that the tourist industry can only benefit if prices fall.

Campaign for Alternative Sources of Energy – CASE

You are not in favour of nuclear power, and are convinced that Tremolo could develop other natural energy resources at far less cost; for example, tidal, solar and wind power. You believe that these systems would provide twice as many jobs as the nuclear programme would.

Trades Union members

You don't like the idea of nuclear power, and you are worried about the risks. But you dislike unemployment even more, and workers in the power stations will be well-paid. You would rather not have to worry about where your next meal is coming from.

Businessmen

You are excited by the nuclear energy programme because you hope to make money out of it. You also think that the production of cheaper fuel will encourage the development of other industries on the island. You are concerned about safety, but you believe that nuclear technology has developed considerably in the last few years, and that the risks are very small.

Proposed Nuclear Energy Development

a) Choose one of the groups, and discuss your attitudes to the government proposals with other members of the group. Decide what you are going to say at the public meeting.

b) Elect a chairman for the meeting.

c) The chairman opens the meeting and asks the government ministers to put their case. Then the other groups present at the meeting should ask questions and argue their cases.

d) The chairman asks the people attending the meeting to vote for or against the nuclear energy programme.

DISCUSSION

What is the main source of energy in your country?
Are there nuclear power stations in your country?
If so, what is the general public reaction to them?
What do you think is the answer to the world energy crisis?

EXAM PRACTICE

PAPER 1: READING COMPREHENSION

Section B *(Suggestions for the exam – see Unit 3)*

In this section you will find after the text a number of questions or unfinished statements about the text, each with four suggested answers or ways of finishing. You must choose the one which you think fits best. For each question, *indicate on your answer sheet* the letter A, B, C or D against the number of the question.

If you want to stay young, sit down and have a good think. This is the research finding of a team of Japanese doctors, who say that most of our brains are not getting enough exercise – and as a result, we are ageing unnecessarily soon.

Professor Taiju Matsuzawa wanted to find out why otherwise healthy farmers in northern Japan appeared to be losing their ability to think and reason at a relatively early age, and how the process of ageing could be slowed down.

With a team of colleagues at Tokyo National University, he set about measuring brain volumes of a thousand people of different ages and varying occupations.

Computer technology enabled the researchers to obtain precise measurements of the volume of the front and side sections of the brain, which relate to intellect and emotion, and determine the human character. (The rear section of the brain, which controls functions like eating and breathing, does not contract with age, and one can continue living without intellectual or emotional faculties.)

Contraction of front and side parts – as cells die off – was observed in some subjects in their thirties, but it was still not evident in some sixty and seventy-year-olds.

Matsuzawa concluded from his tests that there is a simple remedy to the contraction normally associated with age – using the head.

The findings show in general terms that contraction of the brain begins sooner in people in the country than in the towns. Those least at risk, says Matsuzawa, are lawyers, followed by university professors and doctors. White collar workers doing routine work in government offices are, however, as likely to have shrinking brains as the farm worker, bus driver and shop assistant.

Matsuzawa's findings show that thinking can prevent the brain from shrinking. Blood must circulate properly in the head to supply the fresh oxygen the brain cells need. 'The best way to maintain good blood circulation is through using the brain,' he says. 'Think hard and engage in conversation. Don't rely on pocket calculators.'

Matsuzawa's findings show that some professional groups become dullwitted sooner than others, but that it is within anybody's reach to 'save' his brain. Walking on one's hands is not recommended.

1 The team of doctors wanted to find out
- A at what point people grow old.
- B how to make people live longer.
- C the size of certain people's brains.
- D which people are most intelligent.

2 On what are their research findings based?
- A A survey of farmers in northern Japan.
- B Tests performed on a thousand old people.
- C Comparing the brain volumes of different people.
- D Using computer technology.

3 The doctors' tests show that
- A our brains shrink as we grow older.
- B one section of the brain does not shrink.
- C sixty-year-olds have better brains than thirty-year-olds.
- D some people's brains have contracted more than other people's.

4 According to the article, which people have a surprising tendency to age early?
- A People who live in the country.
- B Office clerks.
- C Shop assistants.
- D People who use pocket calculators.

5 Matsuzawa concluded that
- A most of us should take more exercise.
- B it's better to live in the town.
- C the brain shrinks if it is not used.
- D walking on one's hands is bad for the brain.

PAPER 3: USE OF ENGLISH

Section A, Question 2 *(Suggestions for the exam – see Unit 3)*

Finish each of the following sentences in such a way that it means exactly the same as the sentence printed before it.

Example: An American invented the laser.

Answer: The laser was invented by an American.

a) Brazil produces large quantities of coffee.
Large quantities . . . .

b) Air pressure is measured by a barometer.
A barometer is for . . . .

c) Dial 999 to call the police.
You call . . . .

d) Cotton is produced in various countries, including Egypt and India.
Countries which . . . .

e) He didn't let anyone touch the microscope.
No-one . . . .

f) People are doing research into ways of curing cancer.
Research is . . . .

g) The doctor asked me politely to wait outside.
'Would . . . .

h) 'It's because my car has broken down,' she said.
She explained . . . .

i) It's very kind of you to help me.
Thank you . . . .

j) The equipment has probably been damaged.
The equipment is likely . . . .

Section A, Question 3 *(Suggestions for the exam – see Unit 3)*

Complete the following sentences with an appropriate word formed from the word in capitals.

Example: I gave the police a description of the vehicle. DESCRIBE

a) There is scientific . . . . that smoking is harmful. PROVE

b) The meeting began in . . . . , but finally everyone accepted the proposal. AGREE

c) It's not an antique table, but it's a good . . . . PRODUCE

d) The laser has a wide . . . . of uses. VARY

e) Coffee should be kept in an . . . . container. AIR

PAPER 4: LISTENING COMPREHENSION

(Suggestions for the exam – see Unit 1)

Put a tick, as shown in no. 1, against each object needed for the trick.

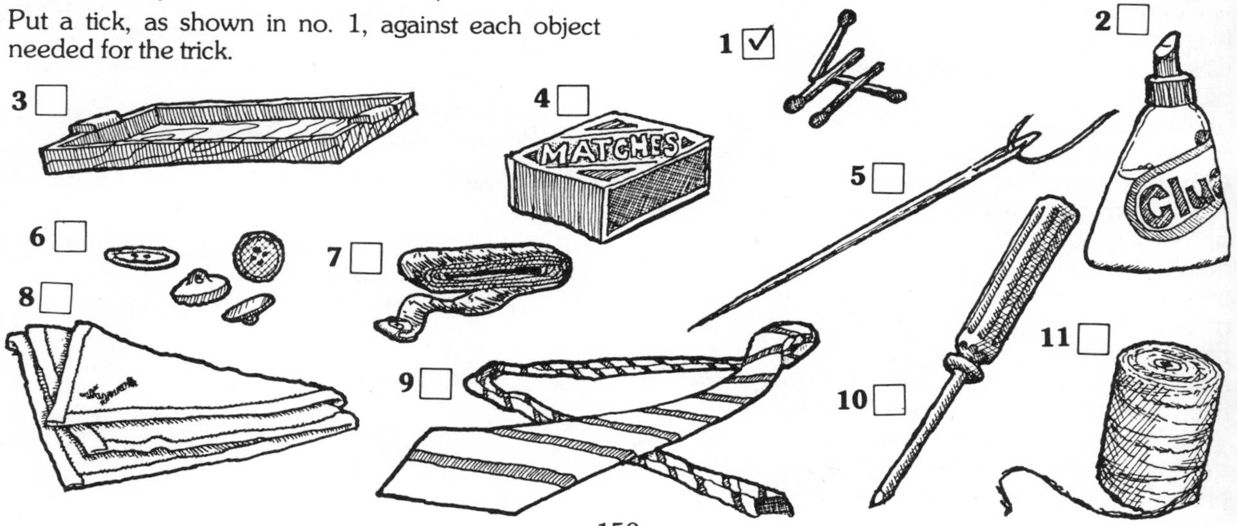

1 ☑ 2 ☐ 3 ☐ 4 ☐ 5 ☐ 6 ☐ 7 ☐ 8 ☐ 9 ☐ 10 ☐ 11 ☐

MATCHES

Glue

PAPER 5: INTERVIEW

Part (i) *(Suggestions for the exam – see Unit 4)*

1 Where do you think this is?

2 What do you think happens here?

3 What do you think it's like to live here?

4 If you lived here, what would you miss most?

5 Would you like to travel in space?

Related topics
Exploration – famous journeys
The possibility of living on another planet
Science fiction – books and films

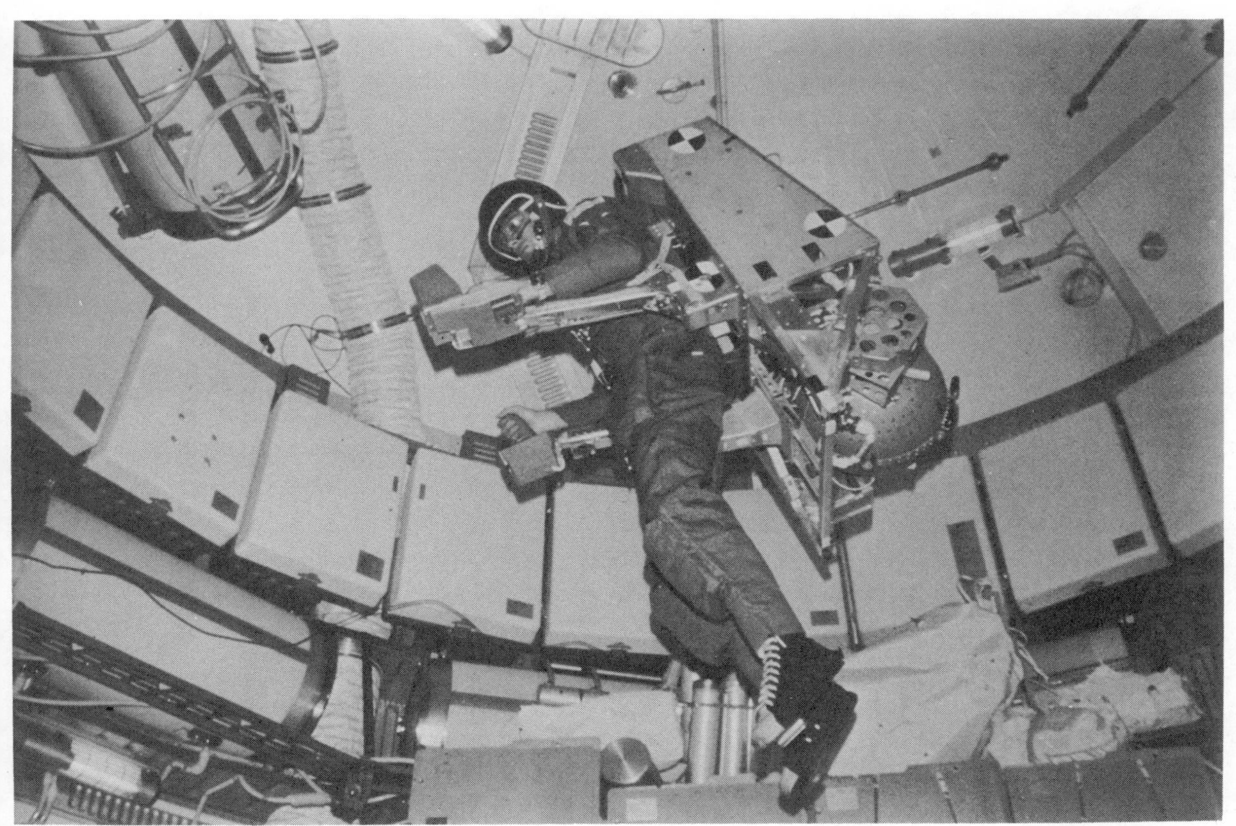

Part (ii) *(Suggestions for the exam – see Unit 4)*

Look through the following text for a few moments.

Stir two tablespoonfuls of flour into the butter, and then stir in a little warm milk until you have a thick paste. Now, over a low heat, you pour in the rest of the milk very gradually. Keep stirring all the time, or the mixture will go lumpy. Then you add salt and pepper, and leave the sauce to simmer for at least ten minutes.

What do you think the situation is?
Who do you think is speaking? To whom?

Now read the text aloud.

Part (iii) *(Suggestions for the exam – see Unit 1)*

1 Work out what household object the examiner is thinking of by asking questions with Yes/No answers.

2 Give a definition for each of the following:

aspirin
chocolate
a clock
a vacuum cleaner
an umbrella

UNIT 10

MIND OVER MATTER

A EXPRESSING SURPRISE AND FEAR

TALKING POINT

These pictures are all connected with English superstitions. Do you know what these superstitions are? What do you think are the origins of these superstitions? Can you think of any others? What popular superstitions are there in your country? Do you have any personal superstitions, such as wearing certain clothes for special occasions, or writing with a special pen for exams?

READING

THE ROOTS OF COINCIDENCE

SOME YEARS ago George D. Bryson, an American businessman, was making a trip from St Louis to New York. He decided to break his journey in Louisville, Kentucky, a town he had never visited before. At the station he inquired for somewhere to stay, and was directed to the Brown Hotel. He went there, found they had a room – number 307 – and registered. Then, just for a joke and because he had nothing better to do, he idly wandered over to reception and asked if there was any mail for him. To his astonishment, the receptionist calmly handed him a letter addressed to Mr George D. Bryson, Room 307. On investigation it turned out that the previous occupant of the room had been another George D. Bryson, who worked with a firm in Montreal.

We have all had similar strange experiences that we put down to coincidence, chance or luck. Because these experiences are so common, scientists and philosophers have begun to wonder

12+1

whether there is more to them than mere chance or coincidence. With this focusing of scientific and philosophical interest, more and more evidence has come to light that both the world we live in and the lives we lead are more mysterious than we might suppose.

Carl Gustav Jung

To shrug off events like these as 'just chance' may be to shut off a significant area of knowledge. The eminent psychologist C. G. Jung certainly thought they were worth serious investigation. Over the years he noticed that both himself and his patients had had many experiences of what he called 'meaningful coincidences'. Many of these involved dreams or premonitions, and he devoted much time towards the end of his life in attempting to explain these experiences. Jung used the term *synchronicity* to describe the phenomenon of incidents that seemed to be connected by time and meaning, but not by cause and effect. He felt that these coincidences, in some way, had their roots in very strong unconscious feelings that came to the surface at certain times of stress or change. He gives several examples of this happening in his own life.

One day, as he was returning home by train, he was overpowered by the image of someone drowning. He was so upset that he was unable to read, and could only wonder whether there had been some sort of accident. When he got home he was met by his grandchildren, and discovered that the youngest had fallen in the lake and had almost been drowned. The little boy had been fished out just in time by his older brother. This nearly fatal accident had happened at exactly the time that the idea of someone drowning had occurred to Jung.

Many of us have had strange dreams and premonitions about our family or friends that have turned out to be true. As a psychoanalyst Jung also had a very close relationship with his patients. One night when Jung was sleeping alone in a hotel after a lecture, he awoke with a start. He was convinced that someone had opened the door and entered the room, but when he switched on the light there was no one to be seen. He then tried to remember what had happened. He had been wakened by a feeling of dull pain as if something had struck his forehead and the back of his skull. The following day he received a telegram informing him that a former patient, with whom he had lost contact after helping through a severe crisis, had shot himself. The bullet had lodged in the back of the skull.

Jung became convinced that synchronistic events of this kind had a deep significance, and he applied his tremendous knowledge, experience and diligence to the task of discovering their meaning. When he died, he was working on the idea that physics and psychology would ultimately come together under a common concept that would be a unifying key to the forces at work in the physical and psychical worlds.

a) 1 Why did Bryson ask for his mail if he was sure there wouldn't be any for him?
2 Why was Bryson astonished when he was given a letter addressed to him?
3 Why do such experiences attract the interest of scientists?
4 How did Jung define this kind of phenomenon?
5 According to Jung, under what circumstances do such coincidences occur?
6 While he was on the train, what made Jung think there had been an accident?
7 Did his grandson actually die?
8 How did Jung foresee the death of his former patient?
9 How did the patient actually die?
10 Why did these coincidences interest Jung so much?

b) Find words in the text which mean:

KEY VOCABULARY

asked	mental tension
concentration	pulled out
appeared	suddenly
dismiss	head
forewarnings	meaning
gave	ability to work hard
origins	in the end

LANGUAGE PRACTICE

1 a) Complete each of the following sentences with a suitable adjective from the list below.

KEY VOCABULARY

shocked	sad	anxious
amazed	surprised	worried
fascinated	astonished	alarmed
curious	puzzled	

1 Bryson was not expecting any mail and he was ________ to be given a letter.

2 He looked at the envelope and he was ________ to see his name.

3 He made enquiries and he was ________ to learn the name of the previous occupant of the room.

4 Jung was returning home one day and he was ________ by the strange image of someone drowning.

5 He wondered whether there had been an accident and was too ________ to read.

6 He met his grandchildren at the station and was ________ to hear of the accident.

7 Then he remembered the image on the train and was ________ by the coincidence.

8 Jung thought that someone had come into his hotel room, and he was ________ when he could see no one.

9 He felt a dull pain in his head and was ________ that he'd been injured.

10 He received a telegram the next day and was ________ to learn of a former patient's suicide.

11 He believed such events were not just coincidences, and he was ________ to find out more about them.

b) Write down the nouns which are formed from the adjectives above.

c) Rewrite the sentences in **a)** using a participle (-ING) clause.

KEY LANGUAGE

Example: Bryson was not expecting any mail and he was surprised to be given a letter.
Not expecting any mail, Bryson was surprised to be given a letter.

d) In each of the sentences above, the present participle clause can be replaced by either *when* + clause, or *because* + clause. Read them again and decide which takes *when* and which takes *because*.

ROLE PLAY

2 a) Role play: In pairs, act out the conversation which takes place when Bryson and Jung each tell a friend about their experiences.

b) Have you ever experienced any strange coincidences? Tell your partner about them.

c) Can you suggest an explanation for 'synchronistic' events of this kind?

KEY LANGUAGE

Expressing surprise:

That's (quite) / *How* — *extraordinary! / surprising! / amazing! / astonishing! / incredible! / unbelievable!*

What an incredible story!

I'm / *I was* *(really)* *amazed / astonished / surprised*

I can't believe it!
I don't believe you!

Expressing fear and anxiety (2):

I'm afraid / frightened / scared of + noun/-ING

I'm (so) uneasy / nervous / worried / anxious / unhappy about + noun/-ING

It really worries/scares/frightens me.
It makes me feel uneasy/nervous/anxious etc.
I've got a nasty feeling that . . . . .

LISTENING ACTIVITY

3 a) Listen to this true story about three people who had the same dream.

b) Rewrite the following extracts from the story using the verbs in capitals.

Example:	Someone knocked at the door of the cabin. *He heard someone knock at the door of the cabin.*	HEAR
1	The door swung open.	WATCH
2	His wife was standing there.	SEE
3	She hesitated for a moment.	NOTICE
4	She crossed the cabin and came towards him.	WATCH
5	She kissed him.	FEEL
6	A strange woman entered the cabin.	SEE
7	Two men were talking in the distance.	HEAR
8	A cold wind was blowing.	FEEL
9	It pushed its way through the enormous waves.	WATCH
10	Something made a noise on the other side of the room.	HEAR
11	There was another man lying there.	NOTICE
12	He turned in his sleep.	WATCH

KEY LANGUAGE

Expressing sensory perception:

see / watch / notice / hear / feel + noun/pronoun +
- -ING (for incomplete actions) — He watched the boys playing football all afternoon.
- infinitive (for complete actions) — He saw her leave the building, cross the road and enter a shop.

c) Make adverbs out of the following adjectives from the text:

KEY VOCABULARY

heavy	stormy
rude	anxious
angry	wild

4 a) How sensitive are you to psychic experiences? Answer the questionnaire below and find out. Score one point for every 'YES' answer. Then check your score below.

b) If you have answered YES to any of the questions above, or know examples of psychic experiences, write a short account of one of them.

If not, make up your own story.

How Psychic are you?

1 Have you ever seen a ghost?
2 Have you ever been in a room where objects fall to the ground or get lost for no apparent reason?
3 Have you ever had a dream which has come true?
4 Have you ever had the same dream more than once?
5 Have you ever made a prediction which has come true?
6 Have you ever foreseen an event before it happened?
7 Do you ever finish people's sentences because you've guessed what they're going to say?
8 Do you ever find yourself thinking about someone just before he or she telephones?
9 Have you ever had a strong intuition about a person or an event which has turned out to be right?
10 Have you ever found yourself able to reveal certain details about a person's life without actually knowing anything about him or her?
11 Have you ever seen something move for no apparent reason?
12 Have you ever tried to make something move or happen just by thinking hard about it?
13 Have you ever been in a strange place which you feel you've visited before?
14 Have you ever felt close to a particular period in the past?
15 Have you ever seen or had contact with a dead member of your family?
16 Have you ever heard yourself speaking in a voice which is not your own?
17 Have you ever tried to cure yourself of an illness, or control pain without medicine or surgery?
18 Have you ever succeeded in doing so?
19 Have you ever been hypnotised?
20 Have you ever had an experience where you seemed to be outside your own body and looking down on it?

How to score

If you got:

0–6	Your feet are firmly on the ground and you don't really believe in the supernatural.
7–11	Your score indicates that you might have some psychic powers but you probably need help from a medium if you want to develop them.
12–16	Very impressive – you should give serious thought to taking your psychic gifts much further to help others as much as yourself.
17 and over	Excellent – you probably knew the results of the questionnaire even before you'd finished it!

DISCUSSION

Which religions or cults involve psychic experiences as part of their faith?

Do you think the people of the twentieth century believe in the supernatural more or less than they used to?

B EXPLAINING CAUSES AND TALKING ABOUT CONSEQUENCES

READING

DAILY GLOBE Dateline: Monday, 20 June 2020

NEW YORK CELEBRATES SOLAR POWER

THE WHOLE of New York was celebrating last night after the official opening of the world's largest power station – which measures 60 miles long by 30 miles wide! Fortunately the Solar Power Satellite has been built 22,400 miles above the city. Here it collects sunlight which is turned into microwaves and sent back to receivers on Earth. These receivers are to be found in the Bronx and only take up the same space as a couple of football fields. The microwaves are used to turn generators which supply all the electricity needs of the city. The SPS can transmit both day and night and even during cloudy weather.

For years the world's increasing demands for energy have caused a shortage of fuel for generating electricity. This has had a depressing effect on industry and has made life difficult for everyone. With the New York SPS, power cuts are now a thing of the past. But best of all, it's extremely cheap to run and New Yorkers are looking forward to lower fuel bills.

Agricultural success in the Sahara

EXPERTS now estimate that over 70% of the Sahara region of Africa is being used to grow crops and is producing enough food to meet the requirements of the world's growing population for at least twenty years. The success of this programme, which was launched in 1995, is due to the discovery of plants which can grow in salt water. A network of pipes has been laid to bring sea water right to the heart of the former desert. Each of these plants only needs 200 millimetres of water a year, yet has more protein per kilogram than either meat or fish. They can be grown on a vast scale and have greatly helped scientists and governments in their struggle against starvation.

New measures for Tokyo motorists

AS FROM midnight, it will be illegal to enter the city of Tokyo by car unless a parking space is free. The City Transport Computer System has in fact been controlling the movement of traffic for years in an attempt to relieve some of the serious problems caused by overcrowding in the city. But now that computers are installed in all cars, the city authorities can do more than simply advise drivers on the best route to take. They can now instruct your car's computer to stop you driving into the city limits if there isn't any room to park. If you decide to ignore the instruction, the computer simply cuts out the electric motor of your car. When a space becomes free, the system directs you straight to it with the minimum of delay. It is hoped that this measure will greatly reduce traffic jams and do away with all parking problems.

10 million homes sold

THE 'Home and Dry' Corporation announced yesterday that it has now sold ten million of its famous 'Living Units' to satisfied customers all over the world. For those of you who are still living in an old-fashioned house with two floors and six or seven rooms, the LU is designed for the two-person family of the twenty-first century, with just one room and a garage below to park your helicopter. Heating and lighting comes from solar and wind power. In the one room, the sleeping area, kitchen, and bathroom are clearly marked off by shelves or curtains, a design which uses the space as efficiently as possible. Asked about their success, a spokesman for 'Home and Dry' said, 'They have answered the need for cheap housing on a large scale. Remember that the world population has doubled since 1990. LUs can be produced very quickly here in our factory in St Louis, USA, and then transported to wherever they're needed. They are effective in even the most uncomfortable climates such as in the Sahara or the Antarctic.'

a) Choose the best alternative to the following words or phrases from the news items.

1 SHORTAGE
A lack B loss C failure D decrease

2 CUTS
A increases B reductions C shortages D breakdowns

3 REQUIREMENTS
A wishes B inquiries C needs D requests

4 ESTIMATE
A notice B calculate C guess D appreciate

5 STRUGGLE
A fight B goal C work D trouble

6 RELIEVE
A support B recover C ease D improve

7 MINIMUM OF
A last B latest C least D lesser

8 "LIVING UNIT"
A shelter B home C flat D building

What do the news items tell us about life in 2020? Choose the best answer.

9 By 2020, solar power will
- A be difficult to use in large cities.
- B be inexpensive and efficient.
- C only operate when it's sunny.
- D be generated by microwaves.

10 In the future, the Sahara will be
- A used as farmland.
- B flooded with salt water.
- C overgrown by 70%.
- D growing ordinary crops.

11 In about thirty years' time, the Tokyo City Transport Computer System will
- A simply give reports on road conditions.
- B advise you not to enter the city if there's no parking space free.
- C be in direct contact with your car's computer.
- D direct you to free parking.

12 'Living Units'
- A will have replaced old-fashioned houses.
- B will be built all over the world.
- C will be distributed all over the world.
- D will only be used in places like the Sahara and Antarctica.

LANGUAGE PRACTICE

1 **a)** Think about your everyday life in the future. What will it be like?

Making predictions about the future (2): KEY LANGUAGE

By (the year) 2010 / *In X years' time* / *In a few years* / *In the future* — *I'll be going to work by helicopter.* / *I'll have retired.*

By the time I'm 60, I'll have been working for about 40 years.

b) What other predictions can you make about the future? Prepare a short talk on one of the following subjects:

fashion	housing
environment	government
holidays	sport and leisure
work	communications
education	transport
city life	shopping

---

2 **a)** Many discoveries and inventions are solutions to problems of some kind. The news items describe future solutions to four serious problems of the world today. Decide what these problems are.

Describing a problem: KEY LANGUAGE

There's a lack/shortage of . . .

There isn't/aren't enough/any more . . .

There 's/are too much/many . . .

There's been an increase/rise / a decrease/drop in + noun (by number)

We're running out/short of . . .

b) Decide what the causes of the problems are.

Explaining causes (2): KEY LANGUAGE

This is owing to / due to / because of / the result of / on account of / caused by . . . .

The reason for this is . . .

c) Decide what the consequences will be, and give examples.

Talking about result (2): KEY LANGUAGE

This has led / will lead to . . .

This has caused / will cause + noun + *to* + infinitive

This means that . . .

If (not) / Unless + present simple, . . . *will/won't* + infinitive

GUIDED WRITING ACTIVITY

Use the guide and the notes opposite to write a paragraph summarising the problems of water pollution as a threat to wildlife. Suggest solutions and sum up at the end.

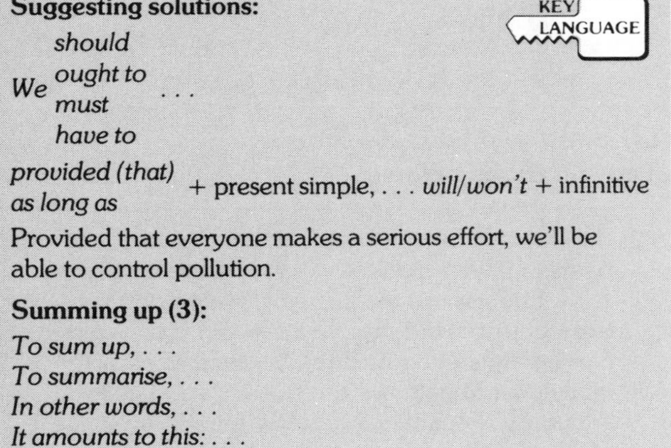

Suggesting solutions:

KEY LANGUAGE

We *should* / *ought to* / *must* / *have to* . . .

provided (that) / *as long as* + present simple, . . . *will/won't* + infinitive

Provided that everyone makes a serious effort, we'll be able to control pollution.

Summing up (3):

To sum up, . . .
To summarise, . . .
In other words, . . .
It amounts to this: . . .

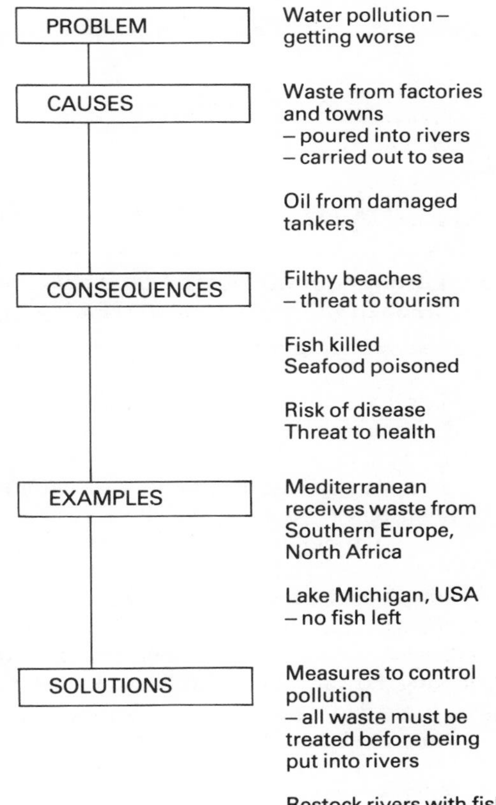

PROBLEM
Water pollution – getting worse
CAUSES
Waste from factories and towns
– poured into rivers
– carried out to sea
Oil from damaged tankers
CONSEQUENCES
Filthy beaches
– threat to tourism
Fish killed
Seafood poisoned
Risk of disease
Threat to health
EXAMPLES
Mediterranean receives waste from Southern Europe, North Africa
Lake Michigan, USA
– no fish left
SOLUTIONS
Measures to control pollution
– all waste must be treated before being put into rivers
Restock rivers with fish

LISTENING ACTIVITY

a) Listen to this radio interview about noise pollution. Take notes using the guide above.

b) Listen to the interview again. What makes each of the following noises?

roar	scream	crash
rattle	bang	

c) What noises would each of the following make? Use the words in **b**).

a door closing loudly
a motor bike
a pile of plates falling to the floor
a button in a wooden box
someone in great pain

d) What would make each of the following noises? Use your dictionary if necessary.

whistle	thump	buzz
click	scrape	rustle
crack	splash	

GUIDED WRITING ACTIVITY

'Noise pollution is a serious problem of the twentieth century, and it's getting worse.' What can we do to change this?

Using your notes and the guide above, give your views on this subject in no more than 180 words.

C MAKING PREDICTIONS ABOUT THE FUTURE

READING

Looking into the Future

Throughout the ages, people have claimed to be able to predict the future. Some of the most dramatic predictions of all are described below.

THE FRENCH doctor and astrologer Michel de Notredame, known as Nostradamus, published his famous book of predictions in 1555. He concentrated mainly on facts about the future rather than dates. He even got the date of his own death wrong! But this did not affect the success of the book which is still in print today. Many of his predictions have come true. For example, he foresaw the Great Fire of London of 1666, the French Revolution of 1789, the abdication of King Edward VIII of Britain in 1936 and the Hungarian Revolution of 1956. He often mentions the United States of America, saying, 'The great man struck down . . .' 'The great one will fall . . .', 'The world put into trouble by three brothers, their enemies will seize the marine city, hunger, fire, blood, plague, all evils doubled.' These words are generally taken as a warning of the assassinations of John Kennedy, President of the USA, and his brother, Robert, but does the 'marine city' refer to New York and its future destruction by fire? And what do we make of his prediction of a Third World War? We'll just have to wait and see, although it's clear that he sees all death and destruction as necessary if the ideal world is to be built on the ruins of the old one.

EDGAR CAYCE was one of the most famous psychic figures of recent times. He was able not only to heal sick people, sometimes from hundreds of miles away, but also to predict the future. By the time of his death, he had foreseen the invention of the laser, the Wall Street Crash of 1929 and the earthquakes, hurricanes and tidal waves that struck California, Japan and the Philippines in 1926. In 1936 he had a vision. In it, he was reborn in the year 2000. He saw himself flying with some companions across North America in an odd-shaped aircraft at high speed. They landed among the ruins of a huge city which was in the process of being rebuilt. He asked what the name of it was. 'New York' was the reply. Along with this vision, he foresaw violent changes throughout the United States and the world. Nebraska had become the west coast after earthquakes had shattered the existing coastal strip, including Los Angeles and San Francisco. Much of Japan was underwater and Northern Europe had been completely altered. New lands had appeared from beneath both the Atlantic and Pacific Oceans.

JEANE DIXON became well-known throughout the United States of America for writing horoscopes which appeared in over 300 newspapers. Her predictions were amazingly accurate; she foresaw the deaths of Roosevelt and Gandhi, Churchill's defeat in the elections of 1945, Marilyn Monroe's suicide, and the fire which killed three young astronauts at Cape Kennedy in 1967. But the most extraordinary were her visions concerning the assassinations of John and Robert Kennedy, and the civil rights leader Martin Luther King. She believes that the years before 1999 will be a time of struggle for humanity, but that a better life for all will follow. This belief is based on a vision she had early one morning in 1962. She rose and looked out of her window in Washington. There, instead of city streets lined with bare autumn trees, she saw a desert scene. Out of the golden rays of the sun stepped Queen Nefertiti of Ancient Egypt, hand-in-hand with her Pharaoh. She carried a new-born baby. A few minutes later the baby had grown to manhood. He was surrounded by worshippers of every colour, race and creed. Mrs Dixon interpreted this vision as the birth of a new religion that will unite the whole world in peace. The leader will be the baby of her vision who will grow in strength until 1999, at which time the peoples of the earth will probably discover the full meaning of the vision.

LANGUAGE PRACTICE

1 a) What are your reactions to the predictions of Nostradamus, Edgar Cayce, and Jeane Dixon? Do you believe that it is possible to predict the future, or is it just coincidence when predictions come true?

b) Do you think it's right to try and predict the future?

> **KEY LANGUAGE**
>
> **Expressing certainty and doubt:**
>
> *I'm (not) / (quite) sure / certain / convinced / positive (that) . . .*
> *I doubt if/that . . .*
> *There's no doubt that . . .*
>
> **Expressing opinions (4):**
>
> *I (don't) believe in . . .*
> *I (don't) think / believe (that) . . .*
> *As far as I'm concerned, . . .*
> *In my view/opinion, . . .*

2 a) Many people read their horoscopes in the newspapers each day. Do you? Do the predictions ever come true? Find your horoscope for yesterday and decide whether its predictions were correct.

b) Find out what another student expects to be doing this time next year. Write his or her horoscope for next year.

> **KEY LANGUAGE**
>
> **Making predictions about the future (3):**
>
> *I expect you'll . . .*
> *It's likely that you'll . . .*
> *You may/could/might . . .*
> *You'll probably / certainly / definitely . . .*
> *You're likely / sure / certain / bound to . . .*
> *As long as you . . ., you'll . . .*
> *There's a good/strong chance that you'll . . .*

3 a) Some people are especially gifted in predicting the future. They use a variety of methods, e.g.

Palm Reading

ASTROLOGY

I Ching

Tarot Cards

Do you know of any other methods?
Choose one method and describe it to a partner.

b) Have you ever had your fortune told? Has it come true?

4 a) Make your own 'Fortune Circle': Each person in the group should write two predictions, one optimistic and one pessimistic. You can make them as amusing or unlikely as you want, e.g.

You'll get top marks in your First Certificate exam.
You'll become rich and famous.
You'll become weak and unable to resist temptation.
You'll become an English teacher.

Place all the predictions in a circle around the table. Place an ordinary kitchen knife in the centre of the circle.

With everyone seated around the table, one person should spin the knife. When it stops turning, the person it points to should spin it again. When it stops for the second time, the person should read the prediction it points to.

b) Use the Fortune Circle to make four or five predictions about your future life.
Imagine the predictions have come true, and write a short story about what has happened.

5 a) Complete the following sentences by choosing the missing word from the list below.

KEY VOCABULARY

superstition	fate	
mystery	symbol	
reflection	dream	
luck	unlucky	trick
fortune	tradition	danger
chance	fantasy	symbol
misfortune	memory	faith

1 It's said to bring bad _______ if you walk under a ladder.

2 With all those clouds, there's a strong _______ it'll rain.

3 No one ever knew what happened to the *Mary Celeste;* it was a complete _______.

4 The dove is a _______ of peace.

5 He had the _______ to break his leg while skiing.

6 In the legend, Narcissus looked in a pool of water and fell in love with his _______.

7 The boys played a _______ on the old man by ringing his doorbell and then running away.

8 I sometimes have this _______ that I've won a million pounds.

9 She was having such a frightening _______ that she woke up screaming.

10 Because of the new motorway, the _______ of the little village is uncertain.

INTERPRETATION ACTIVITY

Read *Looking into the Future* again, and answer the questions below in 40–50 words each.

1 What facts suggest that the predictions about the future might come true?

2 What reason is there to be optimistic about the future?

3 What reason is there to be pessimistic about the future?

D REPORTING AN INCIDENT

READING

IS ANYBODY THERE?

You are here!

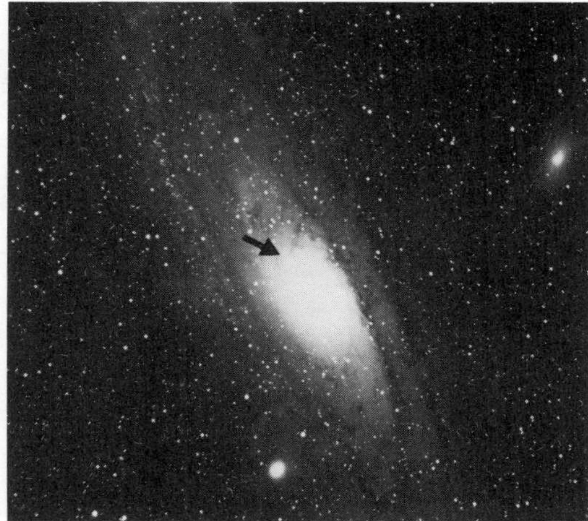

There are approximately 400 billion stars in our universe. Is it possible that Earth is the only planet with any form of life?

Scientists estimate that out of the 400 billion stars, only a quarter have a planetary system, which is necessary to support life as we know it. Only half of those have the ecology to support life. It's possible that nine tenths of those have some form of life, but only one tenth will have intelligence similar to ours. Only a third of these will be able to communicate outside their world. Since we on Earth have been able to communicate for only a few years out of our four and a half billion year existence, only one in 100 billion planets is likely to be able to communicate with us at this very moment. So out of those 400 billion stars, the number that we might be able to contact is about . . . . fifteen.

If there is life out there, why haven't they got in touch with us yet? Is it because it takes so long for a message to reach us? Or is it because they're not as advanced as we are? Or is it because there's no reason why they should be interested in our Earth? Only 200 years ago, there was very little of interest here. Or is it because they're already here but in hiding?

Over the centuries, there have been many stories of strange flying objects in the sky. In the late 1940s and the early 1950s, at the beginning of the Space Age, it was suggested for the first time that these might be forms of life from other civilisations trying to get in touch with us. Since then, more and more Unidentified Flying Objects (UFOs) have been seen all over the world. Are these our neighbours from Outer Space?

DISCUSSION

a) Do you believe there's life elsewhere in the universe?
Do you believe in UFOs?
Ask your partner what he/she thinks.

b) In pairs, prepare a questionnaire on 'Life on other planets.' Use the information in the text above to give you some ideas.

c) Find another student and carry out your questionnaire.

LISTENING ACTIVITY

a) Listen to this account of a strange incident and fill in the report sheet below.

b) Discuss whether you think Colonel Croft really saw a UFO or whether it was just his imagination playing tricks.

UFO REPORT SHEET

Name: ______

Address: ______

______

______

Time of observation: ______

Date of observation: ______

Place of observation (*draw map*):

Description of object (*please sketch*):

Height in sky (*approximate*): ______

General direction: ______

How long was object in view? ______

Visibility: ______

Weather conditions: ______

Was the object seen through anything?
(*e.g. sunglasses, binoculars, car windscreen, etc.*)

______

Outline: Blurred ☐ Clear ☐

Colour: ______

Sound (*please describe*): ______

______

Describe movement: ______

______

Names of witness(es) if any:

______

______

Possible explanation:

______

______

READING ALOUD

a) Look at the following part of the conversation. Can you tell which words are stressed, and on which words the intonation rises or falls? Mark the stress and intonation on your tapescript. Then listen to the conversation again, and check whether you were right.

BELL: Was it making any noise, sir?
CROFT: Well, a kind of whistling sound, a bit like the wind.
BELL: And was there any wind?
CROFT: Well, a little, but not enough to make that sort of noise.
BELL: And you watched from inside your car?
CROFT: Yes.
BELL: Is the windscreen quite clean?
CROFT: Yes, of course it is!
BELL: I mean, the outline was quite clear?
CROFT: Oh yes.

b) Now read the conversation aloud in pairs. Change roles when you have finished.

LISTENING ACTIVITY

a) Listen to another account of the same incident, and take notes.

b) Using the verbs below, put the following sentences into indirect speech.

Example: 'Let's turn the heating on,' she said.
She suggested that they turned the heating on.

1 'No, I'm not moving from here,' she said.
2 'Oh, come on, Jenny, I'll look after you,' he said.
3 'Don't go any closer!' she said.
4 'I'm sure it's burning the grass,' she said.
5 'I'm going back to the car,' she said.
6 'Oh, Mick, please take me home,' she said.
7 'I think we ought to tell the police,' he said.
8 'I'm PC Hackett,' he said.
9 'I'm delighted to see you, officer,' he said.
10 'We were just coming to see you,' he said.
11 'Would you like a cup of tea, ma'am?' he said.
12 'Yes, I'd love a cup of tea!' she said.

c) Write a report of the whole incident using the information given by all the witnesses.

KEY LANGUAGE

Reporting what has been said (3):

Verb + *to* + infinitive	*agree/ask/claim/ decide/hope/offer/ promise/refuse*	He offered to buy me a drink.
Verb + (*that*) clause	*accept/agree/claim decide/explain/hope/ reply/suggest*	She suggested (that) they went to the cinema.
Verb + noun/pronoun	*accept/greet/ introduce/offer/ refuse*	She introduced us.
Verb + noun/pronoun + *to* + infinitive	*ask/invite/ order/persuade/ remind/warn*	He ordered me to sit down.
Verb + noun/pronoun + (*that*) clause	*promise/persaude/ remind/warn*	He warned us that it would rain.

ROLE PLAY

a) In groups of three, use the information in both dialogues, and the questions in the report sheet, to act out the conversation between the policeman and the couple.

b) Another UFO has been spotted and the police want to check that it was not a hoax.

Pair A: You have spotted a UFO and you intend to report the incident to the police. Use the report sheet to establish all the details of what happened, and what you saw. Make sure you both have the same information.

Pair B: You are two policemen who have to investigate yet another sighting of a UFO. Use the report sheet opposite to prepare a list of questions to make sure the people giving evidence are telling the truth. Then interview Pair A separately and check they are both telling the same story!

c) Write a report of this incident.

EXAM PRACTICE

PAPER 1: READING COMPREHENSION

Section A *(Suggestions for the exam – see Unit 1)*

In this section you must choose the word or phrase which best completes each sentence. For each question, 1 to 25, *indicate on your answer sheet* the letter A, B, C or D against the number of the question.

1 People still haven't _______ how dangerous pollution can be.
A remarked B noted C realised D minded

2 There were so many new buildings in the town that she hardly _______ the place.
A distinguished B recognised C made out D identified

3 To be chosen to go to the moon would be the _______ of a lifetime.
A fortune B fate C luck D chance

4 Just try and _______ what life would be like without paper.
A imagine B guess C fancy D suppose

5 In a dream he had a _______ of the future.
A view B vision C reflection D image

6 There are now over four billion people living on _______.
A earth B world C globe D universe

7 We are constantly being _______ of the problems of overpopulation.
A reflected B reminded C remembered D reviewed

8 There was a loud _______ as the cup fell to the floor.
A crash B rattle C slam D tap

9 A flag is usually taken to be the _______ of a country.
A sign B mark C signal D symbol

10 He was extremely _______ to sunlight.
A sensible B sensitive C aware D tender

11 The water looked perfectly clean but _______ it was seriously polluted.
A obviously B apparently C clearly D properly

12 Coming from the kitchen was a wonderful _______ of cooking.
A odour B scent C perfume D smell

13 It's essential to _______ the environment.
A protect B shelter C prevent D restrict

14 The Muslim _______ has many followers throughout the world.
A worship B praise C faith D belief

15 It's unfair to blame the motor car _______ air pollution.
A at B to C in D for

16 Directly _______ the beach was a huge factory.
A beside B besides C nearby D near

17 She had lost her voice and could only speak in a _______.
A whistle B rustle C breath D whisper

18 It was a complete _______ to us how she knew what was happening.
A secret B mystery C trick D magic

19 There has been a huge increase _______ petrol prices.
A of B to C in D by

20 When he finally _______, he couldn't remember what had happened.
A stood back B held back C came round D wore off

21 In the middle of all the panic, she _______ phoned the police.
A silently B calmly C peacefully D mildly

22 He was _______ of sleeping in the old house.
A anxious B worried C afraid D troubled

23 There is no way of knowing _______ what life will be like in a hundred years' time.
A actually B at the moment C currently D presently.

24 He lost his _______ with the post-office official.
A humour B temper C mood D nature

25 She gave _______ doing her shopping in town because it was too crowded.
A up B in C out D over

PAPER 3: USE OF ENGLISH

Section A, Question 1 *(Suggestions for the exam – see Unit 1)*

Fill each of the numbered blanks in the following text. Use only *one* word in each space.

When my mother finally became too old to live alone, we decided that she should stay with us ________ (1) town. I was surprised ________ (2) the amount of furniture she had, but there was no ________ (3) in our flat to store it, so we had to leave it in her house. I always intended to clear it out and sell the place, but somehow I kept putting it ________ (4).

________ (5) night I woke suddenly ________ (6) four o'clock, almost in tears. I was extremely upset ________ (7) a dream in which I saw two men ________ (8) a window, climb ________ (9) my mother's house, and start to take her belongings. Then the burglars must have heard someone's voice outside or a door ________ (10) closed, because they dropped ________ (11) they were carrying and left in a hurry. The dream ________ (12) me feel very guilty that I had not taken better care of the house.

Later ________ (13) morning I received a phone call ________ (14) a lady who lived next door to the house. ________ (15) my astonishment, she told me that it had ________ (16) broken into during the night. Fortunately, something ________ (17) have disturbed the burglars because they left ________ (18) taking anything. I didn't ________ (19) to believe ________ (20) the supernatural, but now I'm not so sure!

Section A, Question 3 *(Suggestions for the exam – see Unit 3)*

Complete the following sentences with *one* appropriate word connected with astronomy.

Example: There are nine . . . . *planets* . . . . in our solar system.

a) It takes 28 days for the . . . . to circle once round the earth.

b) Venus is the brightest . . . . in the northern skies.

c) Many people believe we have received visitors from outer . . . . on Earth.

d) Our solar system is only one of many in the . . . .

e) It takes 365¼ days for the Earth to go round the . . . . once.

Section A, Question 4

Suggestions for the exam
In the exam, you may be given an exercise where you have to transfer direct to indirect speech, or vice versa as below. Read the **whole** *passage through carefully before you write anything. Think of ways to express the* **reporting** *verbs in direct speech, e.g.* **suggested:** *'Let's . . .', 'Why don't we . . .?', 'Shall we . . .?', etc. Make sure that the sequence of tenses in your completed dialogue is* **accurate** *and* **logical.** *You should allow about 15 minutes for this exercise.*

Instructions
Write out the following text in dialogue form, making all necessary changes. Begin as shown:

Jean: Why don't we all go to the cinema this evening?

. . . .

. . . .

Jean sugggested to Patrick and Alison that they all went to the cinema that evening. Patrick asked what they should go and see, and Jean said she was longing to see *E.T. – the Extra-Terrestrial.* Patrick was rather surprised by this because he had assumed that the initials stood for 'English Teaching'. Alison said that he must go round with his eyes closed if he hadn't noticed all the advertising. Patrick replied that if he went round with his eyes closed, it would hardly be worth going to see a film. Jean interrupted at this point to persuade the others to be serious and go with her to the cinema. Patrick asked about the price of seats, as he hadn't been to the cinema for a long time. When Jean told him that they cost over £3, he said he thought English Teaching was much cheaper, and he was going to stay at home! But Alison agreed to go, so she and Jean said goodbye, and left.

Section B, Question 5 *(Suggestions for the exam – see Unit 4)*

Opposite is a horoscope taken from a newspaper, and notes by two people born under the sign of Gemini about various decisions to be taken and things to be done in the near future.

Using the information given in the horoscope continue in about 80 words both of the paragraphs in the spaces provided, giving your reasons.

Gemini *(22 May – 21 June)*
You seem easily worried or annoyed at the moment, but it will help if you speak your mind more often. Don't take any important decisions about your career; things will start to look up at work. It's a good time to make travel plans – go as far as you can, you won't be disappointed! Some minor health problems may become more serious if you don't look after yourself. A chance meeting this month is likely to turn into a close friendship. However, don't neglect your family – they're more important than you realise!

FRAN

Decision about trip to Australia
(It's rather a long way!)
Cancel medical check-up – too busy.
Accept Jim's invitation to opera
(Hate opera but I don't want to hurt his feelings.)
Buy medicine for cough
Ask about pay rise ???

RUSS

Fed-up with boss. Must find new job.
Friday Mrs Sullivan's party.
(Should I refuse? Won't know anyone)
Ring Aunt June – cancel dinner date.
Leaking roof. Tell Landlord?
Summer: Go to Spain or stay at home?

I think Fran should . . . . because . . . . .
I don't think she should . . . . because . . . . .

I think Russ should . . . . because . . . . .
I don't think he should . . . . because . . . . .

ARTICLES

The **indefinite article** (*a/an*) can normally only be used with singular countable nouns. Indefinite reference with plural or uncountable nouns as indicated by **zero article** (see opposite) or **some** (see p. 170).

The **indefinite article** is used:

a) when the noun is mentioned for the first time.
You can get an application form from the Post Office.

b) with nouns (including professions) after the verbs *be* and *become* when the noun has indefinite reference.
I'd like to be a doctor.
It's an interesting book.

c) in emphatic expressions after *what* and *such*.
What an incredible story!
She's such a kind person.

d) in expressions of ratio (price, speed, frequency, etc.)
ten pence a box, fifty miles an hour, twice a day.

e) with certain numbers and expressions of quantity.
a dozen, a hundred, a thousand.
a lot of, a few, a little.

NOTE: *a few apples* / *a little water* = a small amount (neutral meaning)
BUT: *few apples* / *little water* = hardly any (negative meaning)

The **definite article** (*the*) is used:

a) before a noun which has become definite because it has already been mentioned, or when the reference is obvious.
Then fill in the form, and send it off at once.
He turned on the lights.
Pass the sugar.

b) before nouns which are defined by a phrase or clause.
The men with guns were police officers.
Where's the milk I bought?
It led to the invention of photography.

c) before singular nouns to represent a class of things.
The typewriter was invented in 1829.

d) before superlatives, and ordinal numbers.
the oldest man, the first president, the third of June
BUT: *First, let me welcome you.*

e) before names of rivers, seas, and plural names of countries.
the Nile, the Mediterranean, the United States, the USSR, the British Isles.

f) before musical instruments.
He plays the trumpet.

g) in the following phrases:
I'm going to the cinema/theatre/opera/ballet/office.

Zero article. The article is not used:

a) before plural, uncountable and abstract nouns when they are used in a general sense. (Compare **definite article b**)
Women live longer than men.
Milk contains lots of vitamins.
Necessity is the mother of invention.

b) before the names of most countries, towns and streets.
I bought it in New York, near Fifth Avenue.
BUT: *the Congo, the Sudan, the Hague.*

c) before the names of languages and subjects.
I'm taking Spanish and History.

d) in certain idiomatic phrases, e.g.

He went to *prison* (prisoner) / *hospital* (patient) / *school* (pupil) / *university* (student) / *bed* (tired person)

He visited the hospital.
BUT: *They couldn't find the school.*
She put her suitcase on the bed.

I came by *bus* / *car* / *tube* / *boat* / *train* / *plane*

It happened at *dawn* / *noon* / *midday* / *sunset* / *night* / *midnight*

Let's have *breakfast* / *lunch* / *tea* / *supper* / *dinner*

1 Fill in the blanks with the definite or indefinite article, if necessary.

1 _____ neighbours have just bought themselves _____ new car.
2 Football is _____ game played with two teams of eleven.
3 What _____ lovely weather!
4 Could you turn on _____ television?
5 In my opinion, _____ penicillin is _____ most useful medicine ever invented by _____ man.
6 We had to wear _____ uniforms at _____ school I went to.
7 I've been learning _____ English for six years now.
8 Shall we open _____ bottle of wine you bought?
9 At _____ school he was always interested in _____ drama and now he's _____ actor.
10 It's _____ lovely house but did you see how small _____ kitchen was?

11 She really is _____ kindest person I know.
12 I thought I'd buy her _____ plant for her birthday.
13 I've got _____ few eggs, so let's have _____ omelette for _____ lunch.
14 I want to make _____ phone call to _____ Boston in _____ United States.
15 They say that _____ love makes _____ world go round.

some and **any** are used with plural and uncountable nouns (indefinite meaning).
some is used:

a) in affirmative statements.
I'd like some more vegetables, please.

b) in invitations, or questions where the answer 'yes' is expected.
Would you like some tea?
I can hear noises – are there some people upstairs?

any is used:

a) in negative statements, or statements where the sense is negative.
There isn't any tea left.
He's got hardly any furniture.

b) in open questions.
Have you got any ideas?

Uncountable nouns

Uncountable nouns are always singular, but cannot be used with the **indefinite article** (see p. 169).

They usually refer to substances, e.g. *milk, bread, butter, wood, paper, iron, glass.*

Other common uncountable nouns are: *advice, information, news, luggage, furniture, hair, money, weather.*

a) Uncountable nouns are often preceded by words or phrases meaning 'a part of', e.g.

a pint of milk — *a pane of glass*
a slice of bread — *a piece of advice*
some butter — *a bit of information*
a sheet of paper

b) Many nouns can be either uncountable or countable, depending on the meaning.

Uncountable meaning
It's made of glass.
I'd like some coffee.
Iron is a heavy metal.
Paper is made from wood.
a piece of cake.
BUT:
Countable meaning
a glass of milk
I'd like a (cup of) coffee.
My skirt needs pressing but I haven't got an iron.
Have you got a daily paper?
Lets go for a walk in the woods.
a wedding cake

2 Fill in the blanks with *a(n), some,* or *any.*

1 I'd like _____ information about hotels in Paris.
2 Drink _____ pint of milk a day.
3 Have you got _____ washing powder?
4 Would you like _____ boiled egg for breakfast?
5 You rarely spend _____ time with me these days.
6 I need _____ paper to write on.
7 Take _____ glass and pour yourself _____ drink.
8 He's in trouble, isn't he? Do you think he needs _____ help?
9 I haven't got _____ matches.
10 He's just made _____ bread.

TENSES

The **present simple** is used:

a) to describe a permanent state.
He lives in Rome.
She likes curry.

b) to describe repeated or habitual actions (often with adverbs of frequency).
She (always) gets up at 7.30.
He (usually) wears smart clothes.

c) to express general truths.
Two plus two equals four.
Water freezes at 0° C.

d) to give instructions and describe procedures.
Then you dial the number.

e) as the historic or dramatic present to describe past events.
Eliza meets Higgins in the market.
The man pulls out a knife.

f) to express the future when referring to a fixed timetable.
The flight departs at 11.35.

g) in conditional and time clauses referring to the future (see **conditionals**, p. 176 and **future simple** p. 174). (after *if, unless, in case, when, as soon as, after, before, until, etc.*)
If they build new offices, they'll pull down part of the town.
Walk up the hill until you come to a pub.

h) with certain verbs not normally used in continuous forms:

i) Verbs which describe states of mind, emotion, and perception, e.g. *think, believe, understand, know, mean, suppose, remember, forget, trust, like, love, prefer, hate, mind, wish, want, need, see, hear, feel, smell, taste, notice, recognise, seem, appear, look (like), etc.*

ii) Verbs which indicate a permanent state, e.g. *be, have, belong to, contain, consist, cost, equal, fit, own, remain, resemble, deserve, depend,* etc.

I think you're right.
Do you like swimming?
She looks friendly.
The stew tastes delicious.
The box contains little sticks of wood.
How much does it cost?

NOTE: Some of these verbs are used in the continuous form when they describe an activity rather than a state.
What are you thinking about?
The cook is tasting all the dishes.

The **present continuous** is used:

a) to describe an action happening now.
I'm phoning from a call-box.

b) to describe a temporary state or activity.
She is wearing an old coat.
I'm having driving lessons.

c) with *always*, this construction is often used to describe irritating or surprising habits.
She's always breaking things.

d) to describe the background to habitual actions or dramatic events.
I listen to the radio while I'm having breakfast.
It is raining heavily when Eliza meets Higgins.

e) to express future arrangements.
Our son's getting married tomorrow.

3 Read the newspaper article about a rock singer.

DAN TURNER, lead singer with rock band *War Paint*, describes his life-style.

HOME: I live in a tiny apartment in Manhattan. There's no room for any furniture, but I like antiques.
CLOTHES: I always wear casual clothes, but I spend quite a lot of money on them. I buy most of my clothes from a shop round the corner. I like wearing black and white.
FOOD: I eat lots of fruit and salad, but I'm not a vegetarian. I hate hamburgers. I eat in restaurants much too often.
ROUTINE: I get up very early, and work from morning till midnight. I usually go to bed just before I get up.
FREE TIME: I don't have much free time, but I read a lot while I'm travelling. I read thrillers, biographies, poetry, newspapers, telephone directories, anything I can lay my hands on. I don't take enough exercise, but I try to go swimming occasionally. I've given up smoking, I'm glad to say.

a) You are the newspaper reporter who interviewed Dan Turner. Make a list of the questions you asked him, using the present simple.

b) Write a simple description of your life-style, using the headings in the newspaper article.

4 a) People often reveal a lot about their personality by talking about their life-style. Prepare a questionnaire on the following subjects:

Extravagant clothes	Theatre
Letters to friends abroad	Parties
Cook just for yourself	Physical exercise
Novels	Your horoscope
Credit cards	Discos
Concerts	Walks in the countryside
Money to charities	Radio
Taxis	

EXAMPLES: Do you ever buy extravagant clothes?
Do you ever give money to charities?

Fill in the questionnaire by asking three or four people to answer your questions using adverbs of frequency, e.g. *always, usually, often, sometimes, occasionally, rarely, hardly ever, never.*

b) What conclusions can you draw about their personalities? Choose one person and write a short paragraph about his or her personality.

5 Fill in the blanks using the present simple of the verbs below.

be	build	grow	spend
become	die	lose	tell
believe	fill	realise	use

Citizen Kane is often said to be the best film of all time. It ________ (1) the story of a rich little boy who ________ (2) the most powerful newspaper-owner in the USA. Kane ________ (3) his wealth and power for political gain, and in the process, he ________ (4) many friends. As he ________ (5) older, he ________ (6) himself to be a god, and he ________ (7) an enormous palace which he ________ (8) with valuable objects. There he ________ (9) the last years of his life, and he ________ (10) a very sad and lonely man. He ________ (11) too late that money ________ (12) not everything.

6 Fill in the blanks using the present simple of the verbs below.

arrive	end	interview	play
close	fly	leave	start

1 The boat train ________ from Platform 5 in ten minutes.
2 This programme ________ at 10.30.
3 Robin Scott ________ the President in 'Talking Point' at four o'clock.
4 Flight OK 754 ________ in Prague at 14.15.
5 Real Madrid ________ Bayern Munich next week.
6 The bank ________ early this afternoon.
7 He ________ his new job on Monday morning.
8 The Prime Minister ________ to Washington tomorrow.

7 Complete the following sentences with a suitable clause.

1 It will be dark by the time . . .
2 You heat the milk until . . .
3 I'll write to you as soon as . . .
4 He'll finish the work before . . .
5 You'd better write it down in case . . .
6 We'll miss the train if . . .
7 Turn off the lights when . . .
8 You won't find the house unless . . .

8 Put the verbs in brackets in the present simple or continuous.

a) The miners now (ask) for a significant pay-increase. The government (offer) them 6½%, but the miners (think) they (deserve) 10%, and they (do) everything in their power to get it. The union already (prepare) for an all-out strike, and union officials (believe) the government (begin) to get worried. It (look) as if the miners (have) a good chance of getting what they (want). They (know) the country (depend) heavily on coal for its energy – and winter (come).

b) George Forester (go) swimming every day, whatever the weather, (run) for half-an-hour before breakfast, and (play) tennis twice a week. Now he (plan) to get married for the fifth time – at the age of 98. This remarkable man (not look) a day over 50, and he (speak) firmly and without hesitation. 'People always (ask) how I (do) it,' he (laugh), 'so I (write) a book about keeping fit. But I (not have) all the answers. Of course, I (not smoke), but I (have) an occasional glass of brandy. I (suppose) I (be) just lucky.' And the name of the lucky woman? 'I (not tell) you that. We (keep) it a secret until the wedding. We (get) married next month, and I (look) forward to our honeymoon in Capri! After that, we (move) to a cottage in the country which I (buy).'
Well, as the saying (go), you (be) only as old as you (feel).

The **present perfect** is used:

a) to refer to the past in a general way when talking about experience and knowledge (often with expressions of indefinite time e.g. *ever, never, yet, already, before*).
Have you (ever) worked in a shop?
He's been to the USA.

NOTE: The past simple is used to refer to a definite time in the past (see **past simple**, next page).
Yes, I worked in a shop last year.

b) to express the unfinished past when talking about actions or events which continue into the present (often with *for* and *since* (see **prepositions** p. 185) and other expressions of unfinished time e.g. *all my life, etc.*)
He's lived here all his life.
I've worked there for four years/since 1979.

c) to describe recently completed actions or events (with *just, recently* etc.).
I've just left school.

d) to describe recent actions or events with present significance (especially to give news).
I'm sorry, you can't speak to him. He's gone to the USA.
Ten people have died in the storms on the East Coast.

e) to describe a series or number of actions repeated in a period up to the present.
I've written six letters this morning.

NOTE: *go* has two past participles: *been* and *gone.*
He's been to the USA = He's returned.
He's gone to the USA = He hasn't returned (yet).

The **present perfect continuous** is used:

a) to emphasise the duration of actions or events which began in the past and are still happening (often with expressions of unfinished time (see **present perfect**, below left)).
I've been working so hard that I haven't had time to eat.
I've been waiting here for over an hour/since 5 p.m.

b) to emphasise the temporary nature of actions or events which began in the past and are still happening.
She's been living with her parents for the last couple of months.

c) to emphasise the duration of a recently completed action.
I've been looking for my pen all morning, and at last I've found it.

d) to describe a past action or event which has produced a visible result in the present.
The team are playing well this season because they've been training hard.

9 Read the following passage and answer the questions below.

Hat Trick, the latest show by Elliot and Parks, opens tonight at the Duke of Kent's Theatre, and is the fifth musical of this remarkable partnership. They first met at school twenty years ago and they wrote their first musical only a few months later. Even in those days they showed great talent. Geoff Parks learnt to play the piano when he was five and Phil Elliot wrote his first novel when he was fourteen. They still do some work separately. Parks, who is 35, started a jazz band six years ago, and last week was his hundredth concert. Phil Elliot's tenth novel is to be published next week on his thirty-third birthday, after three years of writing and research. A busy month for the brightest stars in Theatre Land!

Ask and answer questions about *how many*.
Example: *How many musicals have they written? Five.*

Ask and answer questions about *how long*.
Example: *How long have they been writing musicals? About twenty years.*

10 Give a suitable response to the sentences below, using the present perfect continuous.

Example: Her eyes are red.
Yes, she's been crying.

1 You look very brown.
2 He looks very tired.
3 His hair's soaking wet.
4 Mmm, there's a lovely smell coming from the kitchen.
5 She's out of breath.
6 What a dreadful cough!

The **past simple** is used:

a) to describe actions or events completed at a definite time in the past.
I started the job four months ago.

b) to describe actions or events completed in the past where the time is understood but not mentioned (typically in narrative).
We flew to Cairo, and then took a local flight to Abu Simbel.

c) to ask questions about definite past time.
When did you leave school?

d) to describe a definite period of time in the past.
I spent three years at the Liverpool Arts Centre.

e) to describe repeated or habitual actions or behaviour in the past (often with adverbs of frequency). (See also **used to** p. 188).
He wrote to her every day.
Rich Harold never spent any of his money.

f) with certain verbs not normally used in continuous forms (see **present simple** p. 170).
She thought she heard voices.

g) in Type 2 **conditional** clauses (see p. 176).
If I had a shorter working week, I wouldn't mind.

h) after
It's time . . . . would sooner/rather . . . .

11 Put the verbs in brackets in the present perfect or the past simple.

Geoff: I (not see) you for a few weeks. Where you (be)?
Jacky: I (go) to the United States on holiday.
Geoff: Oh really? How long you (spend) there?
Jacky: About three weeks.
Geoff: And you (enjoy) yourself?
Jacky: Oh yes, it (be) the best holiday I ever (have).
Geoff: Where you (stay)?
Jacky: Oh, we (fly) to Los Angeles, then we (hire) a car and (drive) to San Francisco, Las Vegas and lots of other places.
Geoff: Wonderful. How many times you (be) to the United States?
Jacky: Twice, but this (be) my first visit to the West Coast.
Geoff: I (stay) in New York once, but it (be) only for a night.
Jacky: Well, remind me to show you the photos I (take) when I (have) them developed.
Geoff: I'd love to see them.

The **past continuous** is used:

a) to describe a continuous activity during a particular period in the past.
They were working in Fiji during the summer.

b) to describe a continuous activity in progress at a particular point in past time. The activity may be 'interrupted' by the past simple.
At ten o'clock, I was sitting in a café.
I was having a quiet drink when the police came in.

c) with *always* to describe repeated (and often irritating) actions in the past.
They were always having noisy parties.

d) to describe simultaneous actions or events in the past.
One team was making a survey while another was diving on the coral reef.

e) to describe the background to past actions or events.
They did research while they were sailing through the Mediterranean.

f) to describe unfulfilled plans and intentions.
I was hoping to go to university, but I went to France.

12 Put the verbs in brackets in the past simple or the past continuous.

1 Columbus (discover) America in 1492.
2 Where you (go) last Saturday when I (see) you in the street?
3 I (plan) to go skiing in February, but I (break) my leg at Christmas.
4 She (hear) the news while she (prepare) dinner.
5 While it (rain) they (stay) in their hotel, but as soon as the sun (come) out, they (go) to the beach.
6 Last year the government (announce) they (intend) to build more houses.
7 While the paint (dry) in the kitchen, they (begin) painting the hall.
8 After he (leave) the bar, he (catch) the bus and (go) home.
9 I (meet) my wife when I (work) in Barbados.
10 John (pay) you back the money he (owe) you?

The **past perfect** is used:

a) to describe the first of two consecutive actions or events.
After they had left Fiji, they sailed to Papua New Guinea.

b) to describe an action or event which happened before a particular time in the past.
She'd gone to bed before midnight.
He'd left home by eight o'clock.

c) in Type 3 **conditional** clauses (see p. 176)
I'd have gone to university if I hadn't gone to France.

NOTE: 1 The following words and phrases are often used with the past perfect:
after, before, when, as soon as, by, by the time, until

2 The past simple is often used instead of the past perfect if it is obvious that the two events are not simultaneous.

After they (had) left Fiji, they sailed to Papua New Guinea.
When she('d) finished her meal, she ordered a coffee.

BUT: *When he'd seen the dentist, he took a taxi to the airport.*

NOT: *When he saw the dentist . . .!*

13 Put the verbs in brackets in the past simple or the past perfect.

For my mother's seventieth birthday we (decide) to send her to visit my brother in Australia, whom she (not see) for over ten years. The evening before she (leave), I (go) round to see her. She (spent) the whole day packing her bags and she (become) too excited to go to bed. I (tell) her to get some sleep and as I (not be able) to take her to the airport in the morning, I (wish) her all the best for a good trip and (say) goodbye. In the morning two hours after the flight (leave), I (receive) a phone call. It (be) my mother! After staying awake most of the night, she (fall) asleep at five a.m. and (not hear) the alarm at seven! She (not know) what to do! Fortunately the airline (be) very understanding and (say) that this (happen) before. So they (find) her a seat on the next flight.

14 Put the verbs in brackets in the correct tense: present perfect, present perfect continuous, past simple, past continuous, or past perfect.

1 You (see) the latest film by Fellini?
2 When she (prepare) the meal for the family, she (go) back to her books.
3 I (wait) for about half an hour and not a single bus (pass).
4 She suddenly (remember) where she (see) his face before.
5 Where you (go) after you (leave) university in 1976?
6 If only you (tell) me that you (come) to London this weekend!
7 We (hope) to go to Spain for a holiday last year, but we (not have) enough money.
8 He (smoke) 20 cigarettes a day since he (be) 16.
9 We just (hear) that the plane (be) delayed.
10 While I (do) the shopping this morning, someone (steal) my wallet.
11 He (spend) the afternoon showing us where he (go) on holiday last year.
12 I (not go) to a restaurant since my father (take) us out to celebrate his birthday.

The **future simple** is used:

a) to make predictions and to express hopes and fears (often after verbs such as *think, expect, suppose, imagine, hope*, and adverbs such as *probably* and *perhaps*).
I expect I'll hear from him soon.
I hope we'll meet again one day.
The flight will probably be delayed.
She'll be 60 on Friday.
You will meet a tall dark stranger . . .

b) often with verbs not normally used in continuous forms (see **present simple** p. 170)
I'll see you tomorrow.
She'll know what to do.

c) for formal announcements, often in news reports.
The Prime Minister will fly to Washington tomorrow.

NOTE: In conversation, we would use the present continuous or *'going to'* future (see below).

d) to express determination (see also note on *'going to'* below).
I will stop smoking. (no contraction)
He won't open the door. (= He refuses to.)

e) in Type 1 **conditionals** (see p. 176), and in sentences with future time clauses (but not *in* conditional or time clauses – **see present simple**, p. 170).
If they build new offices, they'll pull down part of the town.
I'll phone you as soon as I know what's happened.

f) for offers, requests, promises and on-the-spot decisions with *will*.
I'll do the washing-up. (Offer)
Will you give me a lift? (Request)
I won't be late. (Promise)
I'll have a sandwich and a cup of coffee. (Decision – see also note on *'going to'* below)

g) for offers and suggestions with *shall*.
Shall I do the washing up? (Offer)
Shall we meet again tomorrow? (Suggestion)

NOTE: *shall* is normally only used for suggestions and offers (in the first person).

The **future** is also expressed by:

a) the **present simple** for timetables (see p. 170).
The flight departs at 11.35.

b) the **present continuous** for arrangements (see p. 171).
Our son's getting married tomorrow.

c) *going to* + infinitive for plans and intentions, or for assumptions about the future based on the present situation.
We're going to stay for a fortnight.
It looks as if it's going to rain.

NOTE: *going to* may also be used:
1 to express determination.
I'm going to stop smoking.
2 for decisions that have been made earlier.
I'm going to have a salad because I'm on a diet. (Compare with *will* above)

d) *about to* + infinitive for the immediate future.

The space shuttle is about to land . . . and it's landed!

e) the infinitive to describe plans or arrangements.

The Prime Minister is to fly to Washington tomorrow.

The **future continuous** is used:

a) to describe an action which will be in progress at a certain time in the future.

By the year 2010, I'll be going to work by helicopter.

b) to describe an action or event which will take place as a matter of course.

I'll be leaving work at 5.30, so phone me before then.

NOTE: This usage is very similar in meaning to the present continuous, but the present continuous would suggest a specific arrangement.

I'm leaving work early to go to the dentist.

c) for assumptions about the present.

We're having lunch, but they'll be having breakfast in New York.

The **future perfect** is used:

to describe an action or event which will be in the past by a certain time in the future.

In a few years' time, he'll have retired.
The play will have finished by eleven o'clock.

15 Put the verbs in brackets in the future simple or *'going to'* form.

1 I promise I (write) to you every day.
2 Yes, I'd love a drink. I (have) a tomato juice, please.
3 What you (do) when you leave school?
4 I hope I (see) you the next time I come to London.
5 You (come) shopping with me next week? I (buy) some new winter clothes.
6 My boss told me yesterday that he (give) me a rise.
7 I (ring) you as soon as I get there.
8 Oh dear, he (lose) the match.
9 Have you heard the news? Penny and Jack (get) married!
10 I'm sure they (be) very happy together.

16 Make suitable offers/decisions in response to the following statements, using 'I'll . . .'

1 I think I'm going to faint!
2 Oh, it's so cold in here!
3 My cat's stuck up the tree, and can't get down!
4 Poor Mr Jones has just fallen down the stairs. I think he's broken his leg.
5 Oh dear, I seem to have run out of milk.
6 I ought to take my library books back today, but I don't have the time.

17 Make suitable suggestions or offers in the following situations using 'Shall I . . .?'

1 You see an old lady waiting to cross a busy road.
2 A visitor has just arrived, and he's standing in the hall with his coat on.
3 You bump into someone in a café and you spill his tea.
4 A friend suddenly hears a piece of music he likes on the radio.
5 Someone comes into a smoky room and starts coughing.
6 A friend's dog is standing by the back door, wagging his tail.

18 Put the verbs in brackets in the future simple or the future continuous.

1 Just think! This time next week I (lie) on the beach in Majorca.
2 Do you think she (like) the present?
3 By the year 2000, we (do) our shopping by computer. That (make) life much easier.
4 On arrival at Victoria a car (wait) for you which (take) you to your hotel.
5 I expect I (be taken) out to lunch.
6 According to the timetable, the train (leave) at this very moment.
7 I hope you (visit) us in November when we (have) our annual party.
8 Sally (go) to the meeting, so I (speak) to her then.
9 That looks heavy. I (carry) it for you if you like.
10 My son (not come) to school tomorrow because he's still in bed with flu, but I hope he (be) back on his feet by next week.

19 Put the verbs in brackets in the future continuous or future perfect.

1 I hope they (do) the washing-up by the time I get up in the morning.
2 If the river goes on rising at this rate, it (overflow) its banks soon.
3 I expect they (find) an energy source to replace petrol by 1990.
4 This time next year he (be qualified) as a doctor for ten years.
5 By the end of the century, we (use) the space shuttle as often as we take the plane.
6 I wonder what I (do) this time next year.
7 Give him a ring – he (get) back from lunch by now.
8 Just another couple of sentences and I (finish) this exercise.
9 There's eight hours difference in time, so she (get up) as we are going to bed.
10 It's no use expecting the letters to be ready tonight; I (not do) them by then.

CONDITIONALS

Conditional clauses are commonly introduced by *if* or *unless* (= *if not*), and may either precede or follow the main clause.

There are three basic types of conditional sentence.

Type 1

Conditional clause	**Main clause**
if + present tense,	future imperative *must/can/may* etc. +infinitive

This type of conditional is used to indicate open conditions when speculating about the future, often when considering options or discussing consequences. The action or event under discussion is quite likely to happen.

If they build new offices, they'll pull down part c, Crannog.
If you see James, ask him to phone me.
I can give you a lift if it's raining tomorrow.
He won't come to the meeting unless he's finished his report.

NOTE: 1 *Should* may be included in conditional clauses of this type when the action or event is doubtful or unlikely.
If you should see James, ask him to phone me.
In this type of conditional clause the subject and verb may be inverted, and *if/unless* is omitted.
Should you see James, ask him to phone me.

2 *Will* may be used in the conditional clause.
If you'll clear the table, I'll do the washing-up.
Here, *will* means 'are willing to' (see **modals** p. 178)

3 Certain imperative constructions have conditional meaning.
Don't move, or I'll shoot. = If you move, I'll shoot.
Keep quiet, and you won't get hurt. = If you keep quiet, you won't get hurt.

Type 2

Conditional clause	**Main clause**	
if + past tense,	*would* *should* *could* *might*	+ infinitive

This type of conditional is used for:

a) the hypothetical future, where the action or event isn't expected to happen.
I'd be frightened if I lost my job.
If I had a shorter working week, I wouldn't mind.

b) imaginary situations which are contrary to present fact.
If I had my way, schoolchildren would have more freedom.
If I were you, I'd change my job. (Advice)

NOTE: 1 *were* is preferable to *was* in conditional clauses.
2 *would* may occur in the conditional clause.
I should be grateful if you would send me an application form.
Here, *would* means 'were willing to' (see **modals** on next page)

Type 3

Conditional clause	**Main clause**	
if + past perfect tense,	*would* *should* *could* *might*	*have* + past participle

This type of conditional is used to describe completely hypothetical situations which are contrary to past fact, often when referring to unfulfilled plans.

If I'd known you were coming, I could have met you at the station.
I would have gone to university if I hadn't gone to France.

NOTE: In type 3 conditional clauses the subject and verb may be inverted.
Had I known you were coming, I could have met you at the station.

The conditional form is also used after the following words or phrases.

a) *Supposing/What if . . . ?*
Supposing he's late? What shall we do?
What if I failed the exam? I wouldn't get another chance.

b) *provided (that)/as long as . . .*
Provided that everyone makes a serious effort, we'll be able to control pollution.
You'll pass the exam as long as you work hard.

c) *If only/I wish . . .* (Regret)
If only I were tall. (= I'm not tall.)
I wish you could stay longer. (= You can't stay longer.)
If only I hadn't caught flu. (= I *did* catch flu.)
I wish he would stop talking. (= He keeps on talking and I can't make him stop.)

NOTE: *I wish I would . . .* is not possible. For wishes about our personal future, we say *I wish I could . . .*, or *I hope I'll . . .*

d) *in case . . .* (Precaution)
You should take a towel in case you go swimming.
(= Be prepared for the possibility)
Compare:
You should take a towel if you go swimming.

NOTE: If the verb in the main clause is in a past tense, *in case* is followed by the past simple.
He'd given them his home phone number in case they needed to contact him urgently.

20 Write sensible conditional sentences based on the information given.
EXAMPLE: Giles will probably be late.
If Giles is late, we'll go without him.

1 I hope I'll pass my driving test.
2 Have you finished the letter?
3 I think it's going to rain.
4 Don't touch the iron!
5 We'll probably get hungry during the journey.
6 He's determined to give up smoking.
7 I'm thinking of changing my job.
8 I expect John will phone while I'm out.

21 In pairs, ask and answer the following questions:
What would you do if . . .
you won £1 million?
you were shipwrecked on a desert island?
you were trapped in a lift?
you were elected President of your country?
you didn't have to work/go to school?
you saw a flying saucer land?
you saw someone stealing food in a supermarket?
you could choose any job you wanted?

22 Read the following passage.
Last year, Lucy had a disastrous holiday. She was delayed in a traffic jam and missed her flight to Tremolo. As a result, she had to wait at the airport for seven hours. She arrived in Tremolo so late that she missed the last bus to her hotel, and she had to take an expensive taxi ride. She was so tired the next day that she fell asleep in the sun and got badly burnt. The sea was rough so she couldn't go swimming. She wanted to try windsurfing, but the wind was too strong. She didn't like the food because it was so greasy. There weren't any young people in her hotel, so she didn't make any friends. She was planning to go on a sightseeing tour one day, but she changed her mind because it was pouring with rain. She enjoyed the disco on the last evening, and she wanted to dance all night, but she had to leave early in the morning so she went to bed. Fortunately the music was so loud that she couldn't possibly oversleep. This year Lucy thinks she'll stay at home!
Make sentences using Type 3 conditionals.
EXAMPLE: *If she hadn't been delayed in a traffic jam, she wouldn't have missed her flight.*

23 Put the verbs in brackets in the correct conditional form.

1 I wish I (not eat) so much last night.
2 If I (be) you, I (not go) to work tomorrow.
3 As long as nothing (go) wrong, he (fly) home tonight.
4 What (happen) if they (win) the next election?
5 If she (tell) the truth ten years ago, she (not go) to prison.
6 Supposing you (see) a ghost, what you (do)?
7 If you (wait) a moment, I (call) the manager.
8 They (not hear) us unless we (shout) louder.
9 He (buy) a map of the city in case he (get) lost.
10 If we (have) wings, we (not need) aeroplanes.

MODALS

The following verbs are **modal auxiliaries:**
can, could, may, might, shall, should, ought, will, would, must, need

a) There is no -s ending in the third person singular.
b) Questions and negatives are formed without *do*.
c) They are followed by the infinitive without *to* (except *ought*).
d) They have no infinitive or participle forms. Other verbs must be used.

He said he *would be able to* get here before ten.
You need to *know how to* do accounts. = **can**

Will you *let* me borrow your car?
We *were allowed to* buy 200 duty free cigarrettes. = **may**

She *had to* leave by midnight.
If you miss the bus, you'*ll have to* walk home. = **must**

can is used:

a) to express ability (= *be able to, know how to*).
Can you speak Spanish?

b) to express permission (= *be allowed to*).
Can I take photographs?
No, I'm afraid you can't. (Prohibition)

c) to make deductions (see **must**).
He can't be the same person.
They can't have sold the painting.
Whatever can have happened?
Negative for statements

d) to make offers.
Can I buy you a drink?

e) to make requests.
Can you tell me how long the course lasts?

could is used:

a) to express general ability in the past.
He could read when he was two.

NOTE: For particular ability in the past, *was able to* or *managed to* are used.
Were you able to / *Did you manage to* *get the tickets?*

NOT: *Could you get the tickets?* (= Request)
couldn't may be used for both particular and general ability.

b) to ask permission (more formal than **can**).
Could I make a phone call?
Yes, of course you can.

c) to express possibility.
It could be worth a lot of money.
You could have been killed.

d) to make requests.
Could you tell me the time?

e) to give advice or make suggestions.
You could talk to your boss about the problem.

may is used:

a) to express permission (more formal than *can*).
May I sit down? Of course you may.
You may not talk during the examination. (Prohibition)

b) to express possibility.
He may be telling the truth.
The painting may have been stolen.

might is used:

a) to ask permission (very formal).
Might I turn on the television?

b) to express remote possibility.
He might lose his job.
I might have dropped my keys on the bus.

shall is used:

a) to make offers.
Shall I do the washing-up?

b) to make suggestions.
Shall we meet again tomorrow?

should is used:

a) to give advice.
You shouldn't worry so much.

b) to express obligation or criticism.
Everyone should see a dentist regularly.
He shouldn't have said the bag was made of leather.

c) in Type 1 **conditional** clauses (see p. 176).
If you should see James, ask him to phone me.

d) in place of *would* in the first person.
I shouldn't say anything, if I were you.
I should like to take this opportunity to say thank you.

ought to is used:

a) to give advice.
You ought to take more exercise.

b) to express obligation or criticism.
He ought to visit his parents more often.
You ought to have worn a tie.

will is used:

a) in the **future simple** (see p. 174).

b) to express willingness: offers and requests.
If you'll clear the table, I'll do the washing-up.
Will you help me carry the luggage?

would is used:

a) in **conditional** sentences (see p. 176).

b) to express willingness: requests.
Would you close the window, please?
I should be grateful if you would send me an application form.

c) to describe repeated actions in the past.
When we came out of the cinema, we would buy fish and chips to eat on the way home.

must is used:

a) to express obligation or necessity (= *have (got) to, need to*).
We must get onto the plane.

NOTE: 1 *mustn't* = strong prohibition
You mustn't lean out of the window.

2 For absence of obligation or necessity, we use *don't have to, don't need to, needn't.*
As tomorrow is Sunday, I needn't get up early.

When talking about the past:
I *needn't have* booked a table because the restaurant was almost empty. = It wasn't necessary but I *did*.
He *didn't need to* look up the number because he knew it by heart. = It wasn't necessary so he *didn't*.

b) to make deductions.
She must be eighteen.

24 Using the correct form of the modal verb in capitals, rewrite the sentences so that the meaning is almost identical.

EXAMPLE: I'm sure he's forgotten something. MUST
He must have forgotten something.

1	You are not allowed to walk on the grass.	MAY
2	Please stop talking.	COULD
3	Do you have to leave so soon?	MUST
4	I don't believe it's ten o'clock.	CAN
5	You'd better call the police.	SHOULD
6	Perhaps he's lost the address.	MIGHT
7	Why don't you go to the library?	COULD
8	Please sit down.	WILL
9	He apologised, but it wasn't necessary.	NEED
10	I was wrong to say it was your fault.	SHOULD
11	He's bound to have heard the news.	MUST
12	He wasn't able to lift the piano.	COULD
13	It's forbidden to enter the building.	CAN
14	It's just possible that the phone is out of order.	MIGHT
15	He used to smoke his pipe in the evenings.	WOULD
16	Let me help you.	CAN
17	She doesn't work hard enough.	OUGHT
18	I insist that you do as I say.	MUST
19	We didn't call the doctor because it wasn't necessary.	NEED
20	Do you know how to make an omelette?	CAN
21	Why don't we go for a walk?	SHALL
22	Perhaps there's been an accident.	COULD
23	You're not allowed to look.	MUST
24	It's possible that she's visiting her parents.	MAY
25	You are not obliged to say anything.	NEED
26	You can tell he's making a lot of money.	MUST
27	I wish I'd tried harder.	OUGHT
28	Do you mind if I sit here?	MIGHT

THE PASSIVE

The **passive** is formed with the appropriate form of *to be* + past participle.

Nescafé is drunk in most countries. — Present simple
More people are being arrested for speeding every day. — Present continuous
The painting has been removed. — Present perfect
Television was invented in 1926. — Past simple
He stayed with friends while his house was being redecorated. — Past continuous
He said the old man had been knocked down. — Past perfect
In the future, the Sahara will be used as farmland. — Future simple
He didn't expect to be given a letter. — Infinitive
Living units can be produced very quickly. — Infinitive without *to*
The car is likely to have been stolen. — Perfect infinitive
If you cross the road without looking, you risk being run over. — Gerund
The thief regretted having being caught. — Perfect gerund

The **passive** is used:

a) when the person doing the action (the agent) is unknown, or needn't be specified. In such cases, the agent isn't mentioned in the passive.

The painting has been removed. = Someone has removed the painting.
Nescafé is drunk in most countries. = People drink Nescafé in most countries.

If a sentence contains both a direct and an indirect object, e.g.

He gave me the book.

then two passive forms are possible.

I was given the book.
The book was given to me.

(For a list of verbs which take two objects, see **prepositions** p. 184).

b) to emphasise the action rather than the agent. If the agent is mentioned, it is preceded by *by*.

Television was invented in 1926 (by John Logie Baird).

NOTE: If the action is done by something rather than someone, other prepositions may be used, e.g. *with* to express instrument.

The door can be locked with this key.

c) after the introductory *it* with certain verbs, e.g. *believe, consider, expect, feel, find, know, say, think, understand*

It's said that the old city lies underwater.
It's thought that he was very rich.

BUT: a passive + infinitive construction is even more common.

The old city is said to lie underwater.
He's thought to have been very rich.

NOTE: *make, see, hear* and *help* in the passive are followed by *to* + infinitive.

I was made to feel uncomfortable.
She was seen to leave the building.
I was helped to push the car.
(See **infinitives** on next page for comparison)

The past participle is often used with a passive sense as an adjective (see **participles** p. 183).

He's worried about his family.

25 Put the verbs in brackets into the correct form of the passive.

1 I can't lend you my jacket because it (clean).
2 You (not allow) to park here.
3 The lights must (turn out) by the last person to leave.
4 I wish I (teach) to swim when I was younger.
5 The safety pin (invent) by an American.
6 Many people think nurses ought (pay) more.
7 The house (not sell) yet.
8 When the teacher arrived, the room (use) by another class.
9 Should you lose your traveller's cheques, they (replace) by your bank.
10 He doesn't mind (interrupt) while he's working.
11 The letter seemed (write) by a child.
12 Venice (say) to be the most beautiful city in the world.

26 Put the following sentences into the passive.

1 Bad weather has delayed the trains.
2 Someone had informed the police about the planned robbery.
3 People believe the contract is worth £1 million.
4 Charles Dickens wrote *Bleak House*.
5 Someone has stolen my watch!
6 You can make some delicious meals with cheese and eggs.
7 A piece of string held up his trousers.
8 He broke his leg in a skiing accident.
9 Jack is taking Sandra out for a ride in his new car.
10 While we are away, the neighbours will water our plants.
11 People play football in most countries of the world.
12 You have to see it to believe it.

GERUNDS AND INFINITIVES

The **gerund** has the same form as the present participle (-ING). The gerund can be replaced by a noun or pronoun. It is used:

a) after the following verbs:

avoid	*keep* (persist in)
consider (think about)	*mind* (object to)
delay	*miss*
deny	*prevent*
dislike	*regret*
enjoy	*risk*
finish	*stop* (cease)
imagine	*suggest*
include	
involve	

She keeps interfering.
I enjoy playing tennis.
Would you mind opening the window?
He suggested going to the cinema.

b) after **prepositions** (see p. 184) and **compound verbs** (see p. 183).

How about inviting her out for a drink?
He's good at talking to people.
I'm used to working in a team. (See **used to** + Noun/-ING, p. 189).
You can't blame me for being late.
After leaving Fiji, they sailed to Papua New Guinea.
She carried on dancing until midnight.

c) as the subject of the sentence.

Fishing is more relaxing than tennis.
No smoking.

d) after the following expressions

can't stand	*It's (not) worth . .*
can't help.	*It's no good/use . . .*

I can't stand swimming in cold water.
The film isn't worth seeing.
It's no use trying to make her change her mind.

NOTE: The perfect gerund is formed with *having* + past participle.

The manager apologised for having charged us too much.

The passive gerund is formed with *being/having been* + past participle.

If you cross the road without looking, you risk being run over.
The only thing the thief regretted was having been caught!

27 Complete the following sentences with a suitable gerund construction.

1 It's hot in here – do you mind . . . ?
2 I'm annoyed with John. He never stops . . .
3 Can you ask someone else? I'm not very keen on . . .
4 There's a transport strike, so it's no use . . .
5 Do you think politicians enjoy . . . ?
6 She's only just moved to London, and she's not used to . . .
7 Flying is more expensive than . . .
8 As he was hungry, I suggested . . .
9 You can get an application form by . . .
10 He's on holiday soon, and he's looking forward to . . .

The **infinitive** is used:

a) after the following verbs:

i) without an object

afford	*hope*	*plan*
agree	*learn*	*promise*
appear	*manage*	*refuse*
decide	*offer*	*seem*
happen		

He promised to write.

ii) with an object

advise	*forbid*	*remind*
allow	*invite*	*teach*
encourage	*order*	*tell*
force	*persuade*	*warn*

She told him to ask at the baker's.

iii) either with or without an object

ask	*mean* (intend)
expect	*want*
help	*wish*
intend	*would like*

I asked him to sit down.
He asked to leave.

b) after auxiliary verbs (see **modals**, p. 177).

+ *to*, e.g. *have to, need to, ought to, used to* (see **used to** + infinitive, p. 189).

You have to have a valid passport.

without *to*, e.g. *will, should, can, must*

You should be more careful.

c) without *to* after verbs of perception to describe complete actions (see also **participles**, p. 183).

He saw her leave the building.

BUT: *She was seen to leave the building.* (see **passive**, on previous page).

d) without *to* after *make, let, had better, would rather/sooner.*

It made me feel uncomfortable.
They let you take in 200 cigarettes.
You'd better call the doctor.
I'd rather not take the car to work.

NOTE: 1 In the **passive** (see p. 179), *make* is followed by *to* + infinitive.
I was made to feel uncomfortable.

2 *let* has no passive form. Another verb must be used.
You are allowed to take in 200 cigarettes.

3 *help* can also be used without *to*.
The policeman helped me (to) push the car.

e) after *to be*

i) to give orders.
The children are to go to bed early.

ii) to describe plans or arrangements.
The Prime Minister is to fly to Washington tomorrow.

f) as the subject of the sentence.
To find cheap office-space in the centre of town is almost impossible.

This construction is quite formal, and the introductory *it* is more commonly used.
It's almost impossible to find cheap office-space in the centre of town.

NOTE: The gerund is more often used at the beginning of the sentence than the infinitive (see **gerunds**, p. 180).

g) to express purpose.
They planted trees to prevent landslides.

in order (not) to and *so as (not) to* are used to emphasise the idea of purpose.
They modernised the alarm system in order to give better warning of floods.

h)

i) after the following adjectives:

alarmed	*excited*	*puzzled*
amazed	*fascinated*	*sad*
angry	*glad*	*shocked*
anxious	*happy*	*sorry*
astonished	*pleased*	*surprised*
disappointed	*proud*	*upset*
expensive	*hard*	*(un)likely*
cheap	*difficult*	*(im)possible*
easy	*sure*	*important*
simple	*certain*	*interesting*

He was shocked to hear of the accident.
Pleased to meet you.
Is it difficult to get to your flat?
It's simple to organise a package holiday.

ii) after *too* + adjective/adverb, and *enough*.
The case was too heavy (for me) to carry.
The man she married was old enough to be her father.

NOTE: The perfect infinitive is formed with *have* + past participle.
He shouldn't have said the bag was made of leather – it was plastic.
She was proud to have won the award.

The passive infinitive is formed with *be/have been* + past participle
Not expecting any mail, he was surprised to be given a letter.
The car is likely to have been stolen.

Certain verbs are followed by either the **gerund** or the **infinitive**, depending on the meaning.

a) *love, like, prefer, hate, can't bear*
No one likes paying bills. (= general attitude)
I like to pay my bills promptly. (= I think it's a good thing to do.)
I can't bear watching football on TV. (= general attitude)

I can't bear to watch in case they lose the match.
(= specific reaction expressing anxiety)

b) *remember, forget*
I remember seeing the old man last Friday.
I'll never forget meeting Paul McCartney.

Previous action or event ← REMEMBER / FORGET

Did you remember to cancel the milk?
Don't forget to write to me!

REMEMBER / FORGET → subsequent action or event

c) *regret*
I regret telling him about the plan –
I thought he could keep a secret.

Previous action or event ← REGRET

I regret to tell you that the flight is fully booked.

REGRET
↓
Present situation

d) *try*
He tried counting sheep, but he couldn't get to sleep.
(= experiment, not difficult)
Many people have tried to climb Mount Everest, but few have succeeded. (= attempt, difficult)

e) *stop*
He stopped eating. (= He didn't eat any more.)
He stopped to eat. (= He stopped *doing* something *in order to* eat.)
In this case, the action that has ceased is understood, and the infinitive is used to express purpose (see **infinitives,** previous page).

f) *start, begin*
In many cases, either the infinitive or the gerund may be used after these verbs without any difference in meaning. However, the infinitive should be used:

i) in some cases for reasons of style.
It started raining. / to rain. BUT *It's starting to rain.*

ii) after verbs not normally used in continuous forms (see **present simple,** p. 170).
I began to understand what he was talking about.

g) *need, want*
The gerund is often used instead of the passive infinitive after these verbs.

The roof *needs*/*wants* *repairing.* =

The roof *needs*/*wants* *to be repaired.*

28 Pat and Mike are making plans for their holidays. They are looking at the holiday advertisements in the paper.

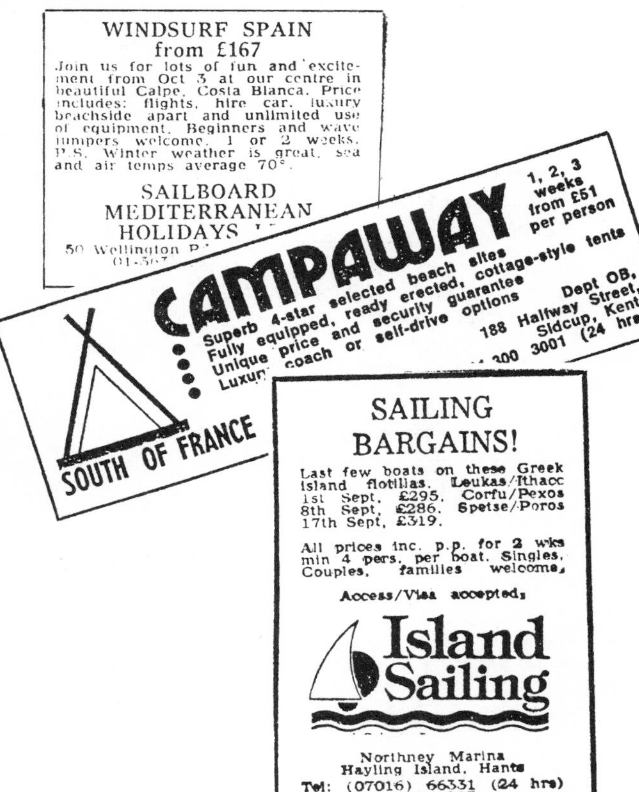

Read the dialogue in pairs.

MIKE: What do you feel like doing this summer?
PAT: I don't mind. Have you got any ideas?
MIKE: Do you like sailing?
PAT: I love sailing.
MIKE: Then why don't we go sailing in the Greek Islands?
PAT: That sounds great – I'd love to!

Now make similar dialogues based on the advertisements.

29 Janet and Paul are discussing what they are going to do this evening. Read the dialogue in pairs.

JANET: How about going dancing this evening?
PAUL: You know I can't stand dancing.
JANET: Well, what would you like to do, then?
PAUL: I'd sooner stay at home and do some decorating.
JANET: Do some decorating? You can't do that all evening. I was looking forward to going out somewhere.

Now act out similar dialogues in pairs. Try and find a partner who shares your interests! Make your own suggestions, or use the ideas below:

go/theatre – write/letters
visit/Peter – watch TV
go/Chinese restaurant – do/work
see/new James Bond film – do/washing

30 Put the verbs in brackets into the correct form of the gerund or the infinitive.

Seventy days after (leave) the USA, David Willoughby, the lone yachtsman, arrives in Plymouth today, having succeeded in (cross) the Atlantic in a boat measuring less than 3 metres in length. He was hoping (reach) port yesterday, but the lack of wind made him (put off) (sail) into harbour until this morning. Pleasure boats waiting for him off Plymouth offered (tow) him, but he prefer (finish) his voyage single-handed. Thousands of people are already waiting on the quayside (see) their hero (step) onto dry land.

When we spoke to David yesterday, he seemed (hesitate) before (answer) our questions, as if he wasn't used to (speak). In fact, his radio had broken down after three days at sea, and he missed (hear) the human voice. But he soon learned (accept) his solitude, and he managed (keep) (go) despite very difficult conditions. He had (steer) his boat for at least sixteen hours a day, and at times he was almost too exhausted (continue). He tried (sing) Beatles' songs (keep) himself awake, and after a couple of weeks, he began (hear) strange noises and (suffer) from nightmares. A passing ship gave him some bread, but this appears (be) the only fresh food he ate during the voyage. A few days before (reach) Plymouth, he only just avoided (collide) with a fishing-boat which had forgotten (post) a look-out on the bridge. As he went by, he remembers (look) with astonishment through the port-hole and (see) the crew calmly eating their dinner. The sight of real food made him (feel) very hungry, but he couldn't help (laugh).

He's obviously very glad (be) home, but his adventures have encouraged him (plan) something even more difficult. He now intends (sail) round the world!

In pairs, act out the conversation which took place between the reporter and David Willoughby.

PARTICIPLES

The **present participle** (-ING) is active in meaning.
The **past participle** (-ED) is passive in meaning.

The **present participle** is used:

a) after verbs of perception to describe incomplete actions (see also **infinitives,** p. 180)

He watched the boys playing football all afternoon.

b) after *come* and *go* with verbs for leisure activities.

Why don't you come dancing with us?
I hardly ever go swimming.

Both **present** and **past participles** are used:

a) as adjectives.

a leaking roof — *broken windows*
fascinating ruins — *He was excited.*

b) in participle clauses, in place of subject + verb.

It's a box containing little sticks of wood. (= It's a box which contains . . .)
It's a 3D image produced by a laser. (= It's a 3D image which is produced . . .)
Not expecting any mail, Bryson was surprised to be given a letter.
(REASON = As he wasn't expecting any mail, . . .)
Looking at the envelope, he was astonished to see his name.
(TIME = When he looked at the envelope, . . .)

31 Put the verbs in brackets into the present participle or the infinitive.

I was standing at the hotel window, listening to somebody (talk) on the radio, when suddenly I saw two men (run) out of the bank opposite, (get) into a car, and (drive) off. Then I heard someone (fire) a single shot. The street was busy, and no-one seemed to notice a woman (fall) to the pavement. I ran out of the hotel and across the road. The woman was unconscious, but I could feel her heart (beat). I could already hear police cars (approach), and in seconds, the street was filled with uniformed officers. One of them noticed me (stand) beside the injured woman. Before I could speak, I felt a heavy hand (grasp) my shoulder, and I heard a voice (say), 'You're under arrest.' A small crowd of curious passers-by watched the police (handcuff) me and (lead) me away.

32 Complete the following sentences with a participle ending in -ING or -ED formed from the word in capital letters at the end of the sentence.

1 It's by far the most ________ film I've ever seen. EXCITE
2 I was quite ________ by your behaviour at the party last night. SHOCK
3 It's not only well-written but also extremely ________. INTEREST
4 She has such a ________ smile that I was prepared to believe her. CHARM
5 My parents get ________ if I'm not home by midnight. WORRY
6 I must say, I'm ________ at those two running away together! SURPRISE
7 I feel really ________ after such a lovely weekend. RELAX
8 He's well-known for his ________ stories. ENTERTAIN
9 What have you put in the soup? It tastes ________. DISGUST
10 I'm slightly ________ by his strange attitude. ANNOY

COMPOUND VERBS

We shall use the general term **'compound verbs'** to describe verbs which form combinations with adverbs or prepositions.

He put his hat on.
My mother is looking after the children.

a) The meaning of a compound verb is often very different from the meaning of the two words taken separately.

He counted on his friends. (He depended on his friends)
He counted on his fingers. (He used his fingers to count)

b) Compound verbs are often used as an informal alternative to single word verbs.

blow up = explode
put off = postpone
put up with = tolerate

c) There are four types of compound verb. It is often difficult to decide whether the verb is followed by an adverb or a preposition, so it is better to try and remember the type when you learn the meaning.

Type 1: Verbs which do not take an object.

My car *broke down* last night.
If you don't put the milk in the fridge, it'll *go off.*

Other examples of Type 1:
catch on (become popular, understand)
come round (recover consciousness)
fall through (fail to happen)
get down (descend)

go back (return)
pass out (lose consciousness)
show up (arrive)
wear off (disappear gradually)

Type 2: Verbs which take a preposition + object. Both the noun and pronoun object are placed at the end of the phrase.
I'm *looking for* Mr Jones.
He cared a great deal *about* her.

Other examples of Type 2:
ask for (request)
come across (find/meet by chance)
count on (depend on)
feel like (be in the mood for)
join in (participate in)
look through (read quickly)
run into (meet by chance)
stand for (represent, tolerate)

Type 3: Verbs which take an adverb + object.
Would you like to *try on* the jacket?
She *held out* the flowers to the passers-by.

NOTE: The *noun* object **may** be placed between the verb and the adverb.
Would you like to *try* the jacket *on?*
She *held* the flowers *out* to the passers-by.

The *pronoun* object **must** be placed between the verb and the adverb.
Would you like to *try* it *on?*
She *held* them *out* to the passers-by.

Other examples of Type 3:
fill in (complete)
give away (reveal)
pull down (demolish)
put off (postpone)
see off (say goodbye to someone at the station etc.)
think out (plan carefully)
turn down (reject, reduce brightness, volume)
wipe out (reduce to nothing)

Type 4: Verbs which take an adverb + preposition + object. Both the noun and the pronoun are placed at the end of the phrase.
The boat *stood up to* the storm extremely well.
I'm *looking forward to* it very much.

Other examples of Type 4:
back out of (withdraw from)
catch up with (draw level with)
do away with (get rid of)
get on with (make progress with)
go down with (become ill with)
make up for (compensate for)
put up with (tolerate)
run out of (exhaust supplies of)

d) When the object is a verb, the -ING form is used (see **gerunds** p. 180)
She carried on dancing until midnight.
I'm looking forward to seeing you.

33 Replace the words in italics with one of the compound verbs below.

show up	hold back
see off	do away with
pass out	wear off
go down with	run into
check in	think out
turn down	stand for

1 During the President's visit, the police had to *restrain* the crowd.
2 It was so hot that I almost *fainted.*
3 I came back from holiday with a wonderful suntan, but it soon *disappeared.*
4 Hitchcock *planned* every shot of his films very carefully.
5 As soon as they got to the airport, they *registered* their luggage.
6 Many people *become ill with* flu during the winter.
7 *By chance I met* an old school friend in town yesterday.
8 I hope he *arrives* on time just for once, as he's usually late.
9 We *said goodbye to* them at the airport.
10 The candidate was *representing* the Conservative party at the elections.
11 We had to *refuse* the invitation to the party as we were busy.
12 The Socialists want to *abolish* private schools.

34 In the following sentences, replace the words in italics with pronouns, making sure that the word order is correct.

1 You should fill in *the form* in block capitals.
2 The night before the exam, he looked through *his notes.*
3 The council decided to pull down *the old houses.*
4 He kept putting off *his visit to the dentist.*
5 The driver ran into *the old man.*
6 He turned off *the light.*
7 After years of research, scientists have managed to wipe out *the disease.*
8 Since the row over the party, it's been difficult to get on with *the neighbours.*

PREPOSITIONS

a) of time

AT a precise time
at ten o'clock, at noon (BUT *at night, at Christmas*)

ON a certain day
on Monday, on 17th December, on New Year's Eve

IN a certain period
in July, in 1984, in the afternoon, in ten days' time

BY a certain time, and usually before it
I'll finish the work by Friday. (= not later than Friday).

FROM a certain time TO a certain time
It's open from 5.30 to 11 p.m.

TILL/UNTIL a certain time (without FROM)
He worked until 5.30 (= up to 5.30).
We didn't get back until midnight. (= not before midnight).

SINCE a starting point in time until the moment of speaking
I've been working here since 1972.
I've known him since my schooldays.

FOR a certain length of time
I've been working here for ten years.
I'm going away for a fortnight next month.

DURING a certain period
He came to stay during the Easter holidays.
She worked in a bar during the summer.

NOTE: the action can last the whole period, or happen at some time within the period.

AT, ON, IN, and DURING are left out before time phrases beginning:
next, last, this, that, yesterday, today, tomorrow, each, every, all, some, any
See you next Monday.
Meetings take place every week.

b) of place

ON a line
Mombasa is on the coast of Kenya.
It's on the road to Cambridge.

ON a surface
You've got a dirty mark on your face.
It's on page 79.

IN a place considered as an area
He works in a restaurant.
Last year we visited our friends in the States.

AT a certain point or position
I live at 34, Patton Street.
Can you pick me up at the airport?

NOTE: *He's waiting at the station.* = probably in front of the station
He's waiting in the station. = inside the station building

BETWEEN two things
Helsinki is between Leningrad and Stockholm.

AMONG more than two things
He shared the money among his four children.

c) of movement

FROM a starting point
How do I get from Gatwick to Victoria?
He comes from Germany.

TO a destination
I'm going to Sweden.

INTO a place
She walked into the room.
You have to turn left into Oxford Street.

OUT OF a place
He fell out of bed.
She drove the car out of the garage.

d) of means

BY *bus/train/car/sea/boat/plane/air/bicycle* etc.

ON *foot/horseback*

BY (MEANS OF) (doing) something
You call the operator by dialling 100.

e) of instrument

WITH something
Lock the door with this key.

f) of agent

BY something or someone (see **passive** p. 179).
The laser was invented by Dr Charles Towney.

g) of purpose

FOR (doing) something
It's for opening tins.

h) indirect objects

A prepositional phrase with TO or FOR can be used instead of the indirect object after certain verbs.
He gave the book to me. = He gave me the book.
I'll make a coffee for you. = I'll make you a coffee.

TO is possible after:
give, take, bring, play, offer, send, lend, hand, pass, throw, tell, show, pay, owe

FOR is possible after:
make, get, find, keep, reserve, build, buy, order, fetch

TO or FOR **must** be used if the direct object is a pronoun.
He passed it to him.
NOT: *He passed him it.*

i) after adjectives

The following adjectives are normally followed by particular prepositions, e.g.

afraid of	*keen on*
famous for	*proud of*
good at/for	*used to*
interested in	*worried about*

j) after verbs

See **compound verbs** (p. 183).
He congratulated me on passing my driving test.

k) in certain expressions

AT	*first*	BY	*accident*	IN	*danger*
	last		*chance*		*the end*
	least		*heart*		*love*
	once		*mistake*		*time*

ON	*business*	OUT OF	*breath*
	fire		*danger*
	the other hand		*sight*
	time		*work*

35 Answer this questionnaire using suitable prepositions.

1 Where do you live?
2 Where are you at the moment?
3 When's your birthday?
4 What time do you get up in the morning?
5 How long have you been learning English?

6 How do you get to your English classes?
7 What's the quickest way of getting to the nearest railway station?
8 Where can you get a bus to the station?
9 When are banks open in your town?
10 When does it rain most in your country?
11 How do you call the police in your country?
12 Where would you like to go for your holidays?
13 When are the next Olympic Games?
14 Where exactly is Benidorm?
15 When do you think you'll have finished this book?

36 Fill in the blanks with suitable prepositions, if necessary.

Reginald Andrews, 29, was standing ________ (1) the subway platform ________ (2) 14th Street, waiting ________ (3) the train to take him back ________ (4) his flat ________ (5) Harlem. He was worried ________ (6) being ________ (7) of work. He had been unemployed ________ (8) a year, and he owed a lot of money ________ (9) the bank. But he had had an interview ________ (10) that morning ________ (11) Jamac Frozen Foods ________ (12) Manhattan, and he was hoping they would offer ________ (13) him a job.

His train pulled ________ (14) the station, and suddenly Andrew's thoughts were interrupted ________ (15) a crisis. David Schnair, 75, a blind war veteran, had fallen ________ (16) two carriages and was lying ________ (17) the rails. ________ (18) less than no time, Andrews climbed down ________ (19) the platform, and he pulled Schnair ________ (20) of danger just as the train was about to move. Neither suffered more than a few cuts and bruises.

President Reagan saw the rescue story ________ (21) a newspaper and rang Andrews to congratulate him ________ (22) his courageous action. He also made a call ________ (23) Jamac Foods' Vice President, and as a result, Andrews now has a job. What's more, all Andrews' debts have been paid ________ (24) an anonymous well-wisher. Said Andrews, 'I'm no hero, but I couldn't stand there and do nothing. I'm just grateful ________ (25) everybody who's helped me get back to work again.'

CHOOSING YOUR WORDS

ADJECTIVES/ADVERBS

a) Adverbs are usually formed by adding *-ly* to the adjective.

entire – *entirely*
proud – *proudly*
equal – *equally*
pitiful – *pitifully*

NOTE: 1 Adjectives ending in *able/ible* drop *e* and add *-ly*.

comfortable – *comfortably*
incredible – *incredibly*

2 Adjectives ending in *-y* usually change *y* to *i* and add *-ly*.

gay – *gaily*
easy – *easily*

3 The adverb for *good* is *well*.

b) The following words are both adjectives and adverbs.

fast, straight, early, late (lately = recently), hard (hardly = almost not), near (nearly = almost)

37 Agree with the statements.

EXAMPLE: Peter is a heavy smoker.
Yes, doesn't he smoke heavily!

1 Baryshnikov is a wonderful dancer.
2 Sue's a sensible driver.
3 Ben is a noisy eater.
4 They're hard workers.
5 Mike is a quick reader.
6 Pam is an imaginative cook.
7 Coe and Ovett are fast runners.
8 Maria is a good designer.
9 John Fowles is a clever writer.
10 Robert is a clear speaker.

DO/MAKE

do is used in certain idiomatic expressions, e.g.
do one's best/well/badly/good/harm/damage/a favour/business

NOTE: *do* usually refers to actions, and often to work.

make is used in certain idiomatic expressions, e.g.
make an appointment/arrangements/a complaint/a decision/friends (with)/love/a mistake/money/a noise/notes/an offer/a phone call/the beds

NOTE: *make* usually suggests creativity or construction.

38 Fill in the blanks in the following sentences using the correct form of *do* or *make*.

1 Karen is very good at ________ dresses.
2 Have you ________ the washing-up yet?
3 ________ me a favour and close the window, would you?
4 By painting the room yellow, she ________ it much more cheerful.
5 In the chalet a maid would come in to ________ the beds and ________ the housework.

6 Pollution has ________ considerable damage to the environment.
7 She ________ me a wonderful cake for my birthday.
8 I've got so much to ________ I don't know where to start!

GET

Get is used:

a) with a direct object to mean 'obtain'.
Did you get the evening paper?

b) with a direct object to mean 'receive'.
I hope you got my letter.

c) with a direct object to mean 'catch' or 'take'.
They must get the 8.15 train to arrive on time.

d) with a direct object to mean 'understand'.
I'm sorry, I didn't get what you said. Would you say it again?

e) with a direct and indirect object to mean 'fetch'.
Would you get me a glass of water, please?

f) in its past participle form with a direct object to express possession or to describe.
Have you got a light?
He's got dark hair.

g) with *to* + object to mean 'arrive in/at'.
You can get to Bristol in 1½ hours by train.

h) with adverbs or prepositions to express movement (see **compound verbs** p. 183 and **prepositions** p. 184) particularly when some difficulty is involved or when we are more concerned with the result than with the action itself.
The burglars must have got in through the window.
I managed to get home before the storm broke.

i) with an adjective or past participle to mean 'become'.
She gets annoyed when people are late.
NOTE: *go* is used for 'colour' words or for permanent change.
Her hair's gone grey.
The television keeps going wrong.
BUT: *get old/tired/ill.*

j) with a direct object + infinitive to mean 'persuade'.
He got me to take him to the station.

k) with a direct object + infinitive to mean 'cause someone to do something'.
They got someone to repair the roof.

l) with a direct object + past participle to mean 'cause something to be done' (see **have**)
I must get the car mended as soon as possible.

m) with a past participle to express the passive, either for an accidental event or for actions we cause ourselves, such as: *get married/dressed/lost.*
His leg got broken while he was playing football.
While I was getting dressed, the phone rang.

n) in its past participle form (got) + *to* + infinitive to mean 'be obliged to' (see **modals** p. 178)
I've got to go now or I'll miss the bus.

39 In the following sentences, decide which verbs can be replaced by *get* or *got.*

1 He became very excited about the Cup Final.
2 You must have your hair cut.
3 I buy my clothes from second-hand clothes shops.
4 Could you give us a bit more time please?
5 If you catch the 9.40, you'll arrive there by midday.
6 She had her windows cleaned by the boy next door.
7 He came home before everyone else.
8 She's looking very well these days.
9 I must have taken the wrong turning.
10 If you tune your radio properly, you can hear the BBC.
11 Pass the salt, please.
12 Do you think we could persuade him to give us a lift?

40 Replace the words in italics with an appropriate phrase made from *get.*

1 Would you try and *return* it to me by the end of the week.
2 How did you manage to *survive* on £30 a week?
3 Just exactly what are you *suggesting?*
4 He left his car in a no-parking zone and he *wasn't caught.*
5 She gave me the telephone number too quickly for me to *make a note of* it.
6 He was *making progress* with his French lessons before he gave up.
7 If there's a fire, *leave* the building as soon as possible.
8 She never managed to *recover from* her illness.
9 The phone was out of order and I didn't *make contact* with him.
10 We must try and *meet* one of these days for a meal.

HAVE

have is used with a direct object + past participle to mean 'cause something to be done'. This 'causative' use of *have* is similar to the more colloquial construction with **get**.

STRUCTURE REVIEW

41 Complete the following sentences using the correct form of *have* and the past participle of the verb in capitals.

EXAMPLE: He writes his reports in English, and then . . . . into French. TRANSLATE
He writes his reports in English, and then has them translated into French.

1 I need to . . . . a passport photo . . . . . . TAKE
2 Your hair looks lovely! When did you . . . .? CUT
3 The car is in the garage because I . . . . SERVICE
4 Your shoes are very down-at-heel. You ought to . . . . MEND
5 I . . . . my eyes . . . . six months ago. TEST
6 We . . . . a new cooker . . . . tomorrow. DELIVER
7 I don't think they . . . . the windows . . . . for years. CLEAN
8 I wish I . . . . the roof . . . . last year. REPAIR

SO/SUCH

so + adjective
such (a) + (adjective) noun } are used to express emphasis

She's so houseproud. (Adjective)
She's such a kind person. (Adjective + countable noun)
He talks such nonsense. (Uncountable noun)

42 Two friends are discussing people at a party.
EXAMPLE: Peter/boring man
Peter is such a boring man!
Actually, he isn't usually so boring.

Make similar exchanges in pairs.
Anna/shy girl
Tom/serious person
Jill/sympathetic listener
David/well-behaved child
Linda/sensible woman
Simon/quiet man

TELL/SAY

tell is used:

a) to mean 'narrate'.
He's good at telling jokes.
He told us about his work.

b) to mean 'inform'.
Can you tell me how to get to Piccadilly Circus?

c) with *how to* + infinitive to mean 'explain'.
She told him how to make a Christmas pudding.

d) to report information in indirect statements.
He told her (that) it was five o'clock.
He told her what the time was.

e) to report orders in indirect commands (with *to* + infinitive)
He told him to go home.

NOTE: 1 *Say* is normally used in preference to *tell* as a reporting verb for direct speech.
2 *Tell* is always followed by an indirect object except in certain expressions where it may be left out, such as: *to tell the truth/a lie/the time/a story*
She's only three, but she can tell the time.
BUT: *Can you tell me the time?*

say is used:
to report statements in direct or indirect speech.
She said, 'I'm cold'.
She said (that) she was cold.

NOTE: *say* is normally used without an indirect object. When the object is used, *say* is followed by *to.*
She said to me that she was cold.
However *tell* is used in preference to *say to* in indirect speech.
She told me that she was cold.

43 Fill in the blanks with *say* or *tell.*
'Excuse me, madam,' ______ (1) the policeman, 'Could you ______ (2) me why you're driving so fast?' I just didn't know what to ______ (3).
'I'm sorry, what did you ______ (4), officer?' I replied innocently.
'You were driving at 50 mph in a 30 mph area. Can you ______ (5) me why?' he repeated slowly.
I ______ (6), 'I'm in a hurry to see my father who's been taken ill and is in the Sloane hospital.'
'Are you ______ (7) me the truth, madam?' he asked.
'Why do you ______ (8) that?' I replied. I had never ______ (9) a lie in my life and I was nervous.
'Because the Sloane hospital is in the opposite direction, madam. Now, perhaps you'd like to ______ (10) me your name and address . . .'

USED TO + INFINITIVE/USED TO + NOUN/-ING

used to + infinitive is used:
to describe a state or habitual action in the past.
The school-leaving age used to be 14. Now it's 16.
There are two negative and question forms:

He *didn't use* / *usedn't* *to be so careless when he was at school.*

Did you use / *Used you* *to play the piano?*

NOTE: *Used to* + infinitive can be seen as a parallel to the present simple for describing a state or habitual action (see **present simple** p. 170)

Used to + noun/-ING is used:

to mean 'accustomed to', and operates as adjective + preposition.

I'm used to working outdoors, since I once worked as a gardener.
When he started work, he wasn't used to getting up early.

NOTE: *get used to* means 'become used to' (see **get** p. 187)
I'd never driven on the left before, but I soon got used to it.

44 Put the verbs in brackets into the correct form (infinitive or -ING).

1 I don't think I'll ever get used to (drink) tea with my meals.
2 Did you use to (do) much sport when you were at school?
3 In the old days, there used to (be) much less traffic on the roads.
4 She used to (smoke) far too much, but she's given up now.
5 Was he used to (play) in front of an audience? He sounded very nervous.
6 People in the USA are used to (drive) long distances.
7 In the 1950s, people used to (go) to the cinema more often than they do today.
8 Sorry I'm late – I'm just not used to (take) the bus to get to work.
9 We usedn't to (spend) our holidays abroad.
10 He never got used to (live) in the city.

UNIT 1

A: Language Practice 4

ASSISTANT: Can I help you, madam?
WOMAN: Yes, I'm looking for something to wear in the summer.
ASSISTANT: Yes, of course. These are our lightweight jackets. What size do you take?
WOMAN: Er – size ten, I think. Oh, this one's lovely. Can I try it on?
ASSISTANT: Yes, of course. You're wearing rather a thick sweater. Do you want to keep it on?
WOMAN: Er – I'm not sure.
ASSISTANT: Well, it *is* meant to be a summer jacket. Why don't you take it off?
WOMAN: Yes, perhaps you're right.
ASSISTANT: Here we are. Let me help you put it on.
WOMAN: Thank you.
ASSISTANT: Yes, it *does* suit you! It goes with your trousers.
WOMAN: But it's much too tight. It really doesn't fit me.
ASSISTANT: Oh, don't worry. It'll be perfect once you've worn it a few times.
WOMAN: How can I wear it a few times if I can't even get it on? Have you got it in a larger size?
ASSISTANT: I don't think so.
WOMAN: Well, this one's no good. It's far too small. Oh, it's just my luck.
ASSISTANT: Never mind, madam. How about this one?

D: Listening Activity

And thanks for the news, Jack. Weather tomorrow should be mainly sunny with some cloud towards the end of the day. This is Island Radio, I'm Johnny Sanders, all the way through to midnight, and if you've just tuned in, you're listening to Night Talk. Give us a ring on 580 0929 if you've got something on your mind, and we'll put you through to Eve Scott, your very own Night Talk counsellor. Now, let's talk to our next caller, Annie, from Portsmouth.
ANNIE: Hallo! Is that Johnny Sanders?
JOHNNY: It certainly is. Go ahead with your question.
ANNIE: Well . . . er . . . it's a bit difficult on the telephone, but . . .
EVE: Hallo, Eve Scott here. Just relax, Annie, and tell us what's on your mind.
ANNIE: Well, I've just left school, and I'm living with my parents. I've got this boyfriend who's a musician and who wants me to go to America with him, and I'm not sure what to do. You see, I'm very fond of my parents, but we're always arguing, – and I think it would be a good opportunity to move away from home and make my life on my own.
EVE: America's a long way from home, isn't it?
ANNIE: Yes, I know, but I've always lived at home, you know, I've never been to college, and I need a bit more personal freedom.
EVE: I see, and what do your parents think about all this?
ANNIE: My mum thinks I'm too young. As for my Dad, I can't even bring the subject up. He's trying to stop me seeing Geoff now – he's my boyfriend. He's very talented, actually, but Dad says he's a hippie and lazy and all that, and not good enough for his daughter, you know. He even tries to make me come home by eleven o'clock when I go out in the evenings.
EVE: How old are you, Annie?
ANNIE: I'm nineteen.
EVE: And Geoff?
ANNIE: Twenty-four.
EVE: And if you go to America, what will you do there?
EVE: Well, Geoff thinks he's got a job. He met some musicians from the States last year when they were over here on holiday. They've stayed in touch, and they've invited him and his friend Mark to join a band they're forming.
EVE: Yes, but what will *you* do?
ANNIE: Well, I'll be with Geoff, and perhaps I'll get a job as a secretary, because I work in an office at the moment. But I'm a bit shy really, and I'm not very good at interviews. I wouldn't mind looking after kids, or something like that.
EVE: What's your job like at the moment?
ANNIE: The boss is very encouraging, and she's offered me promotion in a year or so. But I can't stand the girls I'm working with – they keep gossiping and talking about me behind my back. And I don't really want to stay, because I don't think I've done very much with my life so far. I'd like to make a change, see a bit of the world, you know.
EVE: So why don't you go, then?
ANNIE: Well, I suppose I'm hesitating because I don't want to hurt my parents. I mean, they think the whole thing is completely immoral, quite apart from their dislike of Geoff. My Dad's a bit quick-tempered and my Mum's always so anxious about me, but they're all right, I suppose. After all, they *are* my parents. I'm scared to make the break and leave all my friends. And I'm worried because I think that Mark's a bad influence on Geoff. He's rather irresponsible, and when the two of them are together, they go a bit wild. I don't trust him.
EVE: Have you talked to anyone else about this problem?
ANNIE: Well, there's a neighbour, Mrs Spencer, she's very sympathetic. She thinks I should go to college to train as a teacher for young children. She always listens to my problems when I can't talk to anyone else. But I think her son, Jim, fancies me a bit, so maybe she just wants me to settle down with him, I don't know. He's training to be an accountant, so he's got a degree and he's quite good-looking, I suppose, but . . .
EVE: . . . not your type?
ANNIE: Well, no, not really. He's too cautious.
EVE: Anyone else?
ANNIE: My gran, she's such a kind person, but she's a bit old-fashioned. Oh, and my best friend, Joan. She says I'm stupid to go to America. But I think that's because she's envious – you see, she quite likes Mark . . .
EVE: Ooh, It all sounds very complicated, Annie.
JOHNNY: Thanks for calling, Annie, and stay with us, we're coming back to you after the commercial break. (*Music fade*)

D: Reading Aloud see p. 18

D: Role Play—New information

(*Music fade*)

JOHNNY: Hallo, Annie, are you still there?
ANNIE: Yes, I am.
EVE: Well, Annie, you've got quite a few decisions to make, haven't you?
ANNIE: Yes, I know.
EVE: But you sound like a sensible person, and I'm very optimistic that things'll turn out all right, even though you might not think so immediately. I can't really suggest a solution to all your problems, but I can help you to ask yourself a few more questions. For example, is Geoff really the right person for you? It's such a big step to go to the States with him – are you sure you can depend on him? And even if he stays with you, living with someone is not at all easy, you know . . .
ANNIE: No, I suppose not.

EVE: And you say you like children. One good test of your partner is to ask yourself if he is the person you want to have your children with, that is, if you see any future in the relationship. Does he like children?

ANNIE: (*laughing*) No, he hates them.

EVE: Well, that's not a very good start, is it? Oh, well, he's probably just saying that. I think you should let Geoff go to America and tell him that you'll join him in, say, six months. At least that'll give you time to find out if you still feel the same way about each other. Meanwhile, talk to your boss – she sounds a very reasonable sort of person – she might suggest that you move to another office while you wait for promotion. Save your money, not just for the airfare to the States, but also for a flat somewhere. Maybe you could share with your best friend. And you could get some brochures about teacher training colleges and see if teaching might be a good idea. At least that way you'd be able to leave home.

ANNIE: That's true.

EVE: You've got your whole life in front of you, Annie, and you must open your eyes to all the opportunities that might occur in the future, and not just think about Geoff and America. I *do* appreciate the problems with your mother and father – but their restrictions on you are really only their way of showing they care for you. I think you should try and talk to them again. If you tell them about your plans, and not just a few vague ideas, they might respect your determination and personal freedom. I must admit I don't think your Dad should try and make you come home by eleven every time you go out . . . Is that any help to you, Annie?

ANNIE: Well, yes, that's very good of you. I must think it all over, talk to someone about it . . .

EVE: How about Mrs Spencer?

ANNIE: (*laughing*) Yes, that's an idea. Thanks. Bye.

JOHNNY: Thanks for calling, Annie. Is there anyone else on the line? 580 0929 is the number to call . . . (*Fade*)

Exam Practice

Paper 4 Listening Comprehension

For this part of the test you are going to hear someone talking to an official at the airport. Look at questions 1–9 in your book. For questions 1–6 fill in the form with the information you hear. For questions 7–9 you should tick one of the boxes.

(*At Heathrow airport*)

TAIT: Excuse me, can you help me? I've been waiting for half-an-hour, and my suitcase hasn't come through . . .

OFFICIAL: Now just a minute, sir. You want to report your suitcase missing?

TAIT: Yes, that's right. Everyone else has collected their baggage, but mine . . .

OFFICIAL: All right, sir. Let's take down the details. What's your name?

TAIT: Tait – Peter Tait, that's T-A-I-T.

OFFICIAL: And where have you come from?

TAIT: Toronto – we landed an hour ago.

OFFICIAL: (*Writing*) Toronto International – did you stop on the way, or was it a direct flight to London Heathrow?

TAIT: No, we stopped in Montreal.

OFFICIAL: Flight number?

TAIT: Er, just a moment – AC 865. No, no, sorry, that's the return. It was AC 866.

OFFICIAL: Right. Now you left Toronto yesterday evening – that was April 20th – at what time?

TAIT: We should have taken off at eight o'clock, but we were delayed for fifteen minutes.

OFFICIAL: I see. And what time did you arrive in London this morning?

TAIT: On time, at five past ten.

OFFICIAL: When did you last actually see your suitcase?

TAIT: Well, um . . .

OFFICIAL: For instance, did you see it being loaded onto the aircraft?

TAIT: No. No, I didn't. I suppose the last time must have been at the check-in desk.

OFFICIAL: OK. Now, let's have the details of the case itself . . . What type of suitcase was it?

TAIT: Er, it's a beige case, made of imitation leather . . .

OFFICIAL: Beige – what sort of size?

TAIT: Average, I suppose. And it has buckles over the catches.

OFFICIAL: Fine. What about the contents?

TAIT: Well, mainly clothes and toilet articles.

OFFICIAL: Mm. Can you be more specific?

TAIT: Let me see – there were two jackets, a suit, half-a-dozen shirts . . .

OFFICIAL: Go on.

TAIT: Two pairs of jeans, a couple of pullovers, and then socks and underclothes of course.

OFFICIAL: Uh huh. Any valuables? (*Fade*).

UNIT 2

A: Language Practice 3

1 'I love wandering around markets and looking in junk shops, trying to find things to add to my collection. I only buy things that I like, of course, and then only if they're not too expensive. I collect all kinds of things, I love porcelain, you know plates and cups, but if I know something's rare I'm afraid of using it in case I break it!'

2 'Last year we put in a goldfish pond for the children, and I'm very fond of the flowers and the trees, but it's my greenhouse that I'm most proud of. I keep it at a high temperature so I can grow all sorts of fruit that you can't get in the shops. Sometimes we have so much that we have to give it away to the neighbours!'

3 'I kept falling in at first and I hate getting wet, so I nearly gave up! But after a while, you learn to balance and stay upright, and now I can even do it in a high wind. It really is most exciting once you've learnt to use the sail and the water efficiently. And what's more, when you've bought the essential equipment, you put it on the roof of the car and off you go to the beach!'

4 'I know of someone who was on a business trip in America, and because he was determined not to miss an opportunity like that, he organised his timetable to arrive in certain places at just the right moment of the day in order to have the right light. I'm certainly not as enthusiastic as that but I do love wandering around, just taking whatever I find interesting. But it does get a bit expensive, so I'm trying to save money to buy my own developing equipment.'

B: Language Practice 2

(*Conversation*) . . . Well here we are, in the foyer of the Royal Hotel and all the guests are beginning to arrive for tonight's presentation of the International Entertainment Awards, probably the most important occasion in the showbusiness year. I'm going to ask one or two people which film they think will win this year's Best Film Award.

WOMAN: . . . . Without doubt, *A.D. 1999*. I've never seen such a fascinating film. The writing's excellent, brilliantly imaginative. I loved that bit when Ken-Tobi meets N2B2 again after three centuries. I mean, the look on his face! And the special effects! Absolutely stunning!

MAN: I thought *What Goes Up* was particularly funny. Maggie Philby is such a good actress. And the direction is very clever, especially that scene where she comes home, in through the back door, and they're all waiting for her to come through the front door for a surprise party. And all the characters were marvellous. Highly amusing!

MAN: I think *Two Hearts As One* will get it. All right, you've seen the story in a hundred films before, but the staging of the dance scenes is brilliant and the singing is excellent. It's really enjoyable.

WOMAN: *Western Sunset* . . . without any doubt! Oh, that music, it's wonderful, so haunting. The photography is beautiful and I thought that chap who plays the cowboy coming back to his hometown was very impressive. A wonderfully powerful film.

MAN: Oh, I loved *The Beast In Us All.* I was scared stiff, particularly that moment when he turns into the beast just as the full moon comes through the clouds. The camerawork is remarkable and the design is magnificent, it really does make you think of a deserted old house, with rats and cobwebs and ghosts and things! Very frightening!

WOMAN: I don't know. I thought *The Sicilian Connection* was very good. I mean, the acting is superb and the car chase through the streets of New York in the rush hour is great. The plot's a bit complicated but all in all, it's extremely exciting.

B: Guided Writing Activity 1

(*Music. Applause*)

MAN: Ladies and gentlemen, good evening. It's my great pleasure to be here tonight to welcome you all to the Royal Hotel on the occasion of this year's International Entertainment Awards. It's been a splendid year in the world of entertainment and tonight we celebrate the achievements of all those who worked together to produce such excellent films and plays. And in particular, of course, we're here to announce the winners of this year's awards, and I know we're all dying to hear who they are. Well, I won't go on any longer, except to say that I'm delighted to welcome Lady Gravemere who's here to read the nominations and present the awards.

(*Applause*)

LADY GRAVEMERE: Thank you Peter, and good evening, ladies and gentlemen. The first award tonight is for the best film this year, and the nominations are as follows: *A.D. 1999*, *What Goes Up*, *Two Hearts As One*, *Western Sunset*, *The Beast In Us All*, and *The Sicilian Connection*. And the winner of this year's award is . . . . . . *The Sicilian Connection*!

(*Applause. Cheers*)

Of course there were so many excellent films this year, and it was very difficult to choose the winner. But this thriller was outstanding in every respect, not only the acting and the direction but also the plot and the camerawork. The roles of hero and villain are reversed during the film as the audience's sympathy moves from Kenny, brilliantly played by John Phoenix to Mario, superbly acted by Al Dente. I particularly enjoyed the scene where the two meet by Brooklyn Bridge late one night after the failed bank robbery, neither knowing if he can trust the other. The tension continues to rise until the climax in which Kenny shows us a particularly unusual way of getting through the traffic at high speed! (*Laughter*) In conclusion, ladies and gentlemen, the judges were all agreed that this year's Best Film Award should go to this excellent film and I'd like to ask the director, Mr Paul Ritter, to come forward and receive it.

(*Applause*)

On behalf of this year's committee for the International Entertainment Awards, I'm delighted to present you with this trophy.

(*Applause*)

B: Guided Writing Activity 2

(*Applause*)

PAUL RITTER: Lady Gravemere, ladies and gentlemen, I am very pleased to be able to accept this trophy on behalf of everyone who worked on *The Sicilian Connection*, and I'd like to thank you and everyone who chose it as Best Film of the year. Speaking for all of us, we're delighted to receive this award, particularly as we all enjoyed working on the film. Personally speaking, it was a real pleasure to work with such a talented team of people, and in my opinion, the good working atmosphere is one of the reasons why the film has been so successful. Once again, thank you all.

(*Applause*)

C: Interpretation Activity

STUDENT: 'I'm a student at the university, and it's got all the sports facilities you could ever want. But I have to work quite hard, and I don't seem to have much time for physical exercise. I must admit, I certainly need to do some sport – sitting in a chair all day has made me very lazy! And I think it would help me to relax. Of course, I don't have much money for equipment.'

HOUSEWIFE: 'I'm a full-time housewife at the moment. I had my first child six months ago, but I still haven't got my figure back. So I'd like to do some sport, but the problem is that I must either take my baby with me or leave him with my mother. But she can only look after him for a couple of hours, and it takes me half an hour to get to the Sports Centre. I don't really like competitive sports – I always lost at tennis when I was at school.'

BUSINESSMAN: 'I'm the well-known case of the middle-aged businessman who's overweight, smokes too much, and whose job doesn't allow any time for regular sports. Yesterday I was playing football with my son in the garden, and I was so breathless after five minutes that I've decided to do something about it. I wouldn't mind doing something where I could meet some new people. But during the week, when I get home from work, I'm too tired to do much more than have dinner, watch TV, and go to bed.'

D: Listening Activity (a)

(*Music fade*)

PRESENTER: Hallo, and in today's programme, we'll be looking at walking holidays in Scotland and weekends for golfers, but first of all, we're continuing our series of leisurely visits to cities all over the world. Diana Smith has been to Lyon in France, talking to the Director of Tourism there. Here's her report.

SMITH: Well, I'm standing on the hill overlooking this beautiful city and beside me is the director of Tourism for the city of Lyon, Mr Philippe Duval. This certainly is a remarkable view, Mr Duval.

DUVAL: Yes, most visitors come up here when they arrive, to get a general picture of the city.

SMITH: Can you tell me something about what we're looking at?

DUVAL: Well, at the moment, we're standing beside the Basilica, which was built in 1880 and just below us is the Gothic Cathedral which is in the centre of the fascinating part of town known as the Old District. Walking in the streets down there is like going back three hundred years – you must take a look later. There are some charming little squares and alleys which you just have to visit.

SMITH: I'm told that's where the restaurants are. I've heard they have an excellent reputation.

DUVAL: Yes, as you say, there are lots of very good restaurants down there, offering either the local specialities or the dishes which have made French cooking so famous. There are also a number of more exotic restaurants, Brazilian, West Indian, North African, and so on.

SMITH: I suppose that's where the nightclubs are.

DUVAL: Yes, nightclubs with stage shows and live music, and of course, plenty of discotheques. If you like jazz, try the Hot Club every Wednesday at 9 p.m. It only costs 20 francs for a year's membership.

SMITH: What about the more serious cultural activities?

DUVAL: Well, if you mean classical music, for example, we have an opera which is over there on the far side of the town hall, just the other side of the square. And the round building over there, in the modern part of town, is the Maurice Ravel Auditorium, right by the Commercial Centre. That's the home of the Lyon Symphony Orchestra. They perform two or three times a week during a ten-week season. I think the people of Lyon are as proud of their orchestra as they are of their food.

SMITH: Lyon has its own arts festival, doesn't it?

DUVAL: Lyon has two festivals, one in June, with opera, ballet and concerts as well as plays, jazz and modern dance, and one in September which honours the work of the composer Berlioz.

SMITH: And theatre?

DUVAL: There are theatres everywhere, with some wonderful productions of the great classical plays as well as lots of experimental work. In the distance, straight ahead, you can just see the National Theatre, over there in the east of the city. But its productions are very popular and you have to book tickets a few days in advance.

SMITH: I suppose there are plenty of cinemas.

DUVAL: Of course, and if you walk from the Opera to the main square, Place Bellecour, you'll find not only the main shopping precincts but also most of the cinemas. Oh, and by the way, it's a good idea to go on Mondays because tickets are half price.

SMITH: I'd like to take home something typical from Lyon. What do you suggest?

DUVAL: Well, there's plenty of choice with food and wine, Beaujolais wine, or perhaps some sausages. And then there's silk, which has been made in Lyon for centuries. Any silk clothes would be very acceptable.

SMITH: What about sport in Lyon? What have you got to offer?

DUVAL: If you like running, there's a special track in the park. That's on the river, over there in the trees. The University campus nearby has a swimming pool as well as tennis courts. If you like watersports, sailing, canoeing and so on, you have to go to the park at Miribel, but you can't see it from here. Then there's the sports stadium over there, to the south. It's the home of Lyon football club and it also has professional basketball and tennis fixtures.

SMITH: And what about those rainy days when I just feel like spending an afternoon in a museum or a gallery?

DUVAL: The Museum of Fine Arts is just this side of the Town Hall; it has a fine collection of paintings and sculpture, and entrance is free. Then there's the Gallo-Roman Museum over here to our right, which has all the Roman treasures found in and around Lyon. The amphitheatres are magnificent. Don't forget that it is closed on Mondays and Tuesdays. It costs only 4 francs to visit.

SMITH: Well, since that's close by, I think I'll have a look at that. Thanks very much, Mr Duval.

DUVAL: My pleasure. Enjoy your stay in Lyon.

PRESENTER: That was Diana Smith giving us a taste of life in Lyon.

D: Listening Activity (c)

1 'I must say I was rather disappointed by the place. I was told that I had to go there, particularly as I don't really like the usual tourist sights, you know, churches and museums and so on. There was certainly a great deal of choice, but it's all so expensive. I mean, can you imagine a plain blue skirt costing the equivalent of £40 and of such poor quality! No, tomorrow I think I'll just sit in a café and watch the world go by. I don't ask for much, you know, just something to keep me interested. I'd rather save my money until I get home.'

2 'Wonderful! I've visited a lot of cities in Europe and I'm fascinated by this sort of thing. On this trip we've already done Nôtre Dame in Paris, and Chartres, but I saw nothing quite like this! Looking up at the fabulous ceiling and seeing the sunlight coming in through the stained glass windows, really, I was quite moved by the sight. Apparently, it was begun in the twelfth century and only finished in the fifteenth. I'm sure they took such a long time because they kept stopping to look at their work! We're off to Florence tomorrow, but I shall be sorry to leave Lyon.'

3 'Frankly, I was bored by the performance. Even though I go quite often when I'm back home – I'm a critic, you know – I do like to see what's happening in other countries when I'm on holiday. But I nearly left during the interval. I couldn't hear a word they were saying, and my French is quite good. And the scenery! In the middle of a speech, the lights would change and something would disappear from view! Everyone clapped at the end, but I think they were pleased it was over. No, tomorrow, I think I'll just visit a few museums!

4 'Parts of it I enjoyed and we did have a good dance at the end. I don't go out very much when I'm at home, but I do enjoy listening to live music. I was amused by some of the jokes the comedian told, but the dancing and singing were awful. I'd rather like to try something different tomorrow, perhaps some jazz or something. But no classical music – I just can't bear it!'

5 'After wandering around the Old District, I was too tired to do anything, although we really enjoy sightseeing, particularly when there are so many lovely old buildings to see. But it was about eight in the evening and we found a charming little place where we could sit outside. Very informal and quite relaxing. I have fairly simple tastes but the smell coming from the kitchen was fabulous. I was tempted by the seafood but I was worried that I'd regret it the next day, so I had a delicious steak. It was a bit expensive, but I suppose you have to pay for that kind of service.'

6 'Well, it's very big and you can't see everything in one afternoon. But we spent two hours there and we didn't notice the time going by. I was fascinated by some of the old portraits, although there were others which were a little too abstract and modern for my taste. Tomorrow I think we'll go to the park. Too much culture isn't good for you, you know!'

D: Reading Aloud – see page 36

Exam Practice

Paper 4 Listening Comprehension

For this part of the test you are going to hear a recorded tour of an art gallery. Look at the questions 1 to 9 in your book. For questions 1 to 6, fill in the notes with the information you hear. For questions 7 to 9, you should tick one of the boxes, A, B, C or D. You will hear the piece twice.

'. . . And now you should pass through the door to your right into the next room. Several paintings along on the right-hand side is one of the National Gallery's most famous exhibits. It was painted by Turner, perhaps England's most admired artist of the nineteenth century. He was born in 1775 and died 76 years later in 1851. The painting you are looking at is called *Rain, Steam and Speed* and was finished in 1837. The subject of the painting is a steam train, travelling at high speed and caught in a rainstorm.

Turner was above all famous for his paintings of sunsets, but clearly the subject of this painting, a steam train, is very different. In fact, it's the first major work to show one of the new sights of the nineteenth century. But it also shows Turner's fascination for colour and light which you can see in all his paintings. The new industrial age brought factories, chimneys, and the railways themselves, but it was the effects of light on the smoke and the mist which he loved. Here we see how something as ugly as a steam train is transformed by the painter into something quite beautiful by the rain, the wind, and the movement of the train. Turner usually made many sketches while watching his subjects, before finishing the painting in his studio. He obviously wasn't able to do much work outside in the weather conditions of this picture, but his studies of clouds, rain and mist were certainly very important for the final version of *Rain, Steam and Speed*.

If you leave by the door to your left, you will enter the room containing the paintings . . .'

UNIT 3

B: Listening Activity

SALLY: 435 8447
RICHARD: Hallo. Could I speak to Sally, please?
SALLY: Speaking.
RICHARD: Hallo, Sally. This is Richard.
SALLY: Hi, Richard! How are you?
RICHARD: I'm fine, thanks. How are you?
SALLY: I'm fine too. When are you coming over?
RICHARD: I'm coming the weekend after next.
SALLY: The weekend after next! That's great. How long are you going to stay?
RICHARD: About a week. Is it OK to stay with you?
SALLY: Yes, of course it's OK. My flat's enormous, and there's plenty of room.What time do you arrive in London?
RICHARD: On Saturday at lunchtime—one o'clock.
SALLY: Oh, that's a pity. I'd like to meet you at the airport, but I'm working till lunchtime . . .
RICHARD: Never mind. Is it difficult to get to your flat?
SALLY: No, it's quite easy to get to, but it's a bit complicated to explain over the phone. Look, I'll write to you giving you directions from the airport. By the way, which airport do you arrive at?
RICHARD: Erm, I think it's Gatwick. Yes, Gatwick airport.
SALLY: OK, I'll work out the best way of getting here from Gatwick, and send the letter off today.
RICHARD: Thanks a lot. I'm really looking forward to seeing you again.
SALLY: So am I! Till a week on Saturday, then. Bye.
RICHARD: Bye.

D: Listening Activity

PRESENTER . . . that was the traffic report, and from travelling by road, we move on to travelling by air. Every year, more and more people travel abroad, and more and more travel by air. But who are these people? And why are they travelling? We decided to send an Island Radio reporter to find out . . .

ANGIE: Hallo, I'm Angie Lewis, and I'm in the Terminal 3 departure lounge at Heathrow airport. I'm going to talk to some of the people waiting here. Good morning, madam. May I ask where you're travelling to?
PASSENGER 1: Yes, I'm flying to Rome.
ANGIE: To Rome? Are you Italian?
PASSENGER 1: Yes, I've been studying here, and now I'm going home.
ANGIE: What do you think of England?
PASSENGER 1: I like it very much—but I'm looking forward to some Italian pasta.
ANGIE: Yes, I'm sure you are. And you, madam. Where are you flying to?
PASSENGER 2: I'm off to Amsterdam for a few days.
ANGIE: On holiday?
PASSENGER 2: No, no—you see, I work for a publishing company, and we have connections with a publishing house in Holland, and I'm going to discuss some translations . . .
ANGIE: That's interesting. What kind of translations?
PASSENGER 2: Oh, mostly technical stuff—and some science fiction.
ANGIE: That's quite a combination! What about you?
PASSENGER 3: I'm off to New York . . .
FLIGHT ANNOUNCER: Your attention please. British Airways Flight BA 193 to New York is now ready for boarding. Will passengers please have their boarding cards ready, and proceed to Gate 17. Thank you.
ANGIE: Is that your flight?
PASSENGER 3: No, that must be the Concorde. I'm flight BA 175.
ANGIE: Why are you flying to New York?
PASSENGER 3: Well, er, I'm a journalist. An industrial correspondent. I want to find out what's happening on Wall Street—and talk to the unions. I've got to get a story for tomorrow evening.
ANGIE: Do you travel a lot?
PASSENGER 3: I suppose I do. I've just come back from Tokyo.
ANGIE: I see. Well, good luck with your story!
PASSENGER 3: Thanks.
ANGIE: Now, let me see—there's a gentleman over here with a wonderful sun tan! Where are you going, sir?
PASSENGER 4: I'm flying to Kuwait.
ANGIE: Why Kuwait?
PASSENGER 4: I'm an engineer—and I'm going out for a few months to develop an oilfield.
ANGIE: You look as though you spend a lot of time in the sun. Have you been before?
PASSENGER 4: Not to Kuwait, no. But I've spent a lot of time in the Middle East. It pays the bills you know.
ANGIE: I can imagine.
FLIGHT ANNOUNCER: Your attention please. Pakistan International Airlines Flight PK 702 to Amsterdam and Rawalpindi boarding now at Gate 11. Flight PK 702 boarding at Gate 11.
ANGIE: And here's a very happy-looking couple—where are you off to?
PASSENGER 5: We're going to the States—our son's getting married in New York tomorrow.
ANGIE: How exciting! Have you been over before?
PASSENGER 6: No, we couldn't afford it. But we've saved up for this trip, and we're going to stay for a fortnight. We can't believe it, really.
ANGIE: Well, have a wonderful time—I'm sure you will. And what about you, sir?
PASSENGER 7: Oh, I'm going to Hong Kong.
ANGIE: Are you going for a holiday?
PASSENGER 7: Well, it's not meant to be a holiday! In fact, I'm going to teach English for the British Council.
ANGIE: That should be very interesting.
PASSENGER 7: Yes, I'm looking forward to it.
ANGIE: Are you going to Hong Kong too?
PASSENGER 8: Er, no. I'm going to New York—I hope.
ANGIE: Why do you say that?
PASSENGER 8: Well, they haven't called the flight yet – and it leaves in ten minutes.
ANGIE: Why are you travelling to New York?
PASSENGER 8: I'm an actress, and I start rehearsing tomorrow for a part in a play.
ANGIE: On Broadway?
PASSENGER 8: That's right!
ANGIE: Well let's hope you don't have to wait long.
FLIGHT ANNOUNCER: Your attention please. Will all passengers for British Airways Flight BA 3 to Rome, Bahrain and Hong Kong, please proceed to Gate Number 8, Departure Flight BA 3, proceed to Gate Number 8. Thank you.
ANGIE: Good morning, sir. Where are you flying to?
PASSENGER 9: Er, I'm er to New York, actually.

ANGIE: On business?

PASSENGER 9: Yes, I'm in computers. I'd like to find out what the boys in the States are up to. Quite exciting, really, I'm flying Concorde—for the first time.

ANGIE: I'd love to do that. Wait a minute, you know the flight's been called?

PASSENGER 9: Has it? I didn't hear the announcement. Well, I'd better get moving then! Thanks for telling me!

ANGIE: It would be a pity to miss it! Madam, what about you?

PASSENGER 10: I'm going to New York too, but not on Concorde, unfortunately!

ANGIE: Is it a business trip?

PASSENGER 10: Well, half business, half pleasure. I'm a fashion designer—and I'm meeting some buyers in New York tomorrow, I'm going to try and sell them my designs.

ANGIE: I hope you do well. And you're staying on for a holiday?

PASSENGER 10: Yes, I'm visiting some friends.

ANGIE: And there's a tall young man here. Where are you off to?

PASSENGER 11: Oh, I'm going home to New York.

ANGIE: How long have you been away?

PASSENGER 11: A couple of years—I've been travelling round the world.

ANGIE: Travelling for two years?

PASSENGER 11: Well, yeah. It's been a long time. I can't wait to see the folks back home.

ANGIE: I expect they'll be pleased to see you too!

FLIGHT ANNOUNCER: British Airways regret to announce the delay of Flight BA 175 to New York. This is due to technical problems.

PASSENGER 11: Oh, no. That's all I need.

ANGIE: Don't worry. They'll probably sort it out soon. Are you going to New York too, sir?

PASSENGER 12: No, I'm going to Paris.

ANGIE: On business?

PASSENGER 12: Not exactly, no. I'm going to see, er, a friend—my girlfriend, actually.

FLIGHT ANNOUNCER: Your attention please. Kuwait Airways Corporation Flight KU 162 is now ready for boarding. Will passengers please proceed to Gate 14. Flight KU 162, proceed to Gate 14.

PASSENGER 12: That's my flight!

ANGIE: Have a good holiday!

PASSENGER 12: Thank you, I will!

ANGIE: That's all from Heathrow airport, and this is Angie Lewis reporting back to the studio . . .

D: Reading Aloud – see page 50

D: Role Play—New information

FLIGHT ANNOUNCER: Your attention, please. Will all passengers for British Airways Flight BA 175 departing for New York please proceed to Gate Number 9. Departure Flight BA 175 proceed to Gate Number 9. Will the following passengers please report to the British Airways representative at the gate. Mr Craven, Miss Davis, Mr Goldstein, Mr and Mrs Hatchard, and Miss Temple, please report to the BA representative at Gate Number 9. Thank you.

(*At the gate*)

PASSENGER 8: What's the problem?

BA REPRESENTATIVE: Ah, yes. There are six of you. I'm afraid there is a problem. It turns out that your flights haven't been confirmed, and unfortunately this flight is overbooked . . . there are only three seats remaining, so I'm afraid three of you will have to take a later flight.

PASSENGER 3: When does the next flight leave?

BA REPRESENTATIVE: Er, tomorrow morning . . . I'll let you discuss this among yourselves . . .

UNIT 4

B: Listening Activity

(*Bell, 'Hold tight!', bus moving off*)

GEORGE: Excuse me . . . Sorry . . . Excuse me, is this seat taken?

PAUL: No, it isn't . . . George!

GEORGE: Paul! What a surprise I haven't seen you for ages.

PAUL: No, when was the last time . . .? You look very well. Where did you get that suntan?

GEORGE: Oh, we've just come back from holiday.

PAUL: Really? Where did you go?

GEORGE: We went on a sightseeing tour of Egypt, actually.

PAUL: Oh, how nice! Did you go to Cairo?

GEORGE: Yes and all the other places, like all the tourists. We went on a tour called 'The Treasures of the Pharaohs'.

PAUL: And that's how you got your suntan, then!

GEORGE: Yes, although at times it was *too* hot.

PAUL: And where did you go?

GEORGE: Well, we flew to Cairo, and then took a local flight to Abu Simbel, on Lake Nasser, to have a look at the Temple of Ramesses II.

PAUL: That was the one they had to move when they were building the Aswan dam, isn't it?

GEORGE: That's right. Then we went north to Aswan and took a trip along the Nile on one of those cruise boats.

PAUL: Oh, really? Didn't it get a little boring? I though it was mostly desert.

GEORGE: Well, to the west, yes. It stretches nearly 5.000 kilometres right across North Africa. But the Nile valley is very green because the river floods in August and September, so that's where most of the crops are grown. There are also a few oases in the desert where they grow fruit. And to the east, well, there's a range of mountains and then some rather rocky beaches on the Red Sea.

PAUL: I suppose there are quite a few towns along the river?

GEORGE: Oh, yes, we stopped at a number of places. Luxor was fascinating – the temple there is over 3,000 years old. And nearby there's Karnak, which is huge – full of temples, lakes and avenues. Then there's Thebes, with the Valley of the Kings and the Tomb of Tutankhamun.

PAUL: And did you spend any time in Cairo?

GEORGE: Oh yes, three days at the end of the tour. It's very interesting, you know. The old part of town is more than 3,000 years old.

PAUL: As old as that? I really had no idea. I believe it's the largest city in Africa.

GEORGE: Yes. Now, of course, it's a modern, rather busy place – its strange to see the tall buildings and the traffic surrounding the mosques and the bazaar. And so many people! There are 43 million people in Egypt and I think they're all in Cairo!

PAUL: Did you see the Pyramids?

GEORGE: Oh yes, and the Sphinx! And it was there that we had a ride on a camel!

PAUL: Good heavens!

GEORGE: Yes, one of the tourist traps, you know. We also had a look at the tombs at Memphis. But we certainly didn't see everything, it's such a vast country, you know, over 1 million square kilometres. I'd love to go back again. And apart from the sightseeing, the shopping is very good, and we particularly liked the restaurants. The food is fabulous. Did you get away this year?

PAUL: Yes, we had a week with my wife's parents.

GEORGE: Where was that?

PAUL: Brighton.

GEORGE: Oh, . . . very nice. Oh, this is my stop. Lovely to see you!

We simply must get together again. We took lots of photographs, perhaps you'd like to see them. Anyway, bye for now!
PAUL: Yes, all right. Bye!

D: Listening Activity

EMMA: Phew, I'm exhausted! Shall we stop here for a drink?
CHRIS: Yes, all right. Where are we, anyway?
EMMA: The Kings Arms, Alston. I hope they've got some food, I'm starving.
(Door opening, buzz of conversation)
CHRIS: Right, what will you have?
EMMA: Oh . . . a cider, I think.
CHRIS: A cider and a pint of bitter, please.
LANDLORD: Right away, sir.
CHRIS: Oh, and have you got anything to eat?
LANDLORD: Sorry, sir, you'll have to go to Overmouth for that.
CHRIS: Oh, well, never mind.
LANDLORD: You on holiday then?
CHRIS: Yes, we're on a bike tour of the Keverne Peninsula.
LANDLORD: Are you enjoying yourselves?
EMMA: Oh, it's lovely, really beautiful. And we've had very good weather, too.
LANDLORD: Where are you thinking of going from here?
EMMA: Oh, we don't know yet. Have you any ideas?
LANDLORD: Well, there's lots to see, and plenty of legends around here. The most famous is that the old city of Azuris is said to lie underwater off Ash Kelso, you know, a submerged city, like Atlantis. The legend says that the city was very rich, but the citizens were very greedy, until one day, a violent storm flooded the place and everyone was drowned as a punishment. We still say around here that if anyone is a bit mean or greedy, he lives in Azuris.
CHRIS: Yes, I've heard about Azuris. We'll have to go and see it. How do we get there?
LANDLORD: Oh, there's nothing to see. Once you get there, you can't see anything. But it's meant to lie . . . Have you got a map? . . . . Thanks, well, here it is along the B745 and it's signposted Ash Kelso. Go as far as the cliffs and that's where it's meant to be.
CHRIS: Oh, we'll have a look anyway.
LANDLORD: Then there's Overmouth, there, with the two crossed swords – can you see? To the north-east, not far from here. There was a fight there between the King's soldiers and the rebel army in 1350. The rebels were on the run and were discovered by a passing patrol of soldiers. After a struggle lasting two days, they were captured and hanged at Nettleshaw. You can still see the place where they were hanged.
EMMA: At Nettleshaw, you say? Where's that?
LANDLORD: On the coast, to the north-east of Overmouth. The last man to die there was a local hero called Jack Carver. He used to steal money from the local taxmen in Penberry who were very rich because they used to charge too much and keep the extra money for themselves. Jack was very popular around here but was caught and hanged as well. You can still see the rope hanging from a tree.
EMMA: That sounds awful!
LANDLORD: Oh and I almost forgot. Have a look at Rich Harold's tomb in Overmouth and see if you can find his fortune.
CHRIS: What's this story then?
LANDLORD: Well, Rich Harold, as he's called, died in 1895. He was said to be the richest man in the region, but he never spent anything, so everyone thought he was mean. Perhaps he wasn't rich at all, I don't know. Anyway, on the wall in the church where he was buried, he left a series of clues, a kind of riddle. If you can solve it, you'll find exactly where he left his money. No-one has ever succeeded, though.
CHRIS: Oh, that sounds interesting. We'll have a look at that.
EMMA: Yes, I'd love to solve it.
CHRIS: We could go there now, and have something to eat at the same time.
EMMA: Yes, that's a good idea. Let's go. Bye!
LANDLORD: Enjoy yourselves – and come back here when you've found the treasure!

D: Reading Aloud – see page 67

D: Role Play—New information

CHRIS: Well, this must be the place – 'My sixth is a break from this lengthy chase. Take refreshment and advice from a bird-like place' The Owl Inn. I suppose that must mean we have to ask the landlord. But he can't be the same landlord as the one who Rich Harold might have known.
EMMA: I wouldn't have thought so, no.
CHRIS: Anyway, let's go in. (*Door opening, conversation*) Where's the landlord? Ah, that must be him! Excuse me, we're looking for . . .
EMMA: Chris! Come over here a moment!
CHRIS: What is it?
EMMA: Look at this sketch!
CHRIS: Yes . . . well?
EMMA: Read what it says underneath.
CHRIS: 'This sketch was given to this inn by George Harris the painter who lived with his fellow artists in the village of Kilmere nearby, from 1859 to 1890.' I wonder . . .
EMMA: Read the next bit as well!
CHRIS: 'It shows the Frenchman Henri Laforgue at the moment when he saw the Devil near Lee Forest. He resisted temptation and in thanks he not only built a monument at St Bewli (Beau Lieu in French, or fine place) but also spent the rest of his life as a monk in West Penmarra Abbey.'
EMMA: Chris, don't you think . . .?
CHRIS: Sssh, we must keep this quiet, someone might be listening. Let's sit down and think about this.

UNIT 5

A: Language Practice 2

1 'It's very hard work. The patient is usually nervous, so you have to be bright and cheerful, however you're feeling. And you spend most of the day on your feet. But it's quite creative – making people's teeth look good. And when you do a good job, it's very satisfying. It takes a certain skill – you need to be good with your hands. You can't afford to make mistakes!'

2 'You have to have good, fast, accurate shorthand and typing. You've got to be good at English and spelling – and there are so many other things. You need to be reliable, and loyal to your boss. And you need a sense of humour – particularly in my case, because I work for a TV producer.'

3 'It takes a lot of energy and hard work, and I'm usually exhausted at the end of the day. But I enjoy it. You don't have to have any special talents. I don't have any. But I suppose I do know how to do quite a few things – I'm a cook, and a cleaner, and a nurse when the kids are ill, and I decorate the place, so you could say I'm a painter . . . and I don't get paid for any of it. But I never really thought about a career . . . maybe when the children are grown-up . . .'

4 'You have to be good at working in a team and you've got to be able to make quick decisions. And of course, you need to know how to use the equipment properly. It's funny. When I was a kid, I was scared of heights. And in my job, you've got to go up ten-storey buildings on a ladder. I suppose it takes courage, but when you're saving lives, you don't think about being afraid. I care about people – that's why I do it.'

5 'Well, you have to have a friendly personality, and you've got to look good. And I have to be able to speak Spanish. But it's not as glamorous as you think. You have to look after the passengers and serve drinks and be a waitress and an interpreter, and all the time you have to keep smiling. And that's not easy when you've been in the air for hours, with no time to eat or rest . . .'

D: Listening Activity

(*Fade in*) . . . The Prime Minister will return to London tomorrow. The *Daily Gazette* has announced plans to lay off a hundred print-workers at the end of the month. The chairman of the *Gazette*, Sir Arthur Richardson, blames rising costs for the cutbacks. He has stated that it is no longer economic to employ a staff of three hundred when modern technology can replace at least one-third of the print-workers. The proposed cutbacks will save a million pounds a year in wages alone. It is hoped that a proportion of the redundancies will be voluntary. Our reporter, Angie Lewis, spoke to Sir Arthur this afternoon.

ANGIE: Sir Arthur, why is it necessary to sack so many of the print-workers?

RICHARDSON: Well, basically, the *Gazette* is losing money. Our circulation is quite steady, but rising costs will put us out of business unless we economise. The new technology has given us the chance to do just that. Obviously, I don't like having to take away people's jobs. But I have considered the matter very carefully, and there's just no alternative if we are to save the paper. It would be an absolute tragedy if the *Gazette* had to close.

ANGIE: But surely new printing equipment will be extremely expensive.

RICHARDSON: Yes, of course it will. But, in the long term, it will pay off. It will certainly be cheaper and more efficient to use computer technology than to employ print-workers.

ANGIE: What do you think the print-workers will have to say about your proposal?

RICHARDSON: No doubt I shall hear very soon!

ANGIE: Sir Arthur, thank you for talking to us.

PRESENTER: That was Angie Lewis talking to Sir Arthur Richardson. And, indeed, we shall hear very soon what one print-worker has to say, because with me in the studio are a number of guests, including Paul Rogers from the Print-Workers' Union. Paul, what are your reactions to the announcement we've just heard?

ROGERS: Well, I'm shocked. A lot of the printers have worked on the *Gazette* for years, and now they're – they're to be thrown out on the street. It's incredible. I can't speak for the union, but I don't think they'll stand for it. The management will have to find another solution to their problems.

PRESENTER: But Sir Arthur Richardson has said that there is no alternative.

ROGERS: In that case, I wouldn't be surprised if the union took industrial action.

PRESENTER: You mean, you'd go on strike?

ROGERS: Well, it's a possibility. *I* don't particularly want to – I can't afford to. And my wife would be furious. But it's the principle of the thing. It's not the print-workers' fault that the paper is losing money, it's because of bad editorial policy. I blame the new editor. Ever since he took over, the circulation of the *Gazette* has been falling . . .

PRESENTER: Jonathan Martin, as editor of the *Gazette*, perhaps you would like to comment on that?

MARTIN: Yes, well, of course that's absolute nonsense. The circulation may have dropped slightly, but that's because we've had to increase the price of the paper. You can't blame me for that. But it's true we are losing good journalists because we simply can't afford to pay them enough at the moment. We've got to get more money from somewhere – and the only way to do that is to save on printing costs.

PRESENTER: What if the union calls a strike?

MARTIN: I can't see any point in calling a strike. If they did, the *Gazette* would go bankrupt, and that would be the end of it.

PRESENTER: And it wouldn't be just the print-workers who'd lose their jobs – the journalists would be out of work as well. Polly Mills is a reporter on the *Gazette* – what are your views, Polly?

MILLS: First, let me stand up for Jonathan and say that I don't think he is responsible for the *Gazette's* problems. He's done an excellent job as editor, and it's certainly not his fault that the paper is short of money. As far as the proposed cutbacks are concerned, I'm very worried as are my colleagues. I can see the management's point of view. But I know the print-workers and I don't think they'll accept the proposal. They're quite likely to go on strike if the management doesn't change its mind.

PRESENTER: Do you see any chance of a compromise?

MILLS: Well, I think that the main problem is that most of the printers expect to earn a large amount in overtime pay. Their basic wage is about £230 a week, but with overtime, it goes up to about £300. If they didn't work overtime, the paper could save large sums of money. Now if the union agreed to stop working overtime . . .

ROGERS: There's not much chance of that! We work overtime because we need the money! You can't . . .

PRESENTER: We must leave it there, I'm afraid. Thank you all for talking to us.

D: Reading Aloud – see page 83

D: Role Play—New information

The Print-Workers Union has called an all-out strike in support of the hundred workers on the *Daily Gazette* who have been made redundant. The chairman of the *Daily Gazette*, Sir Arthur Richardson, has announced that the paper will have to close by next Monday unless the strike is called off.

UNIT 6

A: Language Practice 5

1 'I don't know yet but if I get all my 'O' levels, then I'll go into the sixth form and do French and German and probably English. I'm hoping to go to university to do a degree in languages but even if my 'A' level results are not good enough for that, I'd like to do something with my languages, like translating.'

2 'I can't stand school, so I'm thinking of leaving at the end of the spring term in April, when I'm sixteen. I'm very keen on doing things with radios and televisions, so maybe I'd like to work in an electrical shop. I also know how to operate a small computer, so that would interest me as well. But my parents think I should stay on at school and get some qualifications.'

3 'Well, I like school but not the one I'm in at the moment. The teachers treat you just like kids. I've got my 'O' levels and I want to take my 'A' levels because I'm hoping to go to a polytechnic for a business or a secretarial course. My parents are looking for a

sixth form college, where it's not like school at all, but you can still do your exams. But there aren't any in this area so I might have to stay on at school.'

4 'I've decided I want to to teach science subjects but I don't know if I should try for university or if it would be better to do my 'A' levels and go straight to teacher training college. You see, I'd like to leave home, but the college is very close to where my parents live, whereas if I went to university I'd go to Exeter or Manchester or somewhere like that, a long way from home.'

5 'I've gone as far as I need to, and my exam results are quite good, so I could take up the offer of a place at Birmingham University. But I'm not sure if I want to spend three years studying. I want to earn some money! My father runs a small business and he's offered me a job as a trainee accountant. I could study for the accountancy diploma in the evening at the local college of further education.'

D: Listening Activity 1

1 'I wanted to stay on at school and then go to teacher training college, but my father died so I had to get a job to help my mother. I was hoping to do my 'A' levels at evening classes but I was too tired after doing a full day's work as a secretary in an office. I wanted to stay with this firm but there were no prospects of promotion without qualifications. So now I've left and intend to take a part-time course to get an 'A' level, perhaps in French.'

2 'I was intending to go to university to study biology and zoology and I got a place at Birmingham. But when I left school, I went to France – at first for a few months but in the end I stayed for five years and then I got married. I assumed that my student days were over and that I'd stay in France for the rest of my life. Then my husband's firm sent us to Britain. I was going to do some courses, maybe try for a full-time course at the polytechnic nearby, but then we started a family. Now the children are at school and I've got more time. I'd like to do something that uses my mind a bit more.'

3 'I've been with one company as an accountant for fifteen years and I thought I could stay there until I retired. But now they're going to bring in a computer system to make the business more efficient, and this means fewer jobs in the future. I thought my job was safe – after all, I'm now one of the more senior accountants – but I was told that I wasn't trained to use the new technology. I was so cross that I nearly left, but they asked me to retrain for the job or train for a new one, like the legal side of the company's affairs. If I don't, I'll be made redundant.'

4 'My wife and I didn't have much of an education. You just didn't have the same opportunities in those days. But we would've stayed on at school if we hadn't had to go out to work. So now I've retired and we've got more time to ourselves, we thought it would be a good idea to take advantage of the adult education centre just down the road. Neither of us want to do anything too serious; it's more an opportunity to get out of the house and meet some new faces, actually.'

D: Listening Activity 2

INTERVIEWER: What type of people go to classes at the adult education centre?

PRINCIPAL: Well, there are three types really. The first type are the people who want to occupy their leisure time, people who just want to use their minds a bit more. They're usually at work all day and come in the evening once or twice a week.

INTERVIEWER: It must be quite tiring for them to start studying again *and* after a day's work!

PRINCIPAL: Yes, but it's surprising how well most of them manage to attend regularly. And of course, apart from their interest in the course itself, it's a good opportunity for them to make some new friends.

The second type of people who come are those who left school without sitting for their exams and who find that qualifications are necessary to get a job or get promotion in the firm where they work. For these people, the content of the course must be interesting of course, but it's above all the qualification at the end which matters.

INTERVIEWER: So you do 'A' levels?

PRINCIPAL: Yes, and diplomas, but not in all the courses.

INTERVIEWER: And the third type?

PRINCIPAL: Well, it's people who need to study a vocational course of some kind.

INTERVIEWER: What do you mean by vocational?

PRINCIPAL: A vocational course means a training in a specific skill. The content of the course is directly related to a job of some kind. This means studying something like computers or law. If you study English Literature for example, you either do it for personal pleasure or for a qualification. You rarely do it for your job, unless of course you want to teach it. And even then you have to go to teacher training college.

INTERVIEWER: Do you need any qualifications to start a course?

PRINCIPAL: For the majority of courses, none at all, as long as you're interested in the subject. However, some 'A' level or diploma courses require previous qualifications, but if you can prove that you've some experience of the subject and need the course for your job, even this is not always necessary. You should ask the Head of Department about this.

INTERVIEWER: What about the length of the courses?

PRINCIPAL: They usually last from September to May or June. But it depends on the type of course. Often, if you're not taking an exam, you can enrol for just a term to see if you like it or not.

INTERVIEWER: Is there any homework?

PRINCIPAL: Well, 'A' level and diploma courses require some extra work at home and you must make sure that you'll have the time to do this before you begin. It's surprising how difficult it is to study seriously if you finished school several years ago. For other courses there's no homework unless you want to do some.

INTERVIEWER: And the fees?

PRINCIPAL: Well, obviously, that depends on the length of the course, but for a full year it's between £10 and £25, with exam fees extra. But for unemployed people and old age pensioners, it's very much less – about a pound.

INTERVIEWER: Not very expensive!

PRINCIPAL: No, and I think most of our students would say it's very good value.

D: Reading Aloud – see page 100

UNIT 7

D: Listening Activity

(*Footsteps on gravel*)

BOB: You've got an enormous garden, haven't you?

JUDY: Yes, we must get to work before the weeds take over completely!

BOB: It's certainly an impressive building – when did you say it was built?

JUDY: Around 1750, the estate agents said.

BOB: Hmm. I don't like the look of that roof . . . a lot of tiles are missing, up there, below the chimney. You should deal with that pretty quickly. And I expect the drains are blocked with leaves . . . . yes, they'll want cleaning out. Let's see what it's like inside.

JUDY: Hang on, I've got a large bunch of keys here . . . this must be the front-door key . . . yes, that's the one. (*Creaking*) Now, where shall we start?

BOB: Let's have a look at the ground floor first. I must say, you've got a splendid hall, haven't you?

JUDY: Yes, it's huge, isn't it? Here's the lounge.

BOB: Hmm. This has seen better days, hasn't it? But the beams seem to be in good condition . . . And the plaster looks OK. It could do with a coat of paint, though.

JUDY: Yes, it could, couldn't it? Actually, the whole house needs completely redecorating. And it's a pity about the broken windows.

BOB: Yes, you should get those fixed immediately – you don't want the rain coming in, do you? It's like a refrigerator in here. By the way, you're going to put in central heating, aren't you?

JUDY: Ooh yes, I think we'll have to . . . it's the only way of keeping a place like this warm. This door here goes into the kitchen.

BOB: Uh huh. It's a good size. But if you want a decent kitchen, you'll have to strip it completely. I'd throw out that sink for a start – it looks as if it's come from the Stone Age!

JUDY: It isn't exactly a modern practical kitchen, is it? Those steps go down to the cellar, and the dining room's through here.

BOB: That's convenient . . . oh, this looks all right. What a beautiful fireplace! And there must be room for thirty people round that table.

JUDY: Yes, the previous owners left it because they couldn't get it out of the door! It's a bit scratched, and it needs to be polished, but it's a beautiful oak table.

BOB: They must have built the house round it! What's in here?

JUDY: Oh, that's the study.

BOB: Goodness! You could open a bookshop in here, couldn't you? Is, . . . er . . . Is this where the fire started?

JUDY: Yes, you can see . . . some of the shelves are ruined. Still, I suppose it was lucky the whole house didn't burn down, with all this wood about.

BOB: You're telling me. And this goes back into the hall. Well, it's in better condition than I thought. It needs a lot of work, but the structure of the building looks quite sound.

JUDY: Wait till you see upstairs! I hope the staircase won't give way!

BOB: It looks solid enough. How many bedrooms are there?

JUDY: Ten, and there's also an enormous attic. Right – this is the largest bedroom.

BOB: Oh dear. There's a lot to be done in here. It smells very damp. Yes, the ceiling's damp, and the plaster's coming off the wall. The roof must be leaking quite badly. It's done a lot of damage.

JUDY: What a nuisance!

BOB: Ah, one of the bathrooms. Well, this certainly 'requires modernisation'! You'll have to replace the bath, anyway. It's cracked . . . and so is the basin. I warn you, you're going to have to spend a lot of money on this place to get it into shape.

JUDY: Yes, I'm beginning to realise . . . we can go through here into the corridor.

BOB: Wait a minute – let me have a look at the floor . . . yes, just as I thought, some of these floorboards are completely rotten. Look at – Aaaagh! (*Sound of splintering wood, crash*)

JUDY: Bob! Bob?

D: Reading Aloud – see page 116

Exam Practice

Paper 4 Listening Comprehension

For this part of the test you are going to hear an interviewer asking someone about standards of living. Look carefully at the form in your book. You are to fill in the form with the information you hear. You will hear the piece twice.

(*In the street*)

INTERVIEWER: Excuse me, sir!

MAN: Yes?

INTERVIEWER: I'm doing a survey on standards of living in different countries and I was wondering if you'd mind answering a few questions.

MAN: Well, who's it for?

INTERVIEWER: The University of Cambridge.

MAN: Will it take long?

INTERVIEWER: Oh, about three minutes.

MAN: Well, all right then.

INTERVIEWER: Thank you. Well, first of all, are you married?

MAN: Yes, I am.

INTERVIEWER: And do you have any children?

MAN: Yes, I have a baby girl who's just three months old.

INTERVIEWER: Oh, congratulations! Is it the first one?

MAN: Yes.

INTERVIEWER: I don't envy you those sleepless nights! Now, let's see. You must be in your late twenties, early thirties?

MAN: Yes, that's right.

INTERVIEWER: And may I ask what you do for a living?

MAN: I'm a personnel manager for a large insurance firm.

INTERVIEWER: OK . . . personnel manager . . . and have you always worked in this job?

MAN: Well, I started off training to be an accountant, but I didn't like it, didn't really like it very much.

INTERVIEWER: And when did you start working for the insurance firm?

MAN: Oh, I suppose about six years ago.

INTERVIEWER: Fine, thanks very much. Now then, do you live close to your work?

MAN: Well, I wouldn't say close. We live in the suburbs, you see, and I work in town.

INTERVIEWER: How long does it take you to get to work then?

MAN: Well, as long as the train isn't cancelled, just under an hour.

INTERVIEWER: Fine . . . . Now, do you live in a flat or a house?

MAN: A house.

INTERVIEWER: And it's yours?

MAN: It belongs to the bank at the moment! I had to take out a big loan.

INTERVIEWER: What I mean is, you don't rent it?

MAN: No.

INTERVIEWER: OK. How many bedrooms do you have?

MAN: Three. But one of them is a bit small. I use it as a study.

INTERVIEWER: But it is really a bedroom?

MAN: Yes, I suppose so, if you don't mind being boxed in like that.

INTERVIEWER: No, the architects never seem to think about that, do they?

MAN: No, you're right.

INTERVIEWER: We'll call it a bedroom, anyway. Now, is there a living-room and a separate dining-room?

MAN: Not separate, no.

INTERVIEWER: And I assume you don't share your kitchen, bathroom or toilet facilities with another household?

MAN: Oh no.

INTERVIEWER: And how about household appliances? I'm interested in the more expensive items, like televisions, washing machines and so on.

MAN: Yes, we've got a TV and a washing machine.

INTERVIEWER: Anything else?

MAN: A fridge.

INTERVIEWER: Fine . . . and a fridge freezer?

MAN: No, we don't have one of those.

INTERVIEWER: And a telephone?

MAN: Yes, we have to have that because my mother-in-law lives in

the North and she's not very well at the moment.
INTERVIEWER: Oh, I'm sorry to hear that. Now, do you own any motor vehicles?
MAN: Yes, we've got a car.
INTERVIEWER: How old is it?
MAN: Let me see, now. I got it two years ago and it was already three years old then.
INTERVIEWER: Uh huh. Fine. Now, what do you do in your free time? Do you go out much?
MAN: Well, not so much as we used to, because of the baby. But we usually go and see friends once or twice a month. Sometimes we go to the cinema. Not many of our friends like screaming babies!
INTERVIEWER: Oh, they will do when they've got some of their own! And now, last of all, holidays. Do you go away at all?
MAN: Oh, yes, we always try and get away for a summer holiday.
INTERVIEWER: But just once a year?
MAN: Yes, I'm not interested in skiing, or Paris in the spring, or anything like that. I love the sunshine.
INTERVIEWER: Do you usually go abroad?
MAN: If we can yes, but I don't know if we will this year, what with the baby. But we'd like to. You can never be sure of the weather in this country, can you?
INTERVIEWER: No, you certainly can't, although there are some beautiful places to go. I love Devon, for example.
MAN: Oh, yes, so do we. We sometimes go down there for a weekend to see friends.
INTERVIEWER: Right, well, I think that's all I want to ask you. Thank you for giving me your time.
MAN: Not at all, I shall look forward to seeing the results.
INTERVIEWER: Well, I can send you a copy when we've completed the survey if you'd like to leave me your name and address.
MAN: Yes, I would be very interested. Yes, I'm Paul Barrett, that's B-A- double R-E- double T.
INTERVIEWER: And the address is . . .?
MAN: 22 London Road, Croydon, Surrey.
INTERVIEWER: Hold on a minute . . . 22 . . . . London Road . . . . Croydon, Surrey. Fine, well, thanks very much, Mr Barrett.
MAN: Not at all, bye.

UNIT 8

A: Language Practice 1

1 'I was furious! It was an emergency and I left the car in the street in front of the block of flats where one of my patients was having a heart attack. I was only there for about twenty minutes until the ambulance arrived. The traffic warden even saw me taking the man to the ambulance, but she still gave me a ticket for parking in a no-parking area. And what's more, just behind me was a foreign car and he didn't get a ticket. I now have to pay a £10 fine just for doing my job.'

2 'While I was on leave, I was having a quiet drink with friends in a bar when the police came in. They stopped all the young people from leaving and asked to see some proof of our age. I had no papers on me, so they took me down to the police station where I finally admitted that I was only seventeen. So now I have to pay a fine. I think it's really unfair. After all, if I'm old enough to be in the army, I'm surely old enough to drink in a bar.'

3 'We heard that they were going to close down the factory, so we stopped work and went to the front gates to stop people from bringing in supplies and parts for the cars. Then the management called the police and five of us were charged with obstruction and arrested. The whole car plant is on strike now because they're threatening to sack us.'

4 'I've been unemployed for nine months and, OK, I know I'm not supposed to work while I'm getting Unemployment Benefit, but it really isn't enough money to support my wife and children. So I do some window cleaning to get a bit extra. Last week I went down as usual to sign on and get my money when suddenly the whole place was surrounded by officials and police. We were all taken into a special office where they questioned us for three hours. Now I could be sent to prison or at the very least fined.'

A: Language Practice 3

(At a travel agent's)

TRAVEL AGENT: Good morning, can I help you?
MAN: Yes, I'm thinking of going to the United States this summer, and I was wondering what I needed in the way of documents and so on.
TRAVEL AGENT: Well, there's no real problem. Have you got a passport?
MAN: Oh, yes.
TRAVEL AGENT: Well, you'll need to get a visa from the Consular Section of the US Embassy. You'll need to give them a photograph and your passport and fill in a special form. Oh, and can you give them some proof that you will be returning to this country?
MAN: What kind of proof?
TRAVEL AGENT: Oh, just a note from your employer or bank manager or religious minister, or someone like that.
MAN: Oh, I can get that all right. Anything else?
TRAVEL AGENT: No, just take it or send it to the Embassy, and they'll give you your visa in a few days, sometimes even less.
MAN: What about customs?
TRAVEL AGENT: Well, they're quite strict, everyone has to go through them, including US citizens, even if you have nothing to declare. You can take in a couple of bottles of spirits, 300 cigarettes or the equivalent in tobacco.
MAN: What about gifts?
TRAVEL AGENT: Up to $100 worth of gifts duty free. But check with the Embassy if you want to take any fruit, vegetables, plants, seeds or meat. Some are forbidden.
MAN: All right. Do I need any special vaccinations or anything like that?
TRAVEL AGENT: No, unless you come from a country infected by smallpox within the fourteen days before your arrival in the States. But I would advise you to take out medical insurance before you leave just in case you're ill while you're there. It can be very expensive if you're not insured.
MAN: All right. Where can I get that?
TRAVEL AGENT: We can arrange that for you if you like. It might be a good idea to insure your personal luggage at the same time.
MAN: Yes, I suppose it would. Fine. What about driving? I'd quite like to hire a car if it's possible.
TRAVEL AGENT: There's no problem if you're over 25. All you need is your valid driver's licence, and the hire company will do the rest, including organising the insurance.
MAN: What about driving conditions? What are the other drivers like?
TRAVEL AGENT: Oh, very good, they all drive very slowly and carefully. There's a maximum speed limit of 55 m.p.h. on the highways so there's much less risk of accidents. In a way, it's a pity, because the roads are really excellent, but I suppose it's safer that way.
MAN: Yes, I suppose it is.

TRAVEL AGENT: If you're stopped for any reason and fined, whatever you do, don't try and offer to pay the police officer. He might think you're trying to bribe him! You have to go to the local court-house in the nearest town.

MAN: Well, I hope that won't be necessary.

TRAVEL AGENT: Oh, and don't forget to drive on the right-hand side of the road!

MAN: No, I won't. Anything else?

TRAVEL AGENT: No, I don't think so. Oh, one more thing, if you're going with your children they won't be allowed to drink alcohol if they're under 18, and in some states it's 21.

MAN: Well, they're far too young to drink alcohol in any case, so that won't matter. Good, well, I think I've got all that. Thank you very much.

TRAVEL AGENT: Not at all, sir. When you've decided where you're going, come back and see us and we'll make all the necessary arrangements.

MAN: I certainly will. Bye.

TRAVEL AGENT: Bye sir. Have a nice day!

B: Listening Activity

(At the chemist's)

JACK: Good morning. My name's Jack Hunter. I'm sorry to trouble you but I was wondering if you happened to be working here last Friday?

ASSISTANT: Yes, I was here. Why?

JACK: You didn't see what went on outside during the afternoon, by any chance, did you?

ASSISTANT: Oh, you mean the old man?

JACK: Yes, that's right, can you remember anything about it?

ASSISTANT: Well, only that he'd been sitting there for some time, I suppose about twenty minutes in all, and just as the car was leaving, he stood up, walked a few steps and then fell over.

JACK: Do you think he might have been run down?

ASSISTANT: By the car, you mean? Oh no. No, he was about six feet from the car itself. No he fell down right by the bench on the pavement.

JACK: Ah, that's very interesting. You didn't notice anything else, I suppose?

ASSISTANT: No, that's about it. I didn't go out because there was a long queue in the shop, and I was on my own at the time. Anyway, he looked as if he was being well looked after by the people in the car. But I think he was next door in the baker's before he went and sat down. Why don't you have a word with them? They might know something.

JACK: Yes, that's a good idea.

ASSISTANT: Have a word with Betty. She was behind the counter on Friday, I think.

JACK: OK. I'll do that. Well, it's been very useful talking to you, I really am very grateful. Goodbye.

ASSISTANT: Goodbye.

B: Guided Writing Activity

(Doorbell, door opens)

JACK: Excuse me, do you know a Mr Johnson?

NEIGHBOUR: Yes, he's the old man who lives next door. But I don't know if he's in . . . I haven't seen him for a few days.

JACK: Well, actually, he's in hospital.

NEIGHBOUR: Oh dear, I *am* sorry. What's the matter with him?

JACK: He collapsed in the street last Friday.

NEIGHBOUR: Well, I'm not surprised. He's such a nice old man, but he's always having accidents, you know, burning himself on a saucepan, or cutting himself on a tin can. He's not very steady on his feet, you know. I think it's a disgrace that his relatives don't look after him a bit more. They never come round, not even at Christmas.

JACK: Did you see him on Friday?

NEIGHBOUR: No, I didn't. I was a bit worried. He often drops in for a cup of tea in the morning. But I saw him on Thursday, and he was limping and had a nasty bruise on his face. I asked him what had happened and he said he'd fallen down the stairs. Anyway, on Friday evening I knocked to see if he was any better. There was no answer so I came back and fetched the key – he always leaves a key with me, you know – and I went in and found the place empty. I simply thought he'd gone away for a few days . . . he's got some friends in Scotland, you see.

JACK: Well, in fact, he'd been taken to hospital. The fall on Thursday must have made him a bit weak.

NEIGHBOUR: Oh dear.

JACK: Anyway, his son-in-law seems to be taking an interest in him now, at last. I wonder why?

NEIGHBOUR: I couldn't tell you, but the time I met him, I didn't like him at all. Horrible man, he was.

JACK: No, my friends don't like him very much either.

NEIGHBOUR: Your friends? What do you mean?

JACK: Well, it's a long story, but what happened was this . . . *(fade)*

D: Listening Activity 1

NARRATOR: The Paris newspapers called it Black Tuesday, and the whole city was astonished. Nobody ever dreamed that the Mona Lisa could be stolen, and when the news broke, people spoke of little else. In the cafés and restaurants, shops and squares, everyone had his own theory . . .

EXTRA! Mona Lisa stolen, EXTRA!

— I think it's a trick by the government to take our minds off the international crisis.

— It would take a madman to do a thing like that!

— It's probably out of the country by now!

— It's a disgrace! The government should resign!

— How did they manage to do it? It's incredible!

NARRATOR: But it wasn't quite so incredible, and the police soon found out how it was done. They found the hidden storeroom behind the Salon Carré, and a bent key, and they spoke to the plumber . . .

PLUMBER: No, I didn't recognise him. He was a short man with a dark moustache. He was complaining that the doorknob was missing. I didn't ask him any questions, I just thought he worked here. So I let him out with my key.

NARR: . . . and they talked to the guard at the gate . . .

GUARD: Well, I was on my own that day, my assistant was ill. No, I didn't leave the gate. I was washing the steps, cleaning the place like everyone else. Well, maybe I did go in to fetch some water.

D: Listening Activity 1 – New information

NARRATOR: The police began to put two and two together. The thief must have slipped into the storeroom on Sunday afternoon and spent the night there. Then, on Monday morning, during the confusion of the cleaning and repair work, he came out, picked up the Mona Lisa, took it out of its frame and went down to the door. He must have been a bit worried when the key he had didn't work. But he didn't panic and just asked the plumber who happened to be passing by to let him out. And when he got to the gate, he simply waited until the security guard went in to fetch some water, and VOILA, he was out!

So that's how the Mona Lisa was stolen. But the police took a lot longer to learn who stole it, although ironically, the little man with the dark moustache was one of the hundreds of people they questioned.

D: Listening Activity 2

NARRATOR: Well, do you have any ideas who stole the 'Mona Lisa'? Even after months of questioning, the police didn't. Soon the anger and confusion died down and it looked as if the painting was gone forever.

In fact they had almost forgotten about the theft when one day, in Florence, a little man with a dark moustache got off the train from Paris and went to an art dealer's shop with the Mona Lisa for sale. The art dealer took a close look at it, feeling sure that it couldn't be THE Mona Lisa. But he invited his friend, the director of the famous Uffizi Gallery, to come and take a look all the same. They both agreed. The Mona Lisa had been found. But to the anger of the little man, instead of receiving the 500,000 lire he was asking, he received a visit from the police. The world's most hunted criminal had been caught.

At this trial, Vincenzo Perugia, claimed that he'd stolen the Mona Lisa to bring it back to its rightful home in Italy. Fortunately for France, the Italian authorities didn't agree and sent the painting back to the Louvre. They didn't believe him when he claimed that he'd worked completely alone without help from anyone. No, little Vincenzo wasn't really clever enough to have done that. Certainly he stole it and kept it in his Paris flat for two years, but someone must have been the brains behind the whole affair. But who? And why? The police were sure he was telling lies, but they were no nearer to finding out the truth. They might've got closer if they'd remembered two facts. First, there are a number of copies of the Mona Lisa in the world. Part of the painting's fascination is whether the one in the Louvre is genuine or not. There are a number of brilliant artists even today who could make a very good copy. Everyone who owns one of these 'Mona Lisas' claims it's the real one. But how can they be sure? And secondly, what about these rich collectors who'd pay anything for a painting? There may have been several who wanted the Mona Lisa. But why was the Mona Lisa never sold? Could it have been – no, I'll let you think for a moment . . .

D: Reading Aloud – see page 132

D: Listening Activity 2 – New information

'So did you come to any conclusions? Did you guess that Perugia did *not* work alone? And did you discover why he didn't try to sell the painting? In fact, he was only waiting for the organiser of the whole affair to turn up. And this man, someone called Eduardo de Valfierno, just forgot about the Mona Lisa and Perugia. You see he didn't really need the painting itself; all he needed in order to become very rich was the news of the theft. He'd had not *one*, but *six* brilliant copies made. He contacted possible buyers before Perugia did his work. As soon as the theft was announced he sold all six claiming that each one was the original. Of course, the six buyers weren't going to know about each other's purchase, and when the real Mona Lisa turned up again he simply told them that it was a copy; THEY had the real one. So poor old Perugia got tired of waiting for his share of the profits and went to prison, while de Valfierno lived happily ever after.

You might be wondering why the police never discovered the truth, and *I* did. When you listen to this, the whole story can be told as de Valfierno will be dead. You see, it all took place a long time ago. The Mona Lisa was stolen in 1911 and found in 1913. Oh, and perhaps it's a bit strange to introduce yourself at the end of the story, but it seems the right moment to tell you that it was I, Eduardo de Valfierno, who organised the crime of the century!'

UNIT 9

A: Language Practice 4

It's a tall transparent glass container with a narrow neck.

It's a flat circular black plastic object with a small hole in the middle.

It's a small rectangular cardboard box, containing little sticks of wood.

It's a large soft rectangular article, made of cotton and filled with feathers.

It's a long thin cylindrical thing, consisting of a length of string coated in wax.

It's a thick white substance, contained in a flexible tube.

B: Guided Writing Activity

Nescafé is drunk in most countries, and the taste of the soluble coffee obviously depends on the blend of different types of coffee beans. So, first of all, the coffee is carefully blended to suit consumer taste in each different country. This is why throughout the world there are many different types of Nescafé.

Basically, the manufacture of Nescafé is very simple. It starts off with the roasting operation. On leaving the plantation, the coffee is a pale greyish green, known as 'green coffee'. To obtain its beautiful brown colour, and its aroma and flavour, it's roasted at high temperatures in a roasting machine. At 100° C, the beans turn a pale yellow colour, towards 150° C, they begin to turn brown and swell, and start to give out a good coffee smell, and roasting point is reached between 200 and 250° C, by which time the beans, now dark brown, have practically doubled in size and give out a strong aroma. After roasting, the coffee is passed through a machine which removes all foreign bodies which may have become mixed up with the beans when they were harvested.

The next stage of the process is grinding. The coffee goes through a mill and is ground down to fine equal-sized particles. The manufacture then reaches a stage well-known to everyone who makes fresh coffee at home. After grinding the coffee, you pass boiling water through it to extract the liquid coffee. Exactly the same procedure is followed in the factory . . . The freshly ground coffee is put into huge percolators containing circulating boiling water, and a highly concentrated liquid coffee is produced.

After that, the liquid coffee is dried in a current of hot air. This process is known as *atomisation*, and is now – after thirty years of research and progress – widely used in the food industry. The liquid coffee extract is 'atomised' at the upper end of a metal tower which can be as high as thirty metres. The water evaporates instantly, and the fine coffee particles cool upon falling to the lower part of the tower.

Finally the powdered coffee is put into jars under vacuum conditions, so that the coffee can be preserved almost indefinitely. All the consumer has to do is to put a teaspoonful of the powder in a cup, add boiling water, and there's your cup of 'instant' coffee!

Now, are there any questions . . .? (*fade*)

D: Listening Activity

(*Theme music, applause*)

PRESENTER: Thank you, good evening, and welcome to 'That is the Question'. Our first guest tonight is from the Ministry of Energy, and he's here to answer questions from the studio audience about the government plan to build a chain of nuclear power stations throughout the country. Will you please welcome Sir Roland Greave.
(*Applause*)

SIR ROLAND: Thank you.

PRESENTER: And let's have the first question. Yes, you sir.

MAN: In view of the fact that we have considerable reserves of coal, gas, and oil in this country, I should like to ask Sir Roland why he considers it necessary to develop a nuclear energy programme?

SIR ROLAND: Well, there are several good reasons. Firstly, while we are indeed fortunate to have natural energy resources in the form of coal, gas and oil, these resources are limited. There's no doubt that supplies will run out. We must be sure that we can maintain energy supplies to meet the growing demands of the modern world. Secondly, if we can produce enough nuclear power to generate all the energy we need, we won't have to rely on importing fuel. We can be completely independent, which is obviously an advantage today given the rising prices on the oil market. And thirdly, nuclear power production is extremely efficient and clean. It causes far less pollution than energy production from burning coal, for example.

PRESENTER: Another question – yes, madam.

WOMAN: In 1979, there was a nearly disastrous accident at the Three Mile Island nuclear power station in the United States due to a radiation leak. This could have led to a nuclear explosion, with horrifying consequences. There have been many other cases of accidents resulting in the death of workers at power stations, not to mention the countless numbers who have suffered serious ill-health and cancer through exposure to radiation. I wonder if you can give any guarantee that you can prevent accidents and avoid risks of this kind?

SIR ROLAND: Erm, obviously there'll always be risks in nuclear power production. But equally, we must remember that there are serious risks involved in coal-mining and oil-production. We've learned many lessons from the Three Mile Island accident, and our design includes all kinds of automatic back-up security systems should there be a fault. In a real emergency, our nuclear reactors are designed to shut down automatically. I can assure you that safety is being given the highest priority.

PRESENTER: Has anyone else got a question while we're on the subject of safety? Yes, sir. No, the gentleman in the green jacket . . .

MAN: I understand that enormous quantities of radio-active waste have been, and continue to be, dumped in the sea, and that on many occasions, the drums containing the waste have leaked or even burst. May I ask how you intend to dispose of the nuclear waste produced by the power stations?

SIR ROLAND: Yes, well, certainly there have been some unfortunate cases of leaking waste, and as far as dumping at sea's concerned, it is quite likely that this will be internationally banned in the future. At present, we're investigating suitable sites, where there's clay or chalk, for storing the waste underground, and we're developing methods of treating waste and sealing it for storage in blocks of glass or rock. I should add that nuclear waste does decay and eventually turn into non radio-active material. And, you know, reports of dangers have been exaggerated. Let me remind you that a great deal of *chemical* waste products can remain a *permanent* problem. Chemical waste produced by factories causes serious pollution of the air, the rivers and the land, and threatens both animals and people.

PRESENTER: The lady in the second row – yes, madam.

WOMAN: Sir Roland, can you explain why the government is so determined to develop a nuclear energy programme at enormous expense and risk to the lives of millions, when there are so many alternative sources of energy? (*Applause*) I should be interested to know why serious consideration has not been given to the development of renewable energy sources, such as tidal power, solar energy, wind power, and so on, which in the long run would be much cheaper and safer than nuclear power production.

SIR ROLAND: I must point out that we have given serious consideration to alternative sources of energy, and there is continuing research into methods of using these energy sources effectively. However, in our view, it doesn't make economic sense to develop systems of this kind at present.

PRESENTER: One last question – er, yes, the gentleman at the back.

MAN: It seems to me that the nuclear power industry is a dangerous dinosaur and that in the twenty-first century, we'll find that we've created hundreds of useless nuclear reactors and produced millions of tonnes of nuclear waste which we'll have to live with for thousands of years. We're talking about the quality of life, not the short-term profit of industrialists and politicians. Wouldn't it be true to say that you really don't know what the risks of nuclear power production are?

SIR ROLAND: Not at all. On the contrary, I have reason to believe that the risks are negligible, and that nuclear power is an efficient source of energy which we'll be able to rely on for many, many years.

PRESENTER: Well, efficient energy source, or dangerous dinosaur? There we must leave it, and thank you, Sir Roland, for joining us . . . (*applause*)

D: Reading Aloud – see page 147

Exam Practice

Paper 4 Listening Comprehension

For this part of the test you are going to hear someone describing a trick to show your friends. Look at the pictures shown in your book. Put a tick against the objects needed to perform the trick. You will hear the description twice.

Here is a good trick to show your friends. It's simple to perform, and your audience will be amazed.

You start off by showing a matchbox with a length of button thread running through it. If you hold one length of the thread up and let the box run down the thread, there's nothing very magical about that, is there? And the same goes for your next action, which is to reverse the thread, letting the box run to the other end.

But when you do this once more, saying your magic words, the box suddenly stops half-way down the thread! And each time you say your magic spell – the box stops! There seems to be no explanation of how it's done, especially as you can open the matchbox and take out the matches.

But the explanation is quite simple. First you make a hole in each end of the tray of the matchbox with a strong needle. These holes should be in the centre of each end. Then thread about half a metre of strong thread through the holes, and tie a piece of match to each end to ensure that it won't slip right through the box.

Put a layer of matches into the box. Now cut one match to such a length that it's a tight fit when laid *across* the box. It must wedge very firmly across the tray. A spot of glue will help to keep it in place. The thread must go underneath this cross-match, and you must be sure to see that it runs easily backwards and forwards.

Having done this, cover the cross-match with the other matches so that it's quite hidden, and slide the cover on to the tray.

Now, if you hold the thread vertically, the box will slide down, so long as you don't pull the thread tight. The moment you tighten the thread, the box stops, because the cross-match applies friction – just like a bicycle brake – and halts it.

Of course, you must always give another reason for this happening, and as good a reason as any is the power of your magic spell!

UNIT 10

A: Language Practice 3

On 3rd October 1863, the steamship *City of Limerick* set sail from Liverpool on its way to New York. On board was a certain Mr S.R. Wilmot, who was returning to his wife and family in Connecticut, USA. As he was travelling alone, he shared a cabin with a stranger, a Mr Tait. On the night of the thirteenth, there was a heavy storm and the two men spent some time talking because they couldn't sleep. When he finally did fall asleep, Wilmot had a dream in which someone knocked at the door of the cabin. Before he could reply, the door swung open. To his astonishment, his wife was standing there. She hesitated for a moment, as if wondering if she should enter. Then she crossed the cabin, and came towards him. And even though it was a dream, he felt her breath on his face as she kissed him. After that, she turned round and left.

In the morning, Tait was particularly rude to Wilmot for no apparent reason. He asked Tait if he had upset him in any way. Tait explained how angry he was that Wilmot had allowed a woman into their cabin during the night. It seemed that while Tait was lying awake that night, a strange woman entered the cabin, crossed to Wilmot's bed, kissed him and left – in fact, exactly as Wilmot had seen in his dream!

When the ship arrived in New York on 23rd October, the first thing that Wilmot's wife asked him was whether he had received a visit from her ten days earlier. Apparently she had heard about the stormy weather in the Atlantic and had been told of the wreck of another ship which had left Liverpool at the same time. She had gone to bed that night feeling very anxious for her husband's safety. During the night she was awakened by the sound of voices – two men were talking in the distance. She then started shivering as if there was a cold wind blowing, and she seemed to be crossing a wild and stormy sea. She looked down and below was a ship. She watched in horror as it pushed its way through the enormous waves, almost going under at times. Then she seemed to pass through the ship until she came to her husband's cabin. She knocked and opened the door. She was about to go in when something made a noise on the other side of the room and she hesitated. There was another man lying there, and she was almost too afraid to enter. But she quickly crossed the room, kissed her husband on the forehead, watched as he turned in his sleep, and left.

Scarcely able to believe her, Wilmot asked his wife to describe the cabin. She remembered what it looked like almost better than Wilmot did himself!

B: Listening Activity

(*Traffic, car horns, road drills, aeroplane, – muffled as window closes*)

PRESENTER: The roar of the aeroplane, the rattle of a goods train going past, the scream of a police siren in the distance, – most of us have to live with that kind of noise all day long, and sometimes all night too. It can be very annoying but fortunately we *do* get used to it, and accept it as one of the things we have to put up with in today's world. But there are some people who are extremely concerned about the effects of noise on our health. With me today is Dr Peter Moore, from the University of Birmingham. Dr Moore, surely if we get used to all this noise, then it isn't really doing us any harm?

DR MOORE: Well yes, you're right. An American journalist once wrote an article about someone who lived in New York, and who got lost in Central Park one day – and almost died because of the silence! He was saved by a passer-by with a transistor radio! Well, I'm not sure if it's a true story or not, but most people *do* manage to work in busy offices, or sleep near a motorway, because they get used to a steady noise in the background. But this doesn't mean that it's not dangerous. Even if we get used to it, the problem of noise pollution, as we call it, still remains. And even more dangerous are unexpected loud noises, like the bang of a supersonic aeroplane, or the crash of road repair work.

PRESENTER: All of which are caused by man.

DR MOORE: Yes, in fact, the more industry there is, the noisier our lives become. It's man himself who's responsible. And I think it's going to get worse.

PRESENTER: So you're saying that noise pollution is caused by industry?

DR MOORE: Yes, and our desire for those things which industry produces to make our lives more pleasant and efficient: cars, planes and so on.

PRESENTER: . . . which in turn, make life unpleasant because of the noise?

DR MOORE: Exactly.

PRESENTER: What are the consequences of this kind of pollution?

DR MOORE: First of all, there's the psychological effect. It leads to nervous tension and headaches. Above all, it causes stress, and this means that unless we can escape all the noise, it'll actually reduce our efficiency in industry. Secondly there's the environmental effect. There are very few places left in the cities where we can get the peace and quiet that we need. And finally, constant noise can have a physical effect – causing permanent deafness, for example.

PRESENTER: What should be done, do you think?

DR MOORE: It's difficult to say; there are no easy solutions, but we must do something. There are three possibilities. Machines must be designed to function more quietly. They will cost more, and it's the consumer who pays, of course, but they'll be more efficient. Secondly, we have to isolate noise. For example, we must no longer build schools next to airports unless we can isolate the teachers and pupils from the sound of aeroplanes taking off or landing. Thirdly, it's essential to make unnecessary noise illegal. Many governments have forbidden the use of car horns after certain hours and I suggest that we make laws which punish people who go beyond acceptable noise levels.

PRESENTER: It'll be difficult to make everyone co-operate!

DR MOORE: Yes, but it's vital that we do something if we're to avoid all sorts of problems in the twenty-first century.

PRESENTER: Thank you, Dr Moore.

D: Listening Activity 1

(*Telephone ringing*)

JACOBS: Hallo, Barncroft Police Station.

CROFT: Hallo, I'd like some information, please.

JACOBS: Well, I'll see if I can help, sir.

CROFT: I'd like to know if there were any unusual aircraft in the area this evening.

JACOBS: I beg your pardon, sir?

CROFT: I asked if there were any strange aircraft in the area this evening.

JACOBS: May I ask why, sir?

CROFT: Just answer my question, please.

JACOBS: I'm afraid I have to know why, sir.

CROFT: Because if there weren't, I'd like to report an Unidentified Flying Object.

JACOBS: A what?

CROFT: An Unidentified Flying Object, Constable, and will you please hurry up and answer my question.

JACOBS: Just a minute, sir . . . (*turns aside*) Hey, Jack, there's a chap here who wants to report a UFO.

BELL: What? Who is it?
JACOBS: Hang on, I'll ask . . . (*to phone*) Who's calling, sir?
CROFT: Geoffrey Croft, Colonel Geoffrey Croft.
JACOBS: Thank you, sir . . . (*aside*) It's Colonel Croft.
BELL: Croft? Well, he's not likely to bother us for nothing. I'll speak to him. . . . (*to phone*) Hello, Colonel, Sergeant Bell here. I understand you want to know about aircraft movements.
CROFT: Ah, Sergeant Bell, how are you? Yes, that's right. I was down by Hunter's Wood about thirty minutes ago when I saw something flying very low in the sky. We don't usually get any aircraft around this way, so I thought I'd give you a ring to check.
BELL: Can you hang on just half a minute, sir? (*aside*) Vicky, can you do me a favour? In the bottom drawer, under a load of papers is a special form for this kind of thing – you'll have to hunt for it, I've never used it. Then can you give the control tower at Walden Oak airfield a call to see if they know anything about this? Oh, and get PC Hackett and PC Jones on the radio and ask them if they're anywhere near Hunter's Wood at the moment and if so, tell them to take a look. (*to phone*) Right, Colonel Croft, I'll just take down some details, if you don't mind . . . Now, the date is . . .
CROFT: February 13th.
BELL: February 13th . . . and your address is . . .?
CROFT: Smith Lane . . . . Hodding, that's H-O-double D-I-N-G.
BELL: Right, sir, and you saw this about half an hour ago, is that right? That's about a quarter to eleven.
CROFT: That's right.
BELL: And you were just by Hunter's Wood.
CROFT: Yes, I was driving home from the pub; I'd just been having a drink with John Halley.
BELL: Which pub was that, sir?
CROFT: The Rose and Crown.
BELL: So you were driving along the road going northwards from the Rose and Crown.
CROFT: Yes, the pub is on the left-hand side.
BELL: And had you gone over the railway bridge?
CROFT: The one that cuts across the road further up? Yes, I had.
BELL: And Hunter's Wood is on the left?
CROFT: Yes, and I was just between the railway and the river which runs parallel to it.
BELL: I've got you, sir. And opposite the wood . . .
CROFT: . . . is Mackie's orchard. And the road going east runs beside the orchard. I was just by the crossroads where it meets the road I was driving along.
BELL: I'm with you, sir. Now, for how long did you see this object?
CROFT: For about five minutes?
BELL: And what was the visibility like, I mean, how far could you see?
CROFT: Oh, it was very clear, there's a full moon and no cloud at all.
BELL: And what made this object so strange, sir? I mean, why shouldn't it have been a light aircraft, or something like that?
CROFT: Well, first of all, because there were three of them at one point, all of them flashing on and off like torches. But then two of them stopped and flew off in the opposite direction.
BELL: And the one that stayed, can you describe it in detail, sir?
CROFT: Well, it was about . . . I suppose 500 feet up and it looked a bit like a long cigar, you know, fat in the middle, but with a line of windows along the side, all brightly lit, and a trail of bright smoke or vapour coming from the end. It was glowing a kind of gold colour.
BELL: Was it making any noise, sir?
CROFT: Well, a kind of whistling sound, a bit like the wind.
BELL: And was there any wind?
CROFT: Well, a little, but not enough to make that sort of noise.
BELL: And you watched from inside your car?
CROFT: Yes.
BELL: Is the windscreen quite clean?
CROFT: Yes, of course it is!
BELL: I mean, the outline was quite clear?
CROFT: Oh yes!
BELL: And you say it was flying from east to west.
CROFT: Well, it arrived from the east, stopped for a few moments, then flew off again, back to where it came from.
BELL: And were there any other witnesses, sir?
CROFT: Not with me, but it wouldn't surprise me if someone else saw it.
BELL: Fine, well, I think that's . . .
JACOBS: Jack!
BELL: Excuse me, sir. (*aside*) What's up?
JACOBS: I've just had a word with Walden Oak airfield. They close down before night falls, and they've had no emergency landing there for months.
BELL: Mm. That's interesting.
JACOBS: But they do say there have been quite a few shooting stars this week. Maybe he just saw a meteor, or something.
BELL: Mm. Any news from Hackett and Jones?
JACOBS: They're on their way over now.
BELL: Right, let me know when they get there. (*to phone*) Yes, Colonel, now you say you were on your way home from the Rose and Crown and you'd had something to drink . . . (*fade*)

D: Reading Aloud – see page 164

D: Listening Activity 2

(*Noise of car, radio playing '. . . and it's 10.40 here on Island Radio . . .'*)

JENNY: Oooh, it's cold. Let's turn the heating on.
MICK: It's full on already. It must be freezing outside tonight.
JENNY: It's freezing in here as well. Still, it's a lovely clear night.

(*Crackling sound on radio*)

MICK: Oh, what's wrong with the radio?
JENNY: It sometimes does that when we're near electricity cables.
MICK: Well, I can't see any.
JENNY: Perhaps it's that car up there.
MICK: What car?
JENNY: That one up there. Do you see the lights?
MICK: Oh yes. It looks a bit too far away for that, though. (*crackling*) Oh, I can't stand this. I'll try again later. (*turns radio off*).
JENNY: It's a bit strange though.
MICK: What is?
JENNY: Well, that car looks quite high up, as if it's half-way up a hill.
MICK: So?
JENNY: Can you remember any hills over that way? That's where the river is, isn't it?
MICK: Yes, you're right. Look, it's stopped.
JENNY: Mick, I think there are three of them.
MICK: They're very close, aren't they?
JENNY: Is it a plane or something?
MICK: I don't know. It's very strange though. It doesn't look like a plane. I'm going to stop the car and have a closer look.
JENNY: Mick, I'm frightened!
MICK: Don't worry, it's all right. Come on, why don't we take a closer look?
JENNY: No, I'm not moving from here. You can go on your own.
MICK: Oh, come on, Jenny, I'll look after you.
JENNY: Well . . .
MICK: Come on, it'll be all right.

(*They get out*)

JENNY: Look, where are the other two going?
MICK: Did you see how fast they were moving?
JENNY: Yes, I did. But what's this one doing?
MICK: I don't know. Can you hear that whistling sound?
JENNY: How high up is it?

MICK: Oh, about 500 feet, I suppose.
JENNY: Look, it's coming down! Don't go any closer!
MICK: It's very low.
JENNY: It's landing . . .
MICK: No, it's stopping there. Isn't it hot! Just look at that smoke!
JENNNY: I'm sure it's burning the grass.
MICK: I'm going to get as close as possible.
JENNY: I'm not! I'm not staying here. I'm going back to the car.
MICK: Look! Did you see something move! There, look! In that window. There!
JENNY: Oh, it's taking off again. (*noises*)
MICK: Just look at that!
JENNY: Oh, Mick, please take me home.
MICK: Come on, let's go. (*noises fading*) I think we ought to tell the police.
JENNY: But what on earth was it?
MICK: I don't know, I really don't know.
JENNY: I'm sure it was something from outer space . . . Mick?
MICK: What?
JENNY: I think it's coming back. Look! Can you see the lights?
MICK: Where?
JENNY: Over there!
MICK: You're right, it's coming closer. It's coming straight for us.
JENNY: Oh, come on, let's get back to the car. Mick, please!
MICK: All right, I'm coming.

(*Noise of car approaching, slowing down*)

HACKETT: It's all right, it's the police. I'm PC Hackett, from Barncroft.
JENNY: Oh, thank heavens it's the police! Did you see that . . . that thing flying off, officer?
MICK: I'm delighted to see you, officer. We were just coming to see you.
HACKETT: I'm sure you were, sir. You look as if you've had a bit of a fright. Would you like a cup of tea, ma'am? I've got a flask in the back. Then you can tell me what you saw.
JENNY: Oh, thank you, officer, yes, I'd love a cup of tea!

INDEX OF FUNCTIONS

References are to page numbers

INDEX OF FUNCTIONS

INDEX OF STRUCTURES

References are to page numbers

INDEX OF STRUCTURES